LOCAL CODE

LOCAL CODE

NICHOLAS DE MONCHAUX

— 3,659 PROPOSALS ABOUT DATA, DESIGN & THE NATURE OF CITIES

PRINCETON ARCHITECTURAL PRESS, NEW YORK

Published by

Princeton Architectural Press
A McEvoy Group company
202 Warren Street
Hudson, New York 12534

Visit our website at www.papress.com.

Editor: Barbara Darko
Design: Catalogtree

Special thanks to

Madisen Andersen, Janet Behning,
Nicola Brower, Abby Bussel, Erin Cain,
Tom Cho, Benjamin English, Jenny Florence,
Jan Cigliano Hartman, Jan Haux, Lia Hunt,
Mia Johnson, Valerie Kamen, Simone Kaplan-
Senchak, Stephanie Leke, Diane Levinson,
Jennifer Lippert, Kristy Maier, Sara McKay,
Jaime Nelson Noven, Esme Savage,
Rob Shaeffer, Sara Stemen, Paul Wagner,
Joseph Weston, and Janet Wong of
Princeton ArchitecturalPress
—Kevin C. Lippert, publisher

Library of Congress
Cataloging-in-Publication Data

Names: De Monchaux, Nicholas, 1973– author.
Title: Local code : 3,659 proposals about
    data, design, and the nature of cities /
    Nicholas de Monchaux.
Description: First edition. | New York :
    Princeton Architectural Press, 2016.
Identifiers: LCCN 2015039823 |
    ISBN 9781616893804 (paperback)
Subjects: LCSH: City planning—
    Environmental aspects. | Greenways. |
    Vacant lands. | BISAC: ARCHITECTURE /
    Urban & Land Use Planning.
Classification: LCC NA9053.E58 D4 2016 |
    DDC 307.1/16—dc23
LC record available at
    http://lccn.loc.gov/2015039823

CONTENTS

Foreword

For some important books, the structure of the narrative reflects its content, so the act of reading the text in its given framework prompts a habit of mind essential to grasping the evidence within. Against books with parallel chapters and a single species of narrative, Nicholas de Monchaux assembles as *Local Code: 3,659 Proposals about Data, Design, and the Nature of Cities* four case studies and three biographical stories, and invites the reader to make a network of correspondences between texts, images, and maps. Beyond delivering an argument, this book can then be used to engage information more broadly, and in so doing, it models an approach to shaping urban space and actively demonstrates an alternative artistic and architectural endeavor in the city.

In *Local Code*, de Monchaux shares the intellectual underpinnings of the titular series of his projects that have been the subject of exhibitions and short films over the last few years. The projects use GIS mapping techniques to identify, as a special asset, thousands of publicly owned or abandoned sites in major cities, four of which are included here. Observing that these sites are often located in areas of need in the city and rejecting previous models of parks as visible areas of recreation, the projects propose to develop site *networks* into a connective tissue, an "infrastructure for the twenty-first-century city."[1]

In the spirit of these case studies, the other stories in *Local Code* follow three iconoclastic, independent thinkers who each hold a special place in the intertwined histories of information systems and cities in the last century, whose work deeply shapes the fabric of our current one. The first of these figures, the artist and "anarchitect" Gordon Matta-Clark, is the most formative for de Monchaux. In addition to sculpting shape and outline with architectural excisions like *Splitting* (1974) and *Conical Intersect* (1975), in *Reality Properties: Fake Estates* (1973–74) Matta-Clark experimented with a "net-work" of vacant remnant sites in New York City. His is another kind of land art that uses as its raw material urban laws and activities, and it is the chief inspiration for the *Local Code* projects. He even makes a cameo in the second essay, which concerns Jane Jacobs. De Monchaux tells us that Matta-Clark grew up at the edge of the New York neighborhood that Jacobs famously analyzed, and they both worked to counter the prevalent bombast of master plans of architecture and planning. Translating into space her knowledge of biological and cybernetic systems, Jacobs made palpable an active network of urban practices and changing vantage points. And the third essay, about Howard Fisher, an understudied architect who contributed to the development of GIS (geographic information systems), tracks a curiosity and ingenuity about measuring and representing these ecologies of environmental and cultural activities in the urban landscape.

1
Jeff Watson, "An Essential Archipelago of Opportunity," Remote Device (blog), http://remotedevice.net/blog/an-essential-archipelago-of-opportunity/; and Nicholas de Monchaux, Local Code: Real Estates, http://vimeo.com/8080630.

But it is the relationship between these stories that begins to coax out a rare intelligence about architecture and the city. At a moment of ubiquitous computing, it is sometimes difficult to see past all the digital devices that carry information, but in the documents collected here, space itself operates as an information system. Digital information systems only help to identify the potential interaction between properties or Jacobs's "eyes on the street"— that part of an exchange made manifest in the heavy bulk of urban space. And at a moment when space is largely manipulated through econometrics, we are invited to value land networks in ways different from the typical real estate ledger.[2] In crafting a representation of the potentials of these spaces, de Monchaux necessarily draws attention to their linkages, their time-released performance, or their ability to counterbalance each other. Just as this is a book to be used as an exercise in thinking, its form and structure—the book's own architecture—makes it possible to see the designer coax both design possibilities and historical ideas into an intertwined shape, creating not only traditional figures and outlines but also new forms that are active and changing; generating not only things but also the interplay between things, of which the city is truly made.

Keller Easterling, 2016

2
Jane Jacobs,
The Death and Life of
Great American Cities
(New York: Random
House, 1961), 35.

Introduction: Current Location

Let's consider two things.

The first: over the next forty years, we will build as much urban fabric as was built in all the previous ten thousand years of human history combined.[1] The second: every two days—and at a rapidly accelerating rate—we now collect and store more information than the total amount of information captured between the start of recorded history and the last decade. This information is increasingly spatial, and, more than ever, urban in its origins and character.[2]

But an abundance of data is not knowledge. This enormous increase in urban fabric, and in information about it, is inseparable from an equally radical increase in uncertainty surrounding our cities' future, which emerges primarily from the inherent unpredictability surrounding the inevitable effects of man-made climate change. As is already becoming apparent, the coming century will bring cycles of flood and drought, urban damage and civic recovery that will drive dramatic mass population changes—with arriving refugees and departing exiles—as seen in no century before.

The ability of cities to survive and thrive in the face of this kind of predictable uncertainty has been widely termed *resilience*.[3] Yet this word—from the Latin *resiliēns*, describing a mechanical spring's return to form—carries little clue about how such a quality can be achieved. So for all its currency, resilience also implies—through its spring-sprung origin—the impossible. That is, it indicates a near-perfect reprise of a previous state of being and (perhaps worse) a singular and linear means of attempting it.

For what we are beginning to know about how cities actually work tells us that they are not very much like springs. Instead, they resemble, well, us—the complex organisms that collect in and constitute them. Like us, cities are adaptive, self-sustaining systems with interconnected metabolisms. When in good health, they can recover from astonishing injuries. But cities can also—under other circumstances—prove remarkably fragile. And, unlike the lacework of human physiology, the webs of urban metabolisms are only partly physical. They are, most of all, economic and social, and so synthesized out of that most immaterial of substances, information. In this light especially, it is impossible to truly imagine physical resilience without social, cultural, and economic resilience as well.

This book is an attempt to address the question of how information, cities, and resilience can be considered together, and how many different kinds of resilience—all interconnected and each one essential—can be imagined and created in concert. In particular, it proposes an information-inspired, physical resilience that is designed,

1
United Nations, Department of Economic and Social Affairs, Population Division, World Urbanization Prospects: The 2014 Revision, Highlights (ST/ESA/SER.A/352) (New York: United Nations, 2014).

2
Martin Hilbert and Priscila López, "How to Measure the World's Technological Capacity to Communicate, Store, and Compute Information," International Journal of Communication 6 (2012): 956–79.

3
See, for example, Neeraj Prasad, Climate Resilient Cities: A Primer on Reducing Vulnerabilities to Disasters (Washington, D.C.: World Bank Publications, 2009), or Judith Rodin, The Resilience Dividend: Being Strong in a World Where Things Go Wrong (New York: Public Affairs, 2014).

above all, to support its social, cultural, and economic counterparts. The tools for this proposal are the media of architecture and the city—some old, some new, and some crafted specifically in the course of the work. From the Latin "middle element," and originally used to mean "lens," *media* has come to mean, handily, both tools and ways of seeing with them; the work here attempts to be both.

The drawings on these pages speculate about possible futures for 3,659 abandoned and underutilized sites in three large, representative American cities: San Francisco, Los Angeles, and New York. To these are added one small, special European one: Venice. The focus on these spaces arises from a unique yet confluent characteristic of these sites. The same spaces generally abandoned and avoided by normal urban mechanisms of occupation, exploitation, and use turn out to have several very essential qualities in common: from an ecological perspective, they tend to accumulate in parts of the city—downhill, downstream, down-at-heel—where ecological interventions are most transformative, and best buffer the city against physical threats, from floods to heat waves. From a social and economic perspective, such sites are positioned precisely in those communities traditionally denied access to parks and public space. And their remediation is, as a result, also likely to have a remarkable, and predictable, benefit to public health and social well-being.

Before the availability of digital mapping tools, finding and imagining futures for such sites was an exercise in herculean bookkeeping and singular imagination. Before widespread digital information about cities made analysis of their complex qualities possible, speculation on the complex, adaptive qualities of opportunistic urban networks took another, special kind of foresight. Inspired by such visions, this project is indebted to a second kind of media: that of previous ideas, speculation, and experiment. It is in an attempt to trace the possibilities of mechanisms of thought, as well as the making that results, that the 3,659 drawings in this book share space with three essays, examining episodes from the history of ideas that have inspired it.

As the last decades of evolutionary biology have taught us, adaptation and change do not take place through anything resembling optimization. Rather, they take place along what the biologist Stuart Kaufmann has described as a "landscape of adjacent possibility."[4] And if this book is an attempt to trace such a landscape in the fabric of abandoned space in the city, it is also an attempt to trace a similar, related set of transformations in the landscape of ideas that surround this work. For ideas, too, are adapted and transformed things. We forget this as often as we forget that every seemingly new piece of architecture is a remaking—of site, of material, of event—as well. And so the particular focus of these essays is how three fundamental precedents of the design work enclosed here were themselves the product of adaptation, circumstance, and, even, to a large extent, urbane serendipity.

4
See Stuart Kaufmann, **At Home in the Universe: The Search for Laws of Self-Organization and Complexity** (New York: Oxford University Press, 1995).

These stories begin and end, as many do, in New York City. They start with an instrumental, and unfinished, project by the architect and artist Gordon Matta-Clark: *Reality Properties: Fake Estates*, which inspired much of what you now hold.

Between 1971 and 1974, Matta-Clark spent months sifting through phonebook-sized catalogs and attending property auctions in order to locate and purchase fifteen vacant and moribund sites—microscopic fragments of New York real estate—that form the substance of the work. Today, using GIS, the same search can be accomplished in minutes, and locates many thousands of marginal, city-owned vacant lots throughout the five boroughs. When Matta-Clark's *Fake Estates* were first presented together in 1992 (long after the artist's death in 1978), the mere fact of their documentation was alone remarkable. Today, however, *Fake Estates* may be essential in considering how we might respond to a revolution that has occurred since that time: the almost uniform presence of digital information in our encounters with, and designs for, cities.[5] This book's first historical essay, "Fake Estates and Reality Properties," traces the origins of this artwork not as the singular, influential artifact it has become (thanks in part to the assembly by Matta-Clark's widow, Jane Crawford, of the maps and property deeds for the sites into exhibitable artworks) but rather as the unfinished product of the architect-turned-artist's exploratory trajectory, cut short by his death at the age of thirty-five, in property, renovation, and ecology.

Matta-Clark was an adult in New York, but had also been a child in the city; he grew up just a block away from Washington Square Park, which was saved from becoming a traffic circle just as he left for architecture school at Cornell University. This was in large part through the efforts of an architecture critic turned author and activist, Jane Jacobs (née Butzner). The second essay, "Life Attracts Life," moves directly four blocks west from Washington Square, to Jacobs's own home at 555 Hudson Street. It considers not so much her well-known post-1960 career as a public intellectual and activist, the author of the seminal *Death and Life of Great American Cities* (and its four sort-of-sequels considering the complex nature of urban economies). Rather, it chronicles her life before, and how her famous work had its own strikingly evitable origins in the confluence of late nineteenth- and early twentieth-century scientific thinking (taught to Jacobs at Columbia from 1940 to 1941) and a savvy misunderstanding of one of the twentieth century's greatest transformations in science: the understanding of so-called organized complexity. Indeed, some of the most notable recent work in the science of complex systems, emergent networks, and their unpredictable behavior has focused on the statistical nature of cities themselves, work examined in this book's conclusion.

But before that, the third and final essay moves along one of the great infrastructural and intellectual corridors of our age, heading north from New York to Cambridge, Massachusetts. There, the essay

5
See Jeffrey Kastner, Sina Najafi, and Frances Richard, eds., Odd Lots: Revisiting Gordon Matta-Clark's "Fake Estates" (New York: Cabinet Books, in conjunction with Queens Museum of Art and White Columns, 2005), exhibition catalog.

"The Map and the Territory" examines, at its origin, the particular media—geographic information systems, or GIS—that has allowed us to see and engage the city so profoundly through the lens of information. In Cambridge, between 1965 and 1968, building on prior work at Northwestern University in Chicago, and postwar, defense industry–driven innovations in computing and digital map projection, the architect Howard Fisher developed the roots of what was to become the most widespread geographic information software, now used by the government, the military, corporations, and urban planners alike to chart and create strategic interventions in urban fabric worldwide. But this was not the software as Fisher had conceived it—or, in today's open-source era, as it may yet become—but a subtly different animal, with its own habits and preconceptions.

These three stories are presented separately, but they contain another essential character who, like a Brothers Grimm villain, appears in different guises throughout. This is the complex, well-intentioned, and ultimately quixotic encounter between the engineering approaches of systems-based planning, forged in the furnace of the Cold War's first weapons, and brought to bear on the landscape of postwar American cities, sometimes—as in the wholesale clearance of neighborhoods encountered by Jane Jacobs in northern Manhattan in 1955—with sometimes equally devastating effects.

The sudden, seeming efficacy of these techniques in the years from 1943 onward—when they were used first in automatic air-defenses (encountered in "Life Attracts Life"), and then to conceive and build the United States's first intercontinental ballistic missiles, and then to craft the manned space rockets that replaced warheads with astronauts at their tips—led to widespread attempts at their application to complex problems from industry to government. And the information-based strategies that were the lifeblood of systems approaches found application in everything from Title 1–funded slum mapping (encountered in "The Map and the Territory") to academic research on urban systems (as in the Harvard-MIT Joint Center for Urban Studies, encountered in "Life Attracts Life") to, by the late 1960s, a broad acceptance of data-driven approaches as the primary tool of urban design and planning (as encountered in "Fake Estates and Reality Properties").

The specific, systematic failure of these efforts at the scale of the city itself is an epic too enormous for this book, and better told elsewhere. And yet, it is an essential tale to remember in the context of today's reencounter between the city's complexity and computing's power. Underlining these resonances, one of the foremost historians of the transition of defense-honed systems techniques to the urban context, Jennifer Light, begins her 2003 history of the phenomena with the following rhetorical question: "How and why are resources allocated time and again to support the adoption of technical and technological tools whose benefits remain unproven?"[6] Especially in the context of a new generation of claims to the city's tractability through data, this is a fundamental caveat. But this book is not so

6
Jennifer S. Light, From Warfare to Welfare: Defense Intellectuals and Urban Problems in Cold War America (Baltimore: Johns Hopkins University Press, 2003), vii. I first deployed this quote in the conclusion to my 2011 book Spacesuit: Fashioning Apollo, which traced the story of systems engineering mostly in and around the human body, and in the bodies of cities as well—a deeply connected tale. See Nicholas de Monchaux, Spacesuit: Fashioning Apollo (Cambridge, MA: MIT Press, 2011), 311.

much an effort to chart this larger history as it is an attempt to chart essential counterhistories within it.

And so the book's conclusion, after presenting the serendipitous and particular origins of three important threads—the remaking of the abandoned and underutilized in the work of Matta-Clark, the nature of the city as a complex, living network-of-networks in the work of Jacobs, and the visual use of information in the public good in the work of Fisher—charts their interweaving in the work you hold. Thus it also tries to show, through the lens of new and old ideas, how the nature of cities can be better understood, and extended, in our current, uncertain age.

Local Code, and all its embedded and implicated propositions, draws from established, and important, precedents in neighborhood greening at the local scale—such as in Baltimore, Chicago, and Los Angeles—and is deeply indebted to them as well as to the landscape of ideas outlined above.[7] These efforts have so far been justified on mostly social and political grounds; but a much more substantial argument is proposed here: that it is only through understanding and engaging the existing nature of our cities as complex, networked artifacts that we can design for, and imagine, a robust and resilient future for them. Such a future is considered here, socially, economically, ecologically, and, as an inevitable corollary, spatially, materially, and formally—built into and out of the city itself.

A final note concerns this work's future. At the time of writing, several projects are underway, involving myself and others, to address the enormous policy challenges that lie in front of this effort to radically reimagine urban infrastructure alongside social and environmental welfare. These efforts involve local instrumentation, community collaborations, and policy studies. And such unglamorous work is, of course, the real effort of building cities and communities—and will continue long after this book is put to bed. In the story of this project, then, the text you hold is (qua Churchill) not so much the end as it is the end of the beginning.

7
See E. Gregory McPherson, David J. Nowak, and Rowan A. Rowntree, Chicago's Urban Forest Ecosystem: Results of the Chicago Urban Forest Climate Project, General Technical Report NE-186 (Radnor, PA: US Department of Agriculture, Forest Service, Northeastern Forest Experiment Station, 1994); Gary Moll, Urban Ecosystem Analysis for the Washington DC Metropolitan Area (Washington, D.C.: American Forests, 2002), http://www.americanforests.org/downloads/rea/AF_WashingtonDC2.pdf; and Haan-Fawn Chau, Green Infrastructure for Los Angeles: Addressing Urban Runoff and Water Supply through Low Impact Development (Los Angeles: City of Los Angeles Department of City Planning and UCLA Department of Urban Planning, 2007).

San Francisco
Case Study 2009–2010

Mapped from a single spreadsheet kept by the city's Department of Public Works, the sites for the San Francisco case study that follows are so-called unaccepted streets—zoned as rights-of-way but unmaintained by the city.

Hiding in plain sight, the institutional invisibility of these sites becomes clearer when overlaid with other layers of public information. As is the case in many other cities, data on public health and crime in San Francisco reveal abandoned sites to be precisely located in areas most in need of a safe and healthy environment—and off the map of the city's existing investments. Perhaps also unsurprisingly, further data reveal these sites to center on areas most burdened by energy inefficiency, poor water management, and airborne contaminants.

With a distributed surface that rivals that of Golden Gate Park, a locally driven, land-banking renovation of these sites would contain enormous potential to relieve the very same problems the presence of such sites in the city seems to track. Such a system would not only be able to improve urban thermodynamic performance, but its distributed, modular, and incremental nature would vastly increase the resilience of the city's existing, essential infrastructure.

3106000 BREEN PL / DOWNTOWN, TENDERLOIN /
$33,809.84 ESTIMATED SAVINGS PER YEAR

For this design study, a local model of water flow, solar gain, and wind movement parametrically governs the dispersal on each site of a range of hard and soft landscape surfaces, mediating drainage, energy loads, and air quality to enhance not only the site's individual performance, but also that of the city as a whole. Yet these surfaces should be understood as potentials above all; as with subsequent case studies, this analysis attempts to reveal the full possibilities inherent in each site, but does not dictate a specific outcome on it.

What might happen next has been the subject of much thought. In a parallel study, based on existing models of community design, as well as new research on digital democracy, we have envisioned engaging place-based media to gather opinions, engage communities, and even aggregate finances and funding for each site. A prototype interface developed in collaboration with the Berkeley Center for New Media imagines an online system used as a structured forum for each project's development, as well as a resource for design and implementation.

Through parametrically envisioning the energy performance remediative potential of these sites, we make the study's most important argument: that these and other social and political benefits should be funded on the basis of global infrastructural performance. For example, a $1.5 billion bond measure was approved at the same time as our design proposals to upgrade the capacity of San Francisco's combined sewer system to better manage peak flow.[1] Using established engineering metrics and the parametrically derived potential of each of our 1,500+ design proposals, we estimate that between 88 and 96 percent of this investment could be replaced by the surface spending we propose, at half the cost of underground work.[2]

These proposals, then, are not about spending more money but about spending it differently, and so directing it to the communities and ecologies—in San Francisco and elsewhere—that remain most in need.

1
San Francisco Public Utilities Commission (SFPUC), "Final Stormwater Management Plan," 2003, accessed January 29, 2010, http://sfwater.org/Files/Reports/SFPUC_SWMP_Jan_2004_Part1.pdf.

2
This estimate is based on rules of thumb established in the following studies: E. Gregory McPherson, David J. Nowak, and Rowan A. Rowntree, Chicago's Urban Forest Ecosystem: Results of the Chicago Urban Forest Climate Project, General Technical Report NE-186 (Radnor, PA: US Department of Agriculture, Forest Service, Northeastern Forest Experiment Station, 1994); Gary Moll, Urban Ecosystem Analysis for the Washington DC Metropolitan Area (Washington, D.C.: American Forests, 2002), http://www.americanforests.org/downloads/rea/AF_WashingtonDC2.pdf; and Haan-Fawn Chau, Green Infrastructure for Los Angeles: Addressing Urban Runoff and Water Supply through Low Impact Development (Los Angeles: City of Los Angeles Department of City Planning and UCLA Department of Urban Planning, 2007).

4576000 DALE PL / DOWNTOWN, TENDERLOIN / $30,961.56 ESTIMATED SAVINGS PER YEAR

12493000 TENNESSEE ST / BAYVIEW DISTRICT /
$658,424.16 ESTIMATED SAVINGS PER YEAR

1162000 22ND ST / POTRERO HILL /
$616,121.28 ESTIMATED SAVINGS PER YEAR

11025000 RIDGE LN / INGLESIDE /
$256,521.36 ESTIMATED SAVINGS PER YEAR

10354000 PERALTA AVE / BERNAL
HEIGHTS SOUTH / $172,321.12
ESTIMATED SAVINGS PER YEAR

LOCAL CODE

CONTEXT San Francisco Department of Public
Works, Unnaccepted Streets Database, 2009

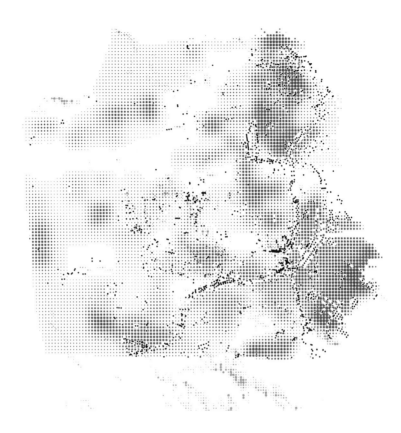

HOUSEHOLDS IN POVERTY
% US Census, 2010

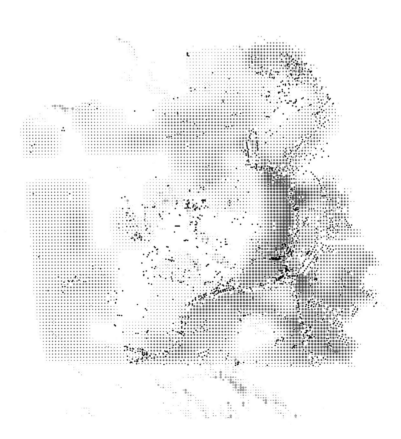

RESPIRATORY AILMENTS
INCIDENCE, % US Census, 2010

CANCER DIAGNOSIS
RISK OF DIAGNOSIS, % US Census, 2010

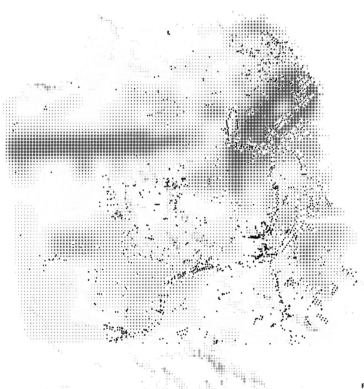

REPORTED CRIME INCIDENT COUNT
San Francisco Police Department, 2011 Data

URBAN HEAT ISLANDS
Landsat Infrared Image Analysis, 2010

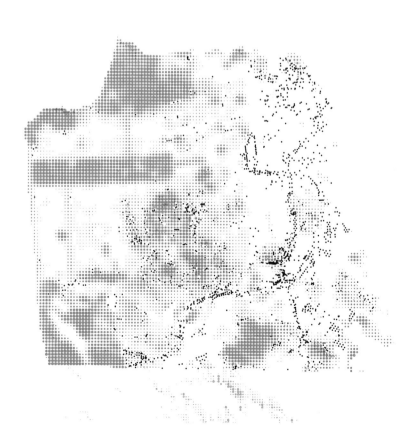

URBAN GROUND COVER
ASTER Image Analysis, 2010

**HISTORIC SHORELINE, CREEKS,
SLOUGHS, AND MARSHES**
San Francisco Public Utilities
Commission, 2010

**SEWER SYSTEM AND
JUNCTIONS/IMPEDANCES**
San Francisco Public
Utilities Commission (PUC), 2010

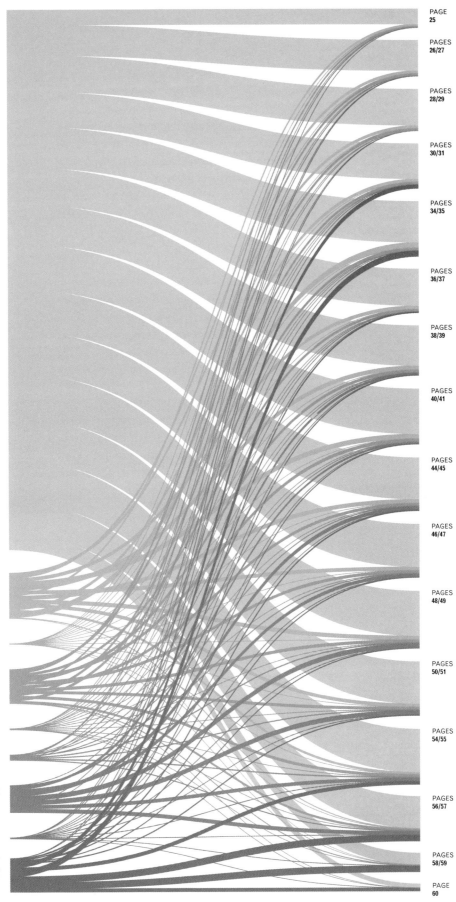

PAGE
25

PAGES
26/27

PAGES
28/29

PAGES
30/31

PAGES
34/35

PAGES
36/37

PAGES
38/39

PAGES
40/41

PAGES
44/45

PAGES
46/47

PAGES
48/49

PAGES
50/51

PAGES
54/55

PAGES
56/57

PAGES
58/59

PAGE
60

PUC
STORMWATER
INITIATIVES
$ 381.5 MILLION

CALTRANS
ENVIRONMENTAL
MITIGATION
$32.6 MILLION

MISCELLANEOUS
NEIGHBOURHOOD
LEVEL HEALTH AND
BEAUTIFICATION
GRANTS $0.4 MILLION

INFILL
INFRASTRUCTURE
GRANTS $24.4 MILLION

EPA BROWNFIELD
REDEVELOPMENT
GRANT $0.8 MILLION

BAY AREA FOCUS
GRANTS PRIORITY
DEVELOPMENT AREAS
$3.9 MILLION

SAN FRANCISCO
REDEVELOPMENT
AGENCY $19.3 MILLION

SF AGENCY MITIGATION
FUNDS $0.8 MILLION

FEDERAL COMMUNITY
BLOCK GRANTS
$23.8 MILLION

LOCAL CODE

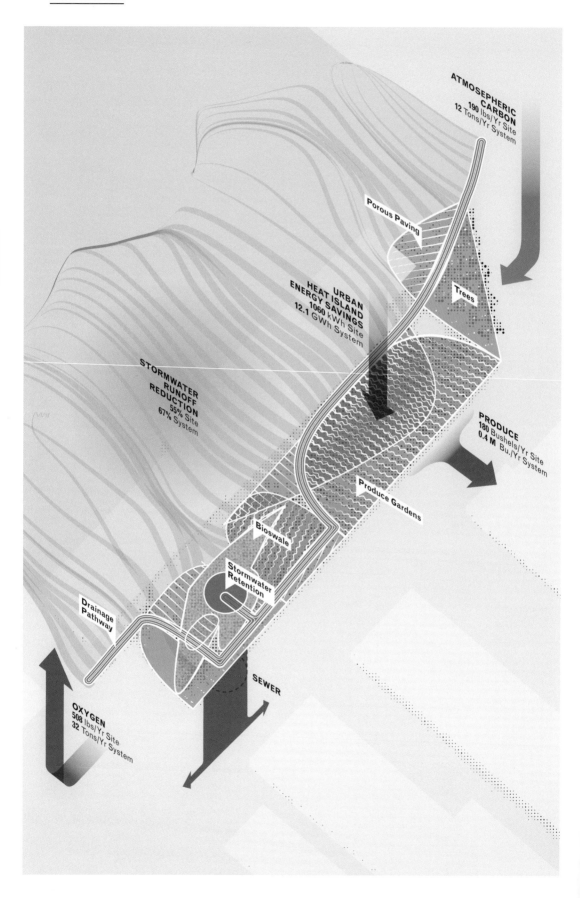

ATMOSEPHERIC
CARBON
190 lbs/Yr Site
12 Tons/Yr System

Porous Paving

Trees

URBAN
HEAT ISLAND
ENERGY SAVINGS
1060 kWh Site
12.1 GWh System

PRODUCE
180 Bushels/Yr Site
0.4 M Bu./Yr System

STORMWATER
RUNOFF
REDUCTION
55% Site
67% System

Produce Gardens

Bioswale

Stormwater
Retention

Drainage
Pathway

SEWER

OXYGEN
508 lbs/Yr Site
32 Tons/Yr System

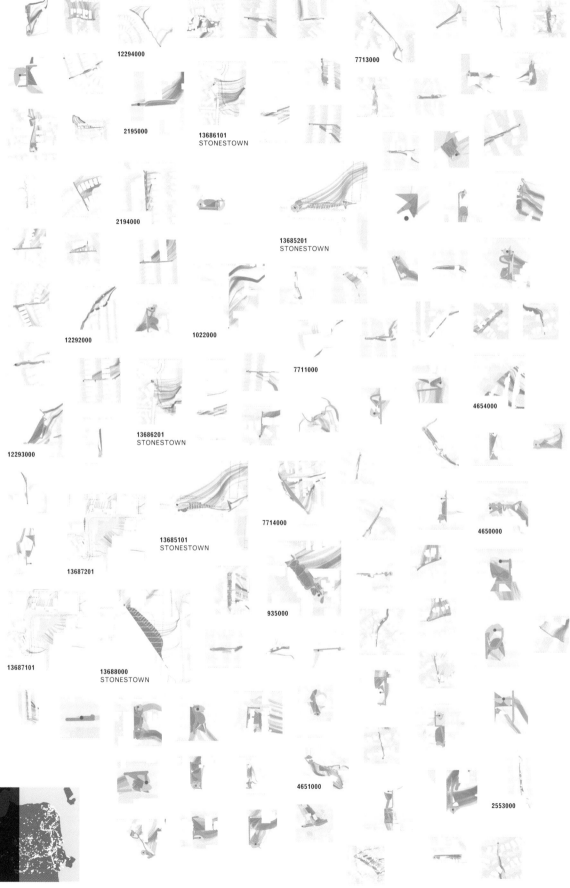

12294000

7713000

2195000

13686101
STONESTOWN

2194000

13685201
STONESTOWN

12292000

1022000

7711000

4654000

13686201
STONESTOWN

12293000

7714000

4650000

13685101
STONESTOWN

13687201

935000

13687101

13688000
STONESTOWN

4651000

2553000

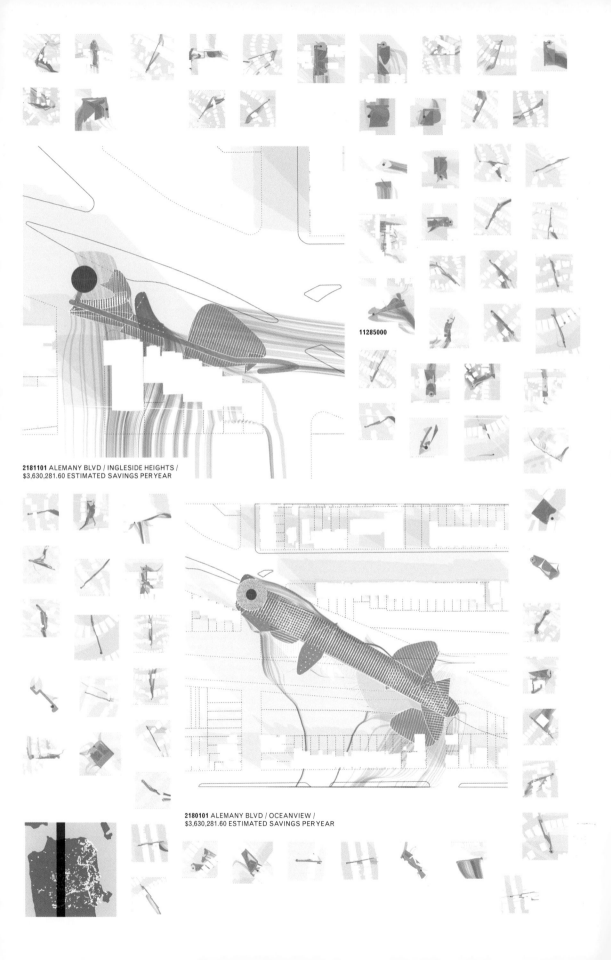

11285000

2181101 ALEMANY BLVD / INGLESIDE HEIGHTS /
$3,630,281.60 ESTIMATED SAVINGS PER YEAR

2180101 ALEMANY BLVD / OCEANVIEW /
$3,630,281.60 ESTIMATED SAVINGS PER YEAR

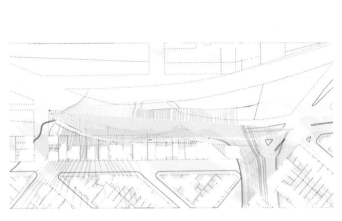

2179101 ALEMANY BLVD / OUTER MISSION /
$3,630,281.60 ESTIMATED SAVINGS PER YEAR

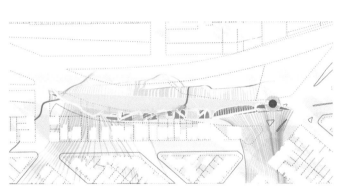

2179201 ALEMANY BLVD / OUTER MISSION /
$3,630,281.60 ESTIMATED SAVINGS PER YEAR

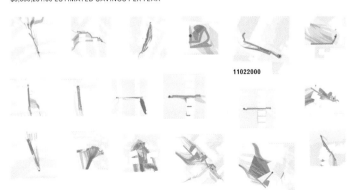

11022000

11019000

11467101 SAN JOSE AVE /
OUTER MISSION / $1,967,047.20
ESTIMATED SAVINGS PER YEAR

11025000   11020000

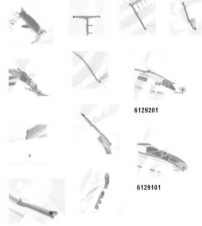

6129201

6129101

11021000

11425000 SAN JOSE AVE /
INGLESIDE / $1,967,047.20
ESTIMATED SAVINGS PER YEAR

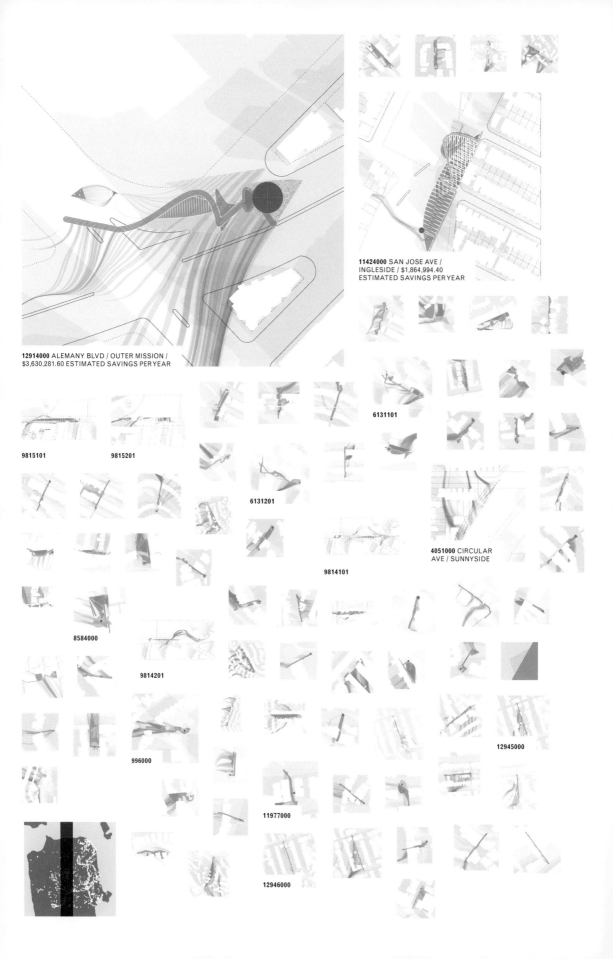

12914000 ALEMANY BLVD / OUTER MISSION / $3,630,281.60 ESTIMATED SAVINGS PER YEAR

11424000 SAN JOSE AVE / INGLESIDE / $1,864,994.40 ESTIMATED SAVINGS PER YEAR

9815101

9815201

6131101

6131201

9814101

4051000 CIRCULAR AVE / SUNNYSIDE

8584000

9814201

12945000

996000

11977000

12946000

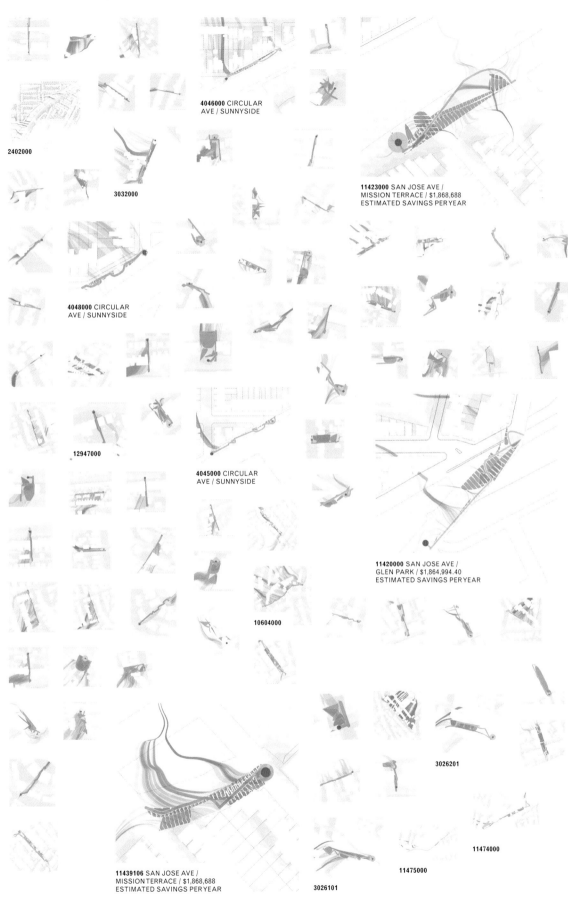

4046000 CIRCULAR
AVE / SUNNYSIDE

2402000

3032000

11423000 SAN JOSE AVE /
MISSION TERRACE / $1,868,688
ESTIMATED SAVINGS PER YEAR

4048000 CIRCULAR
AVE / SUNNYSIDE

12947000

4045000 CIRCULAR
AVE / SUNNYSIDE

11420000 SAN JOSE AVE /
GLEN PARK / $1,864,994.40
ESTIMATED SAVINGS PER YEAR

10604000

3026201

11439106 SAN JOSE AVE /
MISSION TERRACE / $1,868,688
ESTIMATED SAVINGS PER YEAR

3026101

11475000

11474000

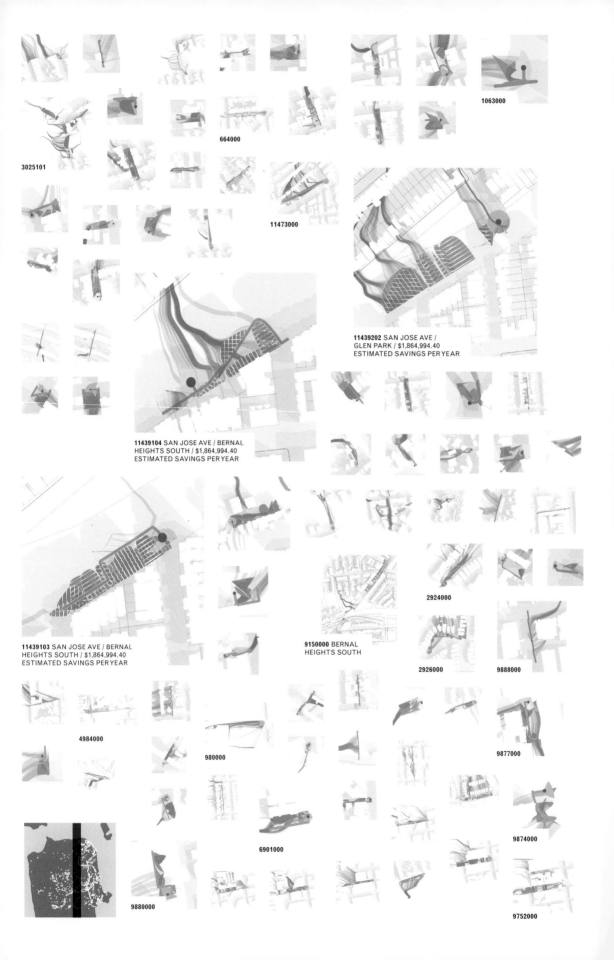

1063000

664000

3025101

11473000

11439202 SAN JOSE AVE /
GLEN PARK / $1,864,994.40
ESTIMATED SAVINGS PER YEAR

11439104 SAN JOSE AVE / BERNAL
HEIGHTS SOUTH / $1,864,994.40
ESTIMATED SAVINGS PER YEAR

11439103 SAN JOSE AVE / BERNAL
HEIGHTS SOUTH / $1,864,994.40
ESTIMATED SAVINGS PER YEAR

9150000 BERNAL
HEIGHTS SOUTH

2924000

2926000   9888000

4984000

980000

9877000

6901000

9874000

9880000

9752000

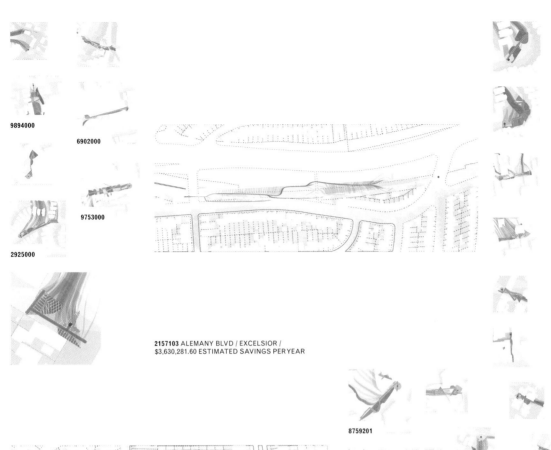

9894000

6902000

9753000

2925000

2157103 ALEMANY BLVD / EXCELSIOR /
$3,630,281.60 ESTIMATED SAVINGS PER YEAR

8759201

6603000

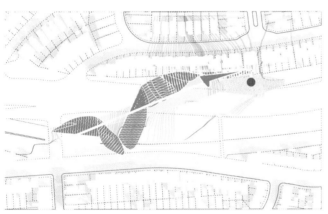

2157204 ALEMANY BLVD / BERNAL HEIGHTS SOUTH /
$3,623,106.08 ESTIMATED SAVINGS PER YEAR

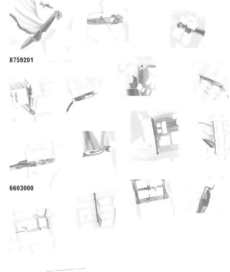

6900000

5139000

8759101

4979000

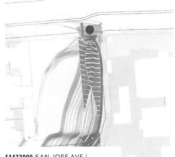

11433000 SAN JOSE AVE /
INNER MISSION / $1,707,879.60
ESTIMATED SAVINGS PER YEAR

10170000

13053000

10168000

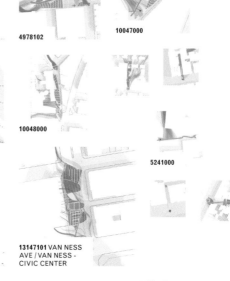

4978102

10047000

10048000

5241000

13147101 VAN NESS AVE / VAN NESS - CIVIC CENTER

2157102 ALEMANY BLVD / EXCELSIOR / $3,630,281.60 ESTIMATED SAVINGS PER YEAR

4978201

9112201 MISSION ST / INNER MISSION / $1,418,886.40 ESTIMATED SAVINGS PER YEAR

9112101 MISSION ST / INNER MISSION / $1,418,886.40 ESTIMATED SAVINGS PER YEAR

13146201 VAN NESS - CIVIC CENTER

13145202 VAN NESS - CIVIC CENTER

13146101 VAN NESS - CIVIC CENTER

9111001 MISSION ST / SOUTH OF MARKET / $1,418,886.40 ESTIMATED SAVINGS PER YEAR

9111000 MISSION ST / SOUTH OF MARKET / $1,418,886.40 ESTIMATED SAVINGS PER YEAR

13145101 VAN NESS - CIVIC CENTER

551102 13TH ST / INNER MISSION

10046000

13143103 VAN NESS - CIVIC CENTER

13143102 VAN NESS - CIVIC CENTER

9909000

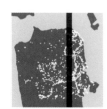

2933000

12019101

6811000

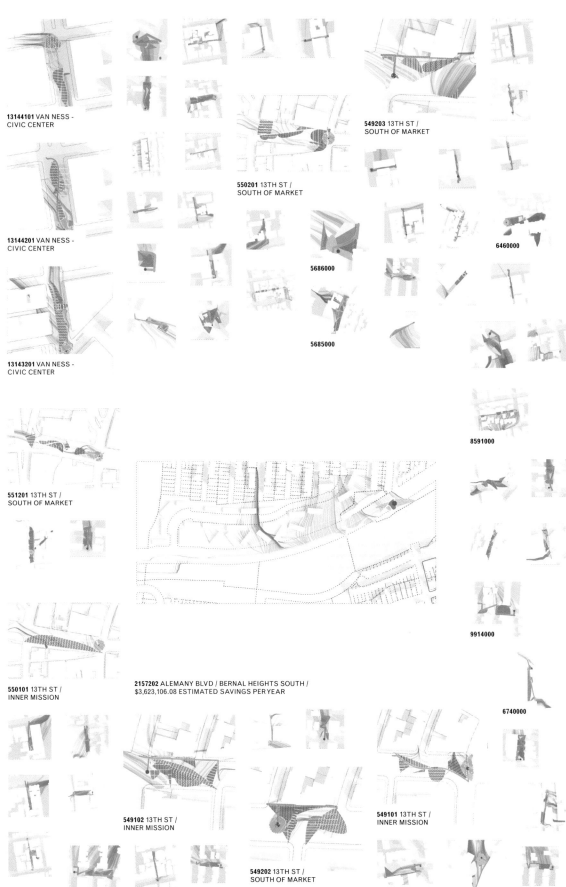

13144101 VAN NESS - CIVIC CENTER

13144201 VAN NESS - CIVIC CENTER

13143201 VAN NESS - CIVIC CENTER

551201 13TH ST / SOUTH OF MARKET

550101 13TH ST / INNER MISSION

550201 13TH ST / SOUTH OF MARKET

5686000

5685000

549203 13TH ST / SOUTH OF MARKET

6460000

8591000

9914000

6740000

2157202 ALEMANY BLVD / BERNAL HEIGHTS SOUTH / $3,623,106.08 ESTIMATED SAVINGS PER YEAR

549102 13TH ST / INNER MISSION

549202 13TH ST / SOUTH OF MARKET

549101 13TH ST / INNER MISSION

9912000

6459000

6739000

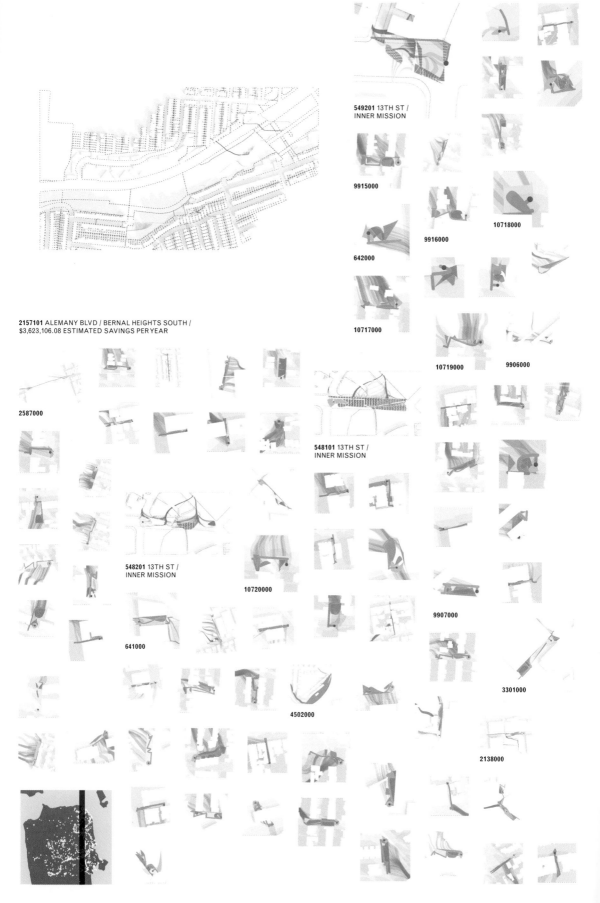

549201 13TH ST / INNER MISSION

9915000

642000

10717000

9916000

10718000

10719000   **9906000**

2157101 ALEMANY BLVD / BERNAL HEIGHTS SOUTH / $3,623,106.08 ESTIMATED SAVINGS PER YEAR

2587000

548101 13TH ST / INNER MISSION

9907000

548201 13TH ST / INNER MISSION

10720000

3301000

641000

4502000

2138000

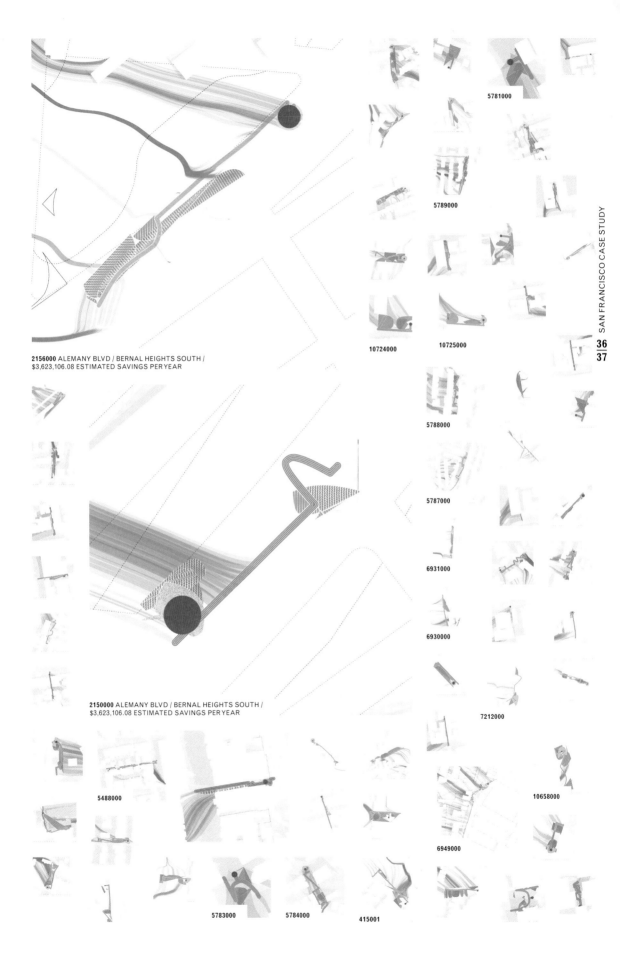

2156000 ALEMANY BLVD / BERNAL HEIGHTS SOUTH /
$3,623,106.08 ESTIMATED SAVINGS PER YEAR

2150000 ALEMANY BLVD / BERNAL HEIGHTS SOUTH /
$3,623,106.08 ESTIMATED SAVINGS PER YEAR

5781000

5789000

10724000

10725000

5788000

5787000

6931000

6930000

7212000

10658000

6949000

5488000

5783000

5784000

415001

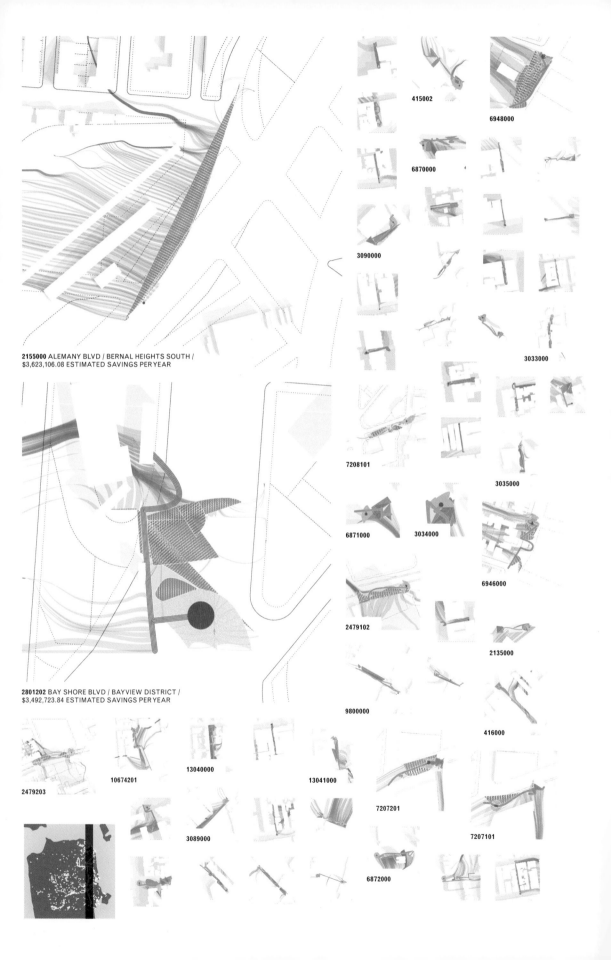

2155000 ALEMANY BLVD / BERNAL HEIGHTS SOUTH /
$3,623,106.08 ESTIMATED SAVINGS PER YEAR

2801202 BAY SHORE BLVD / BAYVIEW DISTRICT /
$3,492,723.84 ESTIMATED SAVINGS PER YEAR

415002

6948000

6870000

3090000

3033000

7208101

3035000

6871000

3034000

6946000

2479102

2135000

9800000

416000

2479203

10674201

13040000

13041000

7207201

3089000

7207101

6872000

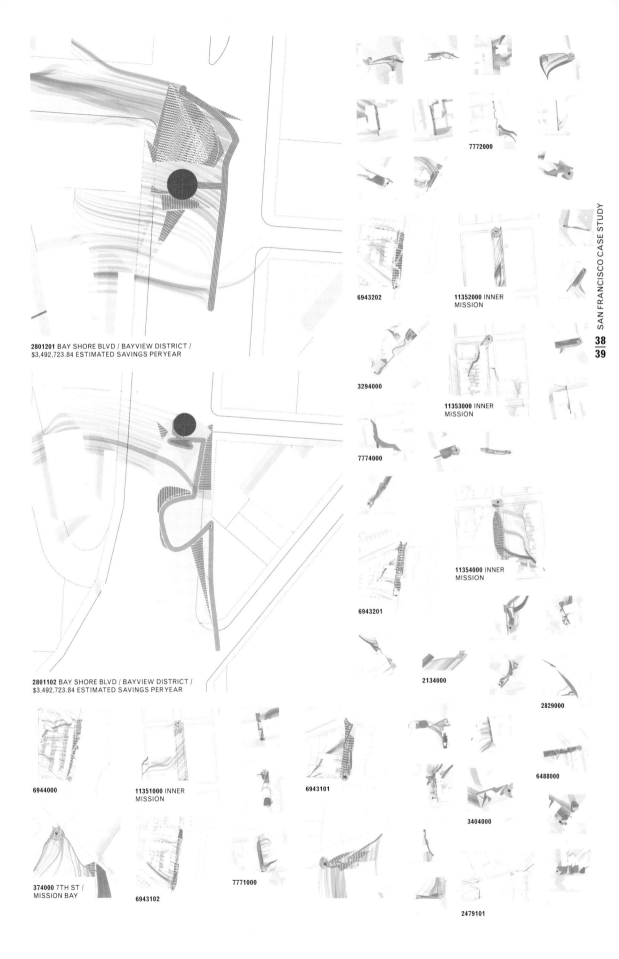

2801201 BAY SHORE BLVD / BAYVIEW DISTRICT /
$3,492,723.84 ESTIMATED SAVINGS PER YEAR

2801102 BAY SHORE BLVD / BAYVIEW DISTRICT /
$3,492,723.84 ESTIMATED SAVINGS PER YEAR

7772000

6943202

11352000 INNER MISSION

3294000

11353000 INNER MISSION

7774000

11354000 INNER MISSION

6943201

2134000

2829000

6488000

6944000

11351000 INNER MISSION

6943101

3404000

374000 7TH ST / MISSION BAY

6943102

7771000

2479101

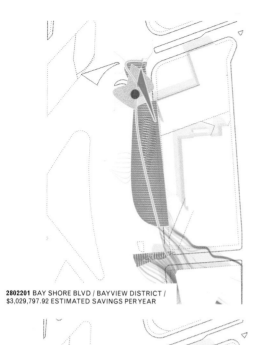

2802201 BAY SHORE BLVD / BAYVIEW DISTRICT /
$3,029,797.92 ESTIMATED SAVINGS PER YEAR

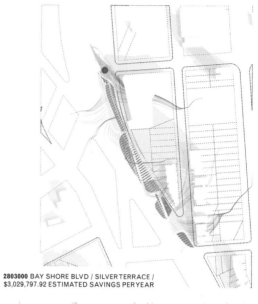

2803000 BAY SHORE BLVD / SILVER TERRACE /
$3,029,797.92 ESTIMATED SAVINGS PER YEAR

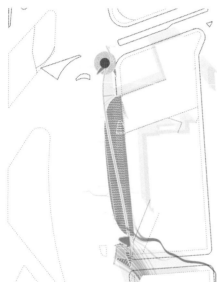

2802101 BAY SHORE BLVD / BAYVIEW DISTRICT /
$3,189,588.48 ESTIMATED SAVINGS PER YEAR

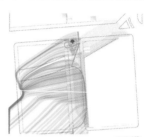

13208000 VERMONT ST /
MISSION BAY

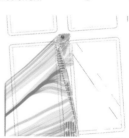

13209000 VERMONT ST /
MISSION BAY

374002 7TH ST /
MISSION BAY

11362000 INNER
MISSION

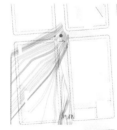

13210000 VERMONT ST /
MISSION BAY

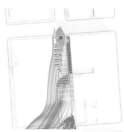

13211000 VERMONT ST /
POTRERO HILL

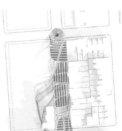

13212000 VERMONT ST /
POTRERO HILL

2800202 BAY SHORE BLVD / BAYVIEW DISTRICT /
$3,492,723.84 ESTIMATED SAVINGS PER YEAR

2800102 BAY SHORE BLVD / BAYVIEW DISTRICT /
$3,492,723.84 ESTIMATED SAVINGS PER YEAR

13219000 VERMONT ST /
INNER MISSION

13221000 VERMONT ST /
INNER MISSION

13220000 VERMONT ST /
INNER MISSION

418000

2579000

10844000

7089000

7505000 JERROLD AVE /
BAYVIEW DISTRICT

338000

375000 7TH ST /
MISSION BAY

1248000

1326000

13222000 VERMONT ST /
INNER MISSION

8700000

13223000 VERMONT ST /
INNER MISSION

1509000

6487000

1419000

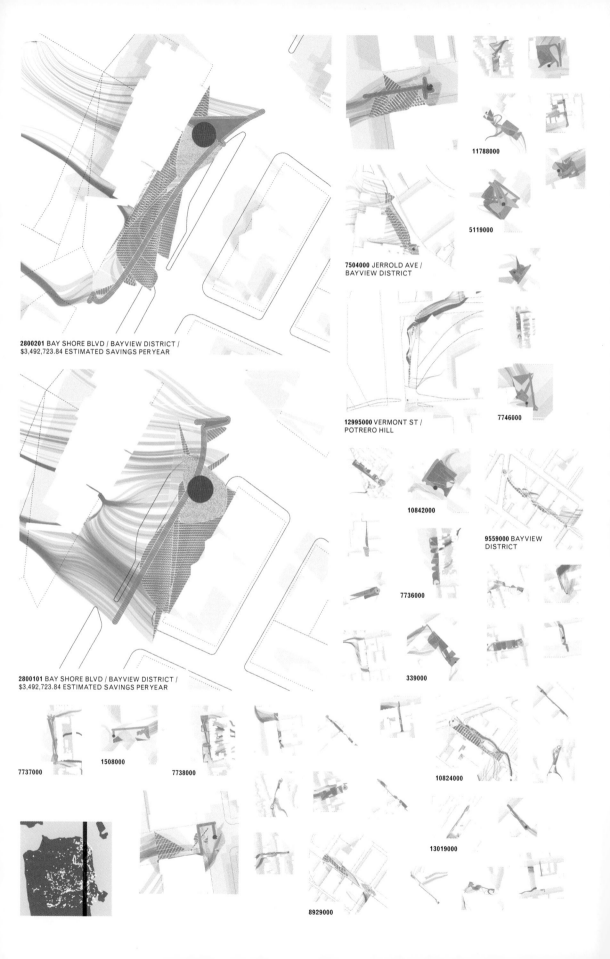

2800201 BAY SHORE BLVD / BAYVIEW DISTRICT /
$3,492,723.84 ESTIMATED SAVINGS PER YEAR

2800101 BAY SHORE BLVD / BAYVIEW DISTRICT /
$3,492,723.84 ESTIMATED SAVINGS PER YEAR

11788000

5119000

7504000 JERROLD AVE /
BAYVIEW DISTRICT

12995000 VERMONT ST /
POTRERO HILL

7746000

10842000

9559000 BAYVIEW
DISTRICT

7736000

339000

7737000

1508000

7738000

10824000

13019000

8929000

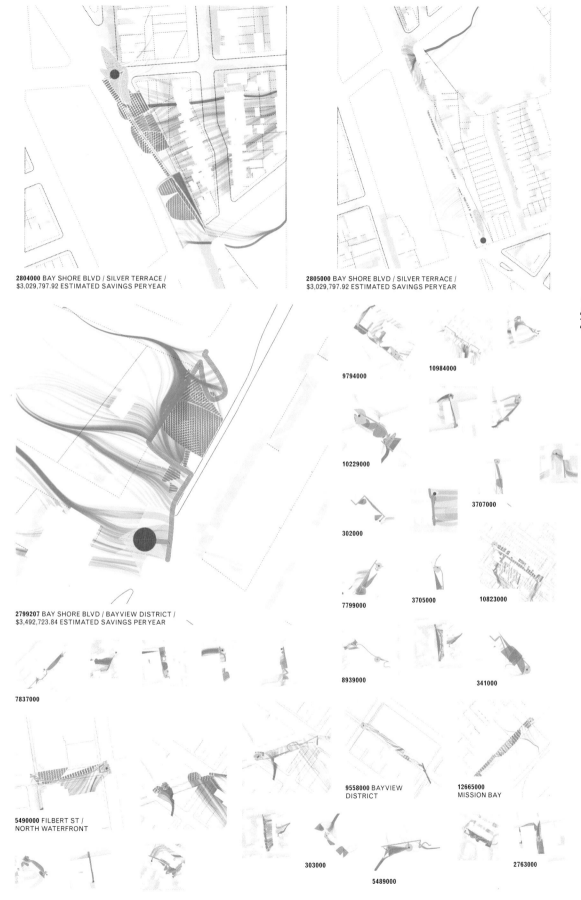

2804000 BAY SHORE BLVD / SILVER TERRACE /
$3,029,797.92 ESTIMATED SAVINGS PER YEAR

2805000 BAY SHORE BLVD / SILVER TERRACE /
$3,029,797.92 ESTIMATED SAVINGS PER YEAR

2799207 BAY SHORE BLVD / BAYVIEW DISTRICT /
$3,492,723.84 ESTIMATED SAVINGS PER YEAR

7837000

5490000 FILBERT ST /
NORTH WATERFRONT

9794000

10984000

10229000

3707000

302000

7799000

3705000

10823000

8939000

341000

9558000 BAYVIEW
DISTRICT

12665000
MISSION BAY

303000

2763000

5489000

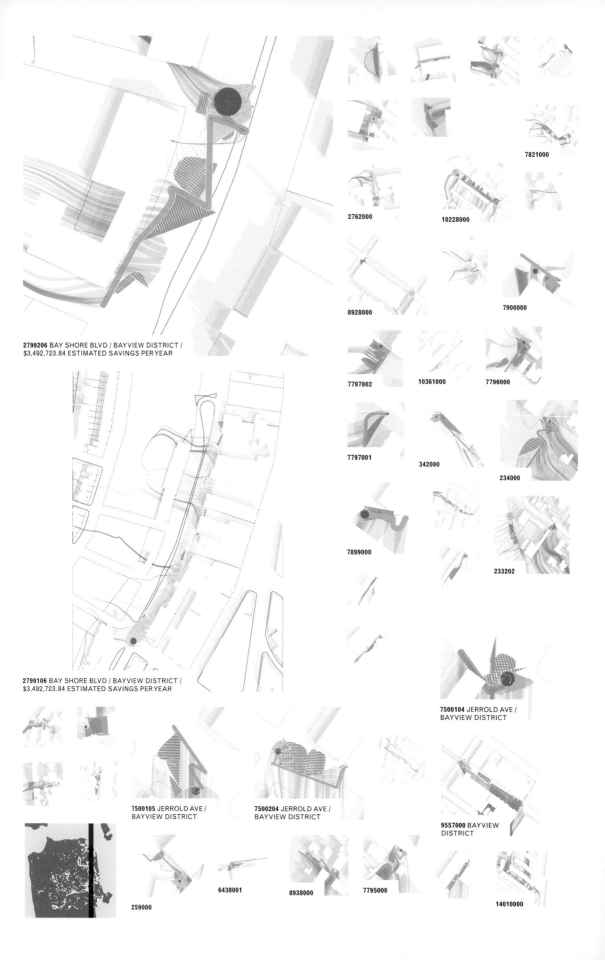

2799206 BAY SHORE BLVD / BAYVIEW DISTRICT /
$3,492,723.84 ESTIMATED SAVINGS PER YEAR

2799106 BAY SHORE BLVD / BAYVIEW DISTRICT /
$3,492,723.84 ESTIMATED SAVINGS PER YEAR

7821000

2762000

10228000

8928000

7900000

7797002

10361000

7796000

7797001

342000

234000

7899000

233202

7500104 JERROLD AVE /
BAYVIEW DISTRICT

7500105 JERROLD AVE /
BAYVIEW DISTRICT

7500204 JERROLD AVE /
BAYVIEW DISTRICT

9557000 BAYVIEW
DISTRICT

6438001

8938000

7795000

259000

14010000

2799205 BAY SHORE BLVD / BAYVIEW DISTRICT /
$3,029,797.92 ESTIMATED SAVINGS PER YEAR

12556202 THE EMBARCADERO / NORTH WATERFRONT /
$2,860,703.28 ESTIMATED SAVINGS PER YEAR

2806000 BAY SHORE BLVD / SILVER TERRACE /
$3,195,588.96 ESTIMATED SAVINGS PER YEAR

7898000

7468000

14009000

2956001

7500103 JERROLD AVE /
BAYVIEW DISTRICT

7794000

4611000

10932000

12556102 THE EMBARCADERO / NORTH WATERFRONT /
$2,860,703.28 ESTIMATED SAVINGS PER YEAR

8927000

344000

12664000
MISSION BAY

261000

7434000

7500203 JERROLD AVE /
BAYVIEW DISTRICT

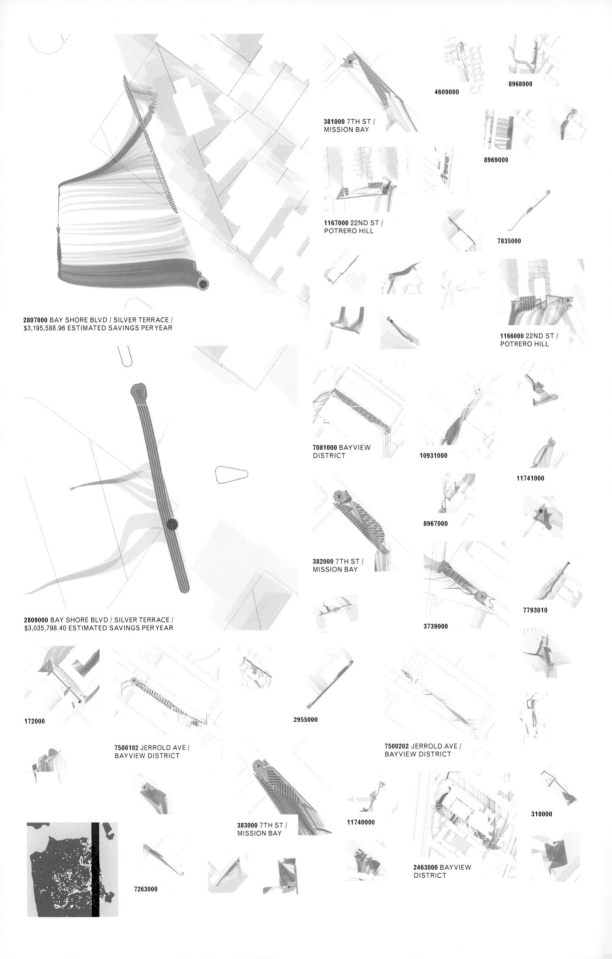

2807000 BAY SHORE BLVD / SILVER TERRACE /
$3,195,588.96 ESTIMATED SAVINGS PER YEAR

2809000 BAY SHORE BLVD / SILVER TERRACE /
$3,035,798.40 ESTIMATED SAVINGS PER YEAR

381000 7TH ST /
MISSION BAY

1167000 22ND ST /
POTRERO HILL

4609000

8968000

8969000

7835000

1166000 22ND ST /
POTRERO HILL

7081000 BAYVIEW
DISTRICT

10931000

11741000

8967000

382000 7TH ST /
MISSION BAY

3739000

7793010

172000

7500102 JERROLD AVE /
BAYVIEW DISTRICT

2955000

7500202 JERROLD AVE /
BAYVIEW DISTRICT

11740000

310000

383000 7TH ST /
MISSION BAY

7263000

2463000 BAYVIEW
DISTRICT

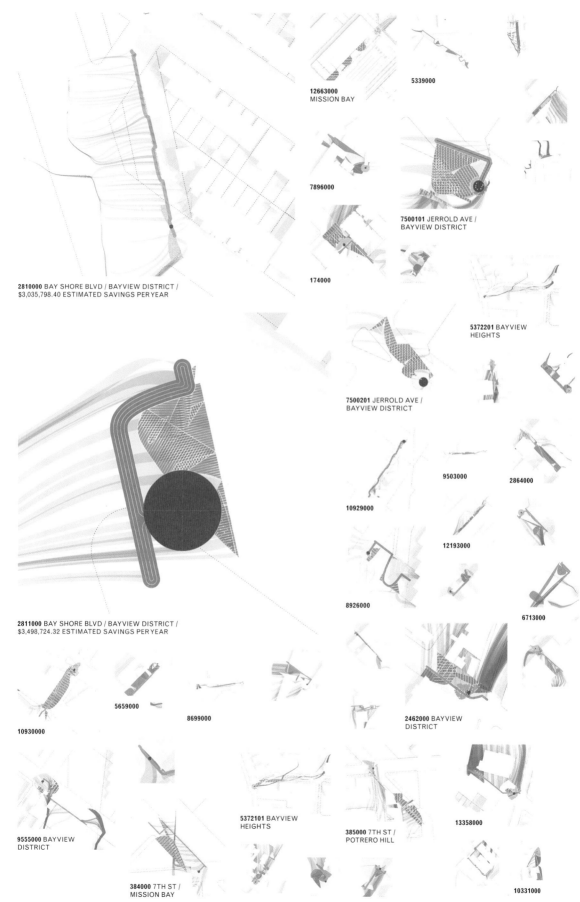

12663000
MISSION BAY

5339000

7896000

7500101 JERROLD AVE /
BAYVIEW DISTRICT

174000

5372201 BAYVIEW
HEIGHTS

7500201 JERROLD AVE /
BAYVIEW DISTRICT

9503000

2864000

10929000

12193000

8926000

6713000

2810000 BAY SHORE BLVD / BAYVIEW DISTRICT /
$3,035,798.40 ESTIMATED SAVINGS PER YEAR

2811000 BAY SHORE BLVD / BAYVIEW DISTRICT /
$3,498,724.32 ESTIMATED SAVINGS PER YEAR

5659000

8699000

2462000 BAYVIEW
DISTRICT

10930000

9555000 BAYVIEW
DISTRICT

5372101 BAYVIEW
HEIGHTS

385000 7TH ST /
POTRERO HILL

13358000

384000 7TH ST /
MISSION BAY

10331000

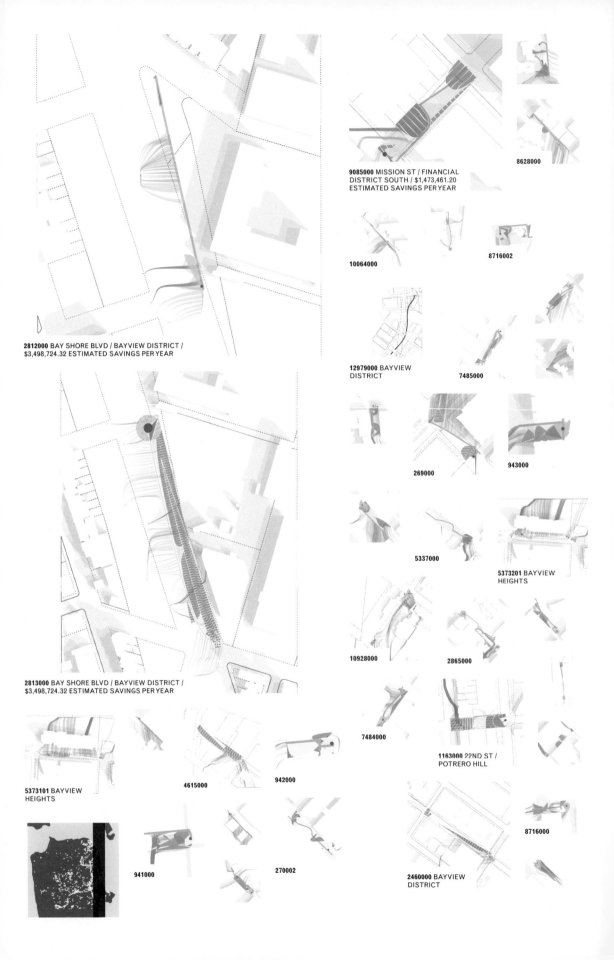

2812000 BAY SHORE BLVD / BAYVIEW DISTRICT /
$3,498,724.32 ESTIMATED SAVINGS PER YEAR

2813000 BAY SHORE BLVD / BAYVIEW DISTRICT /
$3,498,724.32 ESTIMATED SAVINGS PER YEAR

5373101 BAYVIEW
HEIGHTS

4615000

942000

941000

270002

9085000 MISSION ST / FINANCIAL
DISTRICT SOUTH / $1,473,461.20
ESTIMATED SAVINGS PER YEAR

8628000

10064000

8716002

12979000 BAYVIEW
DISTRICT

7485000

269000

943000

5337000

5373201 BAYVIEW
HEIGHTS

10928000

2865000

7484000

1163000 22ND ST /
POTRERO HILL

8716000

2460000 BAYVIEW
DISTRICT

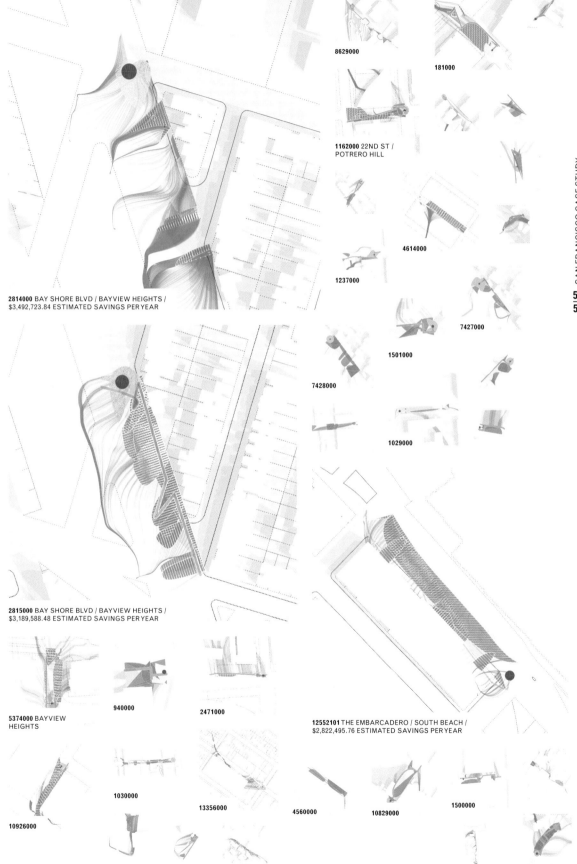

8629000

181000

1162000 22ND ST /
POTRERO HILL

4614000

1237000

7427000

1501000

7428000

1029000

2814000 BAY SHORE BLVD / BAYVIEW HEIGHTS /
$3,492,723.84 ESTIMATED SAVINGS PER YEAR

2815000 BAY SHORE BLVD / BAYVIEW HEIGHTS /
$3,189,588.48 ESTIMATED SAVINGS PER YEAR

5374000 BAYVIEW
HEIGHTS

940000

2471000

12552101 THE EMBARCADERO / SOUTH BEACH /
$2,822,495.76 ESTIMATED SAVINGS PER YEAR

10926000

1030000

13356000

4560000

10829000

1500000

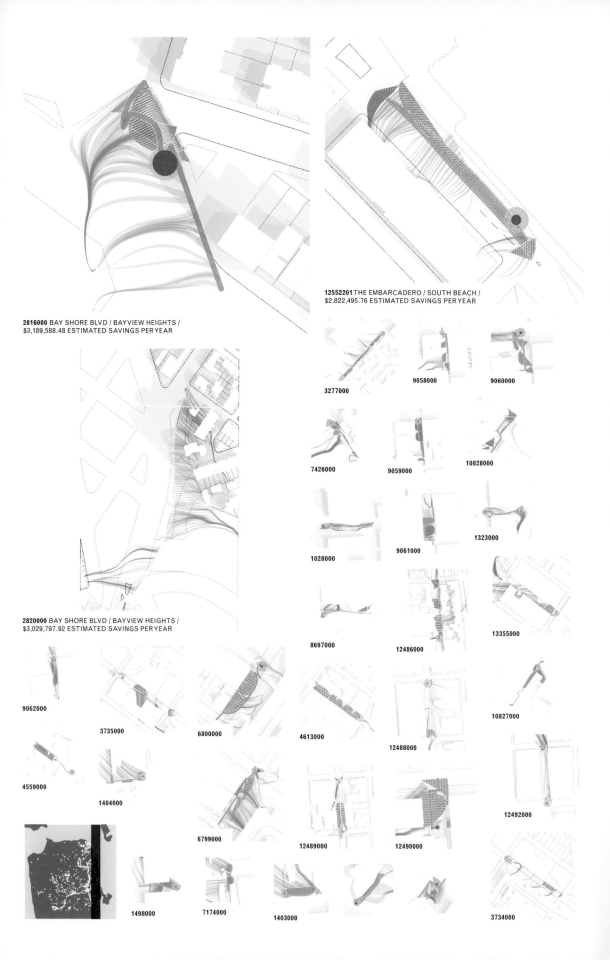

2816000 BAY SHORE BLVD / BAYVIEW HEIGHTS /
$3,189,588.48 ESTIMATED SAVINGS PER YEAR

12552201 THE EMBARCADERO / SOUTH BEACH /
$2,822,495.76 ESTIMATED SAVINGS PER YEAR

2820000 BAY SHORE BLVD / BAYVIEW HEIGHTS /
$3,029,797.92 ESTIMATED SAVINGS PER YEAR

3277000

9058000

9060000

7426000

9059000

10828000

1028000

9061000

1323000

8697000

12486000

13355000

9062000

3735000

6800000

4613000

12488000

10827000

4559000

1404000

6799000

12489000

12490000

12492000

1498000

7174000

1403000

3734000

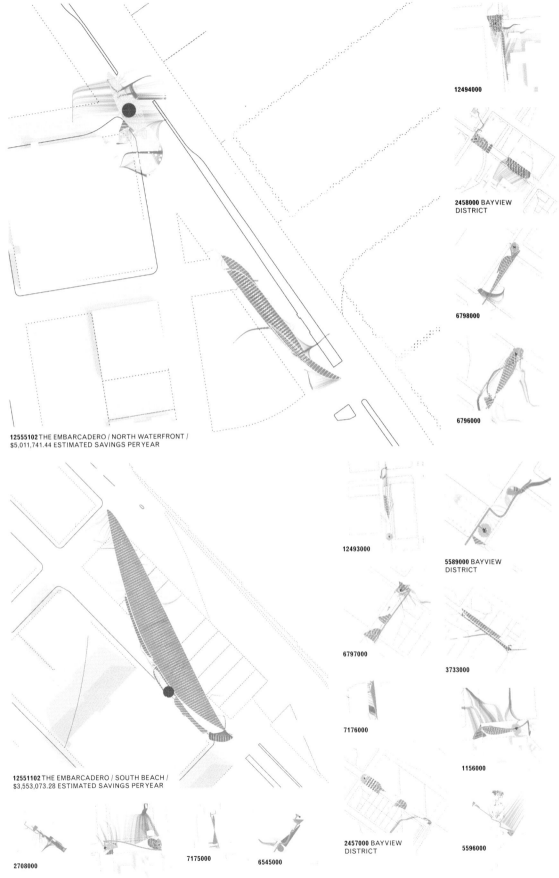

12494000

2458000 BAYVIEW DISTRICT

6798000

6796000

12555102 THE EMBARCADERO / NORTH WATERFRONT /
$5,011,741.44 ESTIMATED SAVINGS PER YEAR

12493000

5589000 BAYVIEW DISTRICT

6797000

3733000

7176000

1156000

12551102 THE EMBARCADERO / SOUTH BEACH /
$3,553,073.28 ESTIMATED SAVINGS PER YEAR

2708000

1157000

7175000

6545000

2457000 BAYVIEW DISTRICT

5596000

6794000

1319000

6793000

5595000

1318000

4900000

12555202 THE EMBARCADERO / NORTH WATERFRONT / $5,011,741.44 ESTIMATED SAVINGS PER YEAR

5113000

1399000

12935000

5112000

10971000

12551202 THE EMBARCADERO / SOUTH BEACH /
$3,553,073.28 ESTIMATED SAVINGS PER YEAR

5584000 BAYVIEW
DISTRICT

10216000

10808000

10215000

6531000

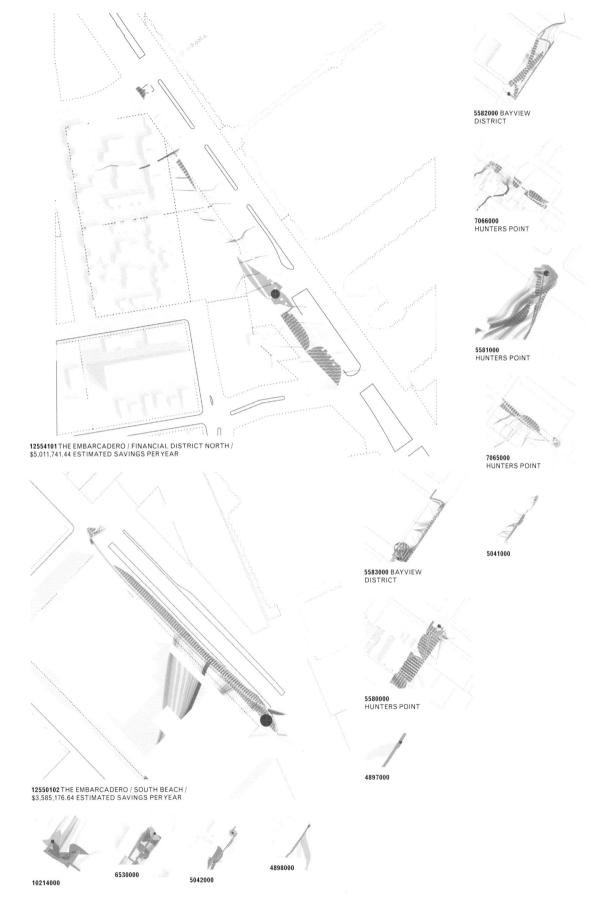

5582000 BAYVIEW DISTRICT

7066000 HUNTERS POINT

5581000 HUNTERS POINT

7065000 HUNTERS POINT

5041000

12554101 THE EMBARCADERO / FINANCIAL DISTRICT NORTH / $5,011,741.44 ESTIMATED SAVINGS PER YEAR

5583000 BAYVIEW DISTRICT

5580000 HUNTERS POINT

4897000

12550102 THE EMBARCADERO / SOUTH BEACH / $3,585,176.64 ESTIMATED SAVINGS PER YEAR

10214000

6530000

5042000

4898000

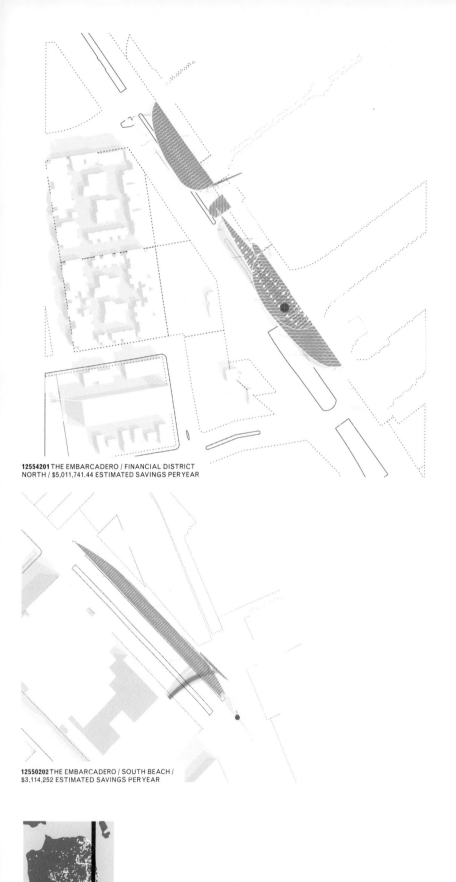

12554201 THE EMBARCADERO / FINANCIAL DISTRICT
NORTH / $5,011,741.44 ESTIMATED SAVINGS PER YEAR

12550202 THE EMBARCADERO / SOUTH BEACH /
$3,114,252 ESTIMATED SAVINGS PER YEAR

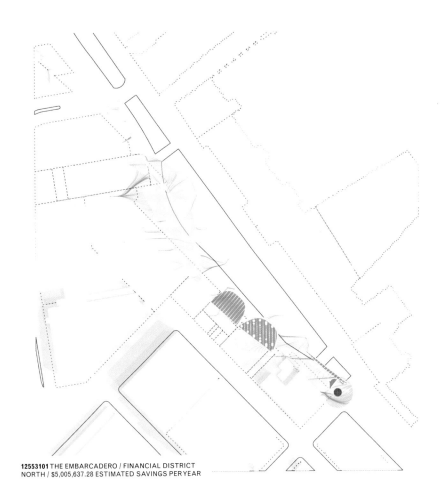

12553101 THE EMBARCADERO / FINANCIAL DISTRICT
NORTH / $5,005,637.28 ESTIMATED SAVINGS PER YEAR

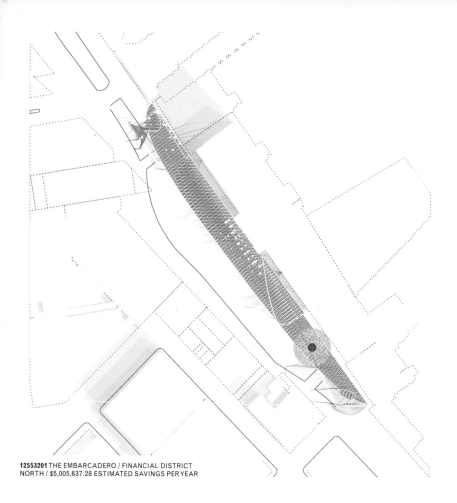

12553201 THE EMBARCADERO / FINANCIAL DISTRICT
NORTH / $5,005,637.28 ESTIMATED SAVINGS PER YEAR

Fake Estates and Reality Properties

LOCAL CODE

A half-dozen acid-free boxes in a Montreal archive house the collected papers of Gordon Matta-Clark. These are the chronologically ordered contents of his truncated life, and disordered desk, as collected by his widow, Jane Crawford. Near the end of the papers, prior to the hand-lettered condolences, is the death certificate itself, terse and tragic; his age, thirty-five. And just before are the wedding photos, from three months prior. Matta-Clark sits with Crawford in a Buddhist ceremony, orange magnolias and everyone cross-legged on the floor. The bride young and vital, the groom sallow and sick but still, it seems, elated.

Before this, in the traces of months and years of life preceding, lie other papers, other unfinished beginnings. These are tragic in a different way. Plans for uncompleted projects and half-begun adventures, these papers trace an ambitious outline. Much like the initial, geometric outlines that preceded Matta-Clark's own monumental cuttings, they document an essential future not yet come to pass.

FAKE ESTATES

Fake Estates was fifteen tiny, vacant parcels of New York City real estate purchased and documented by Gordon Matta-Clark, enfant terrible and ex-architect artist. This project is examined here as both precedent and provocation to the current work, as well as a deep and unfinished essay in its own right, on the catalytic interplay of form, order, community, and renovation in the life of cities.

Fake Estates is also simply this: the posthumously ordered contents of one of Matta-Clark's own files—although according to those who knew him, more often actually "piles."[1] In 1976 or 1977 he gave the box to his friend Norman Fisher to keep; it returned to Jane Crawford after both Matta-Clark and Fisher were dead, in 1979 or 1980, whereupon, after a brief glance at the disorder within, it was "stuck...away in a closet."[2]

1
"You have to understand his study was just piles. It looked like he never went in there, but he knew where stuff was." Betty Sussler, interview by Frances Richard et al., in Odd Lots: Revisiting Gordon Matta-Clark's "Fake Estates," ed. Jeffrey Kastner, Sina Najafi, and Frances Richard (New York: Cabinet Books, in conjunction with the Queens Museum of Art and White Columns, 2005), 47.

2
Jane Crawford, interview by Frances Richard et al, in Kastner, Najafi, and Richard, Odd Lots, 52.

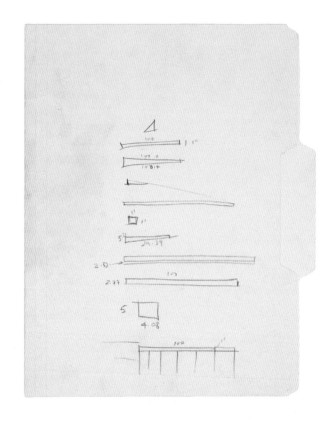

Fig. 1 — The folder holding the deeds to eleven properties in New York City, with their outlines sketched on the exterior
© The Estate of Gordon Matta-Clark. Courtesy of the Canadian Center for Architecture (CCA).

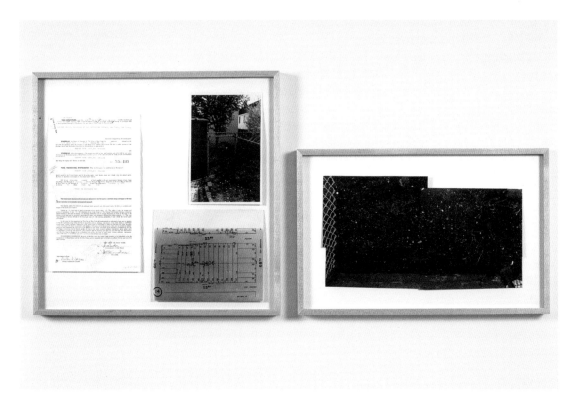

Fig. 2 — Gordon Matta-Clark, *Reality Properties: Fake Estates*—
"Long Island City" (grassy parking place), Block 556, Lot 103,
1973 (assembled 1992). Collage: 18 black-and-white photographs,
21 x 9 ½ in.; deed, 14 x 8 ½ in.; map, 8 x 10 in. © The Estate of
Gordon Matta-Clark/Artists Rights Society (ARS). Courtesy of
David Zwirner Gallery.

3
See Frances Richard et
al., "Spaces Between
Places: The Evolution of
Fake Estates, Part 1," in
Ibid., 38–48.

4
Frances Richard et al.,
"Mythology: The Evolution
of Fake Estates, Part II,"
in Ibid., 51–59, interview
with Jane Crawford, 52.

5
Gordon Matta-Clark,
Gordon Matta-Clark:
[IVAM Centre Julio
González, Valencia
3 diciembre 1992/31 enero
1993: Musée Cantini,
Marsella, 5 marzo/
23 mayo 1993: Serpentine
Gallery, Londres 30
junio/15 agosto 1993]
(Valencia: Institut
Valencià d'Art Modern
Centre Julio González,
1993), 183.

The box contained unsorted photographs, maps, and a folder of papers. The folder—a standard, off-white manila ⅓-cut file—remains decorated with eleven annotated shapes in pencil: two squares, two triangles, a trapezoid, and the rest long rectangles. These were the outlines of eleven of fifteen vacant and unused parcels of New York City real estate that Matta-Clark purchased and assembled in 1973 and 1974. (The artist's friend Manfred Hecht purchased several of them; perhaps Matta-Clark arrived at his first city real estate auction without even the thirty-five dollars necessary to pay for the otherwise unwanted parcels that he wanted, or maybe he was merely out of town at the time—records, memories, and the order of events are all today unclear.[3])

Papers relating to the parcels and their respective tax status and photographs of thirteen of them were enclosed in the file and an accompanying cardboard box. These—minus real estate receipts—were organized and assembled by Crawford (by then a well-established writer and filmmaker) in 1992 for an exhibition at the Institut Valencià d'Art Modern (IVAM) in Valencia, Spain, at the suggestion of the curator, Corinne Diserens.[4] In the catalog for that show, however, the work was dated to 1973.[5] Several of Matta-Clark's contemporaries recall an exhibition of portions of the material, held in 1974 at the 112 Greene Street gallery, although there is no surviving documentation of such an event.

As a direct result of this indirect history, *Fake Estates* becomes (at least) two different artworks.[6]

The first encompasses the lifetime of this documentary box after 1978: fourteen very private years in a closet, several decades of very public life as a matted and framed set of specimens, understood and endlessly interpreted as a speculation on real estate, property, ownership, and territory. This work has been critiqued, presented, discussed, and dissected at enormous length.[7]

The second is as a much more unfinished, unsettled, and discontinuous adventure. Historically and physically, this second *Fake Estates* is not so much things or places, but a network of objects, thoughts, speculations, and experiments, all tracing interconnected, tangent trajectories in Matta-Clark's contemporaneous oeuvre. This second version is also not so very different from the first; the themes of territory, ownership, modernity, and meaning are much the same. But the unresolved ambition of the undertaking, along with its interconnected, nascent neighbors in the folders of the archive (not to mention the folds of the artist's imagination and intelligence), prompt a set of speculations of which the documentary evidence of *Fake Estates* circa 1992 is only one constituent part.

"JUST GIT YOU THE GOOD BOOK"

Matta-Clark's encounter with architecture began, in some ways, before his birth. His father, the painter Roberto Matta, worked for two years in the studio of Le Corbusier—helping to draft the *Ville Radieuse*—before rejecting the master's work as suitable only for a (presumably nonexistent) "creature that lived in perfect harmony with the society and his work."[8] Matta père abandoned his young family in turn only a few months after Gordon and his twin brother, John Sebastian (known as Batan), were born in 1943, in New York, though he remained in their social circle. He returned to Europe in 1948.[9] After several "unstable" years, Matta-Clark's mother, Anne Clark, would marry the writer Hollis Alpert, who became a surrogate father to her boys.[10]

Matta-Clark's relationship with his father—both literal and intellectual—had all the resulting complexity one would expect. He was, in the opinion of those around him, perpetually and simultaneously following, competing with, and disdaining Matta.[11] "Matta was his psychological drive," his onetime partner Carol Goodden would reflect years later.[12] After moving to New York, where his ambitions in art mirrored Matta's, Matta-Clark would deliberately add his mother's maiden name to his own, for the first time.[13]

Some seven years prior—also in the steps of his father, and still carrying only his last name—Gordon Matta entered his career through the door of architecture, arriving at Cornell University's undergraduate professional program in 1962. Painting, his father would declare, "has one foot in architecture and the other in the dream."[14] At Cornell, his first-year grades were unremarkable (his grade in introductory English bested all of his grades in drawing,

6
See the recollections of Carol Goodden and Jeffrey Lew, the proprietor of 112 Greene Street in Frances Richard et al., "Spaces Between Places," in Kastner, Najafi, and Richard, Odd Lots, 40.

7
See in particular the volume cited above.

8
"Gesprach mit Matta," in Matta, Katalog Kestner-Gesellschaft, 1974, 4 (Hanover: Kestner-Gesellschaft 1974), 22–37. Translated and quoted in Nancy Miller, Matta: The First Decade (Waltham, MA: Rose Art Museum, Brandeis University, 1982), 19, exhibition catalog. By Matta's telling, the Surrealists greeted him by asking, "What, are you with Corbusier? How terrible!" "The masochistic and protestant Le Corbusier," Salvador Dalí was later to write, "is the inventor of the architecture of self-punishment." See Salvador Dalí, Dalí on Modern Art: The Cuckolds of Antiquated Modern Art (New York: Dial Press, 1957), 29.

9
His departure was precipitated by his official expulsion by the then New York–based Surrealists, related in turn to his role in precipitating the suicide of his friend, the proto-abstract painter Arshile Gorky, through a very public affair with his wife. See Miller, Matta, 35.
10
Pamela M. Lee and Gordon Matta-Clark, Object to Be Destroyed: The Work of Gordon Matta-Clark (Cambridge, MA: MIT Press, 2000), 5. I am greatly indebted to this incisive and erudite history.

11
Ibid.

design, and architectural history). In 1963 Matta-Clark was the driver in a car crash that proved fatal for one of his friends; a withdrawal from school followed, with a year abroad in Paris, in Matta's direct orbit. On his return to Cornell, Matta-Clark's grades did not so much improve as become more interestingly inconsistent: a raft of Ds in structures, but also the occasional strong grade (as in sculpture and junior design studio), mixed in with a sea of Bs and Cs until his final year, which merited high Bs, As, and an A+ in his final design studio.[15] His performance may well have been a symptom of his own elliptical intelligence and aversion to authority. But it also likely resulted from the intersection of his strong personality and Cornell's own transforming pedagogy.

For many years prior, there had been a tug-of-war within the School of Architecture at Cornell between its own Beaux-Arts history and the influence of the Bauhaus, whose methods had influenced pedagogy as early as 1929. By the 1960s, this conflict had essentially been resolved, broadly in favor of the latter, only to be in turn upset during Matta-Clark's tenure by a conflict with the sudden, enhanced influence of Corbusier, arriving through intense reinterpretation and advocacy at the hands of the theorist and historian Colin Rowe. Rowe arrived at Cornell in the fall of 1962, at the same time as Matta-Clark.[16] (For Rowe, this was the final, decades-long stop at the end of a peripatetic itinerary that included two years at the University of Liverpool, a year in New York, six at the University of Texas at Austin [UT], a previous year at Cornell, and then three at Cambridge in England.[17]) Colin Rowe's career was bookended by two deeply influential sets of architects of which he was the historical and critical figurehead. The first were his Austin colleagues, the so-called Texas Rangers, whose name draws from the title of a Cornell undergraduate doggerel, from Matta-Clark's freshman year, set to the tune of "Streets of Laredo":

> Oh I am a Ranger and I come from Texas
> Oh I am a Ranger and I'm teaching you
> We are Lee, John, and Werner and
>   we are all Rangers...
> Just git you the good book and you'll
>   be one too.[18]

The "book," in this case, refers to Corbusier's own *Ouvre Complet*, published in eight volumes between 1929 and 1970, and "Lee, John, and Werner" to Rowe's fellow refugees from UT then teaching studio at Cornell: Lee Hodgden, John Shaw, and Werner Seligman. These three and Rowe, as well as John Hejduk, Bernard Hoesli, the painter Robert Slutzky, and several others, had been brought to Austin by

12
Adding, "Batan was his guilt." Goodden to Corinne Diserens, in "Gordon Matta-Clark: The Reel World," in Gordon Matta-Clark, ed. Corinne Diserens (London: Phaidon, 2003), 213.

13
The critic Thomas Crow presents an alternative explanation, asserting that the name Gordon Matta-Clark is also that which would have been given to Matta-Clark had he been born in his father's native Chile, where a matronymic follows the traditional paternal surname. However, this is somewhat unstably grounded; as a hyphen is never used in Chile, nor anywhere where this Spanish tradition is followed, Matta's father was thus officially Roberto Matta Echaurren, not Matta-Echaurren. See Thomas Crow, "Gordon Matta-Clark," in Ibid., 44. See, by contrast, Carol Goodden's memory, "Gordon began to change his identity...He didn't want to be identified with his father, Matta, so he played with different names...He settled on Matta-Clark, and never seemed displeased with that" (ibid., 195). On balance, this author is inclined to imagine that Matta-Clark would have enjoyed both interpretations, and particularly the conflict between them; a very public rejection of the father in his own, American identity hiding a private, Latin-inflected tribute.

14
Matta quoted in Miller, Matta, 21.

15
Cornell University, Academic Transcript of Gordon Robert Matta-Echaurren, Gordon Matta-Clark Archive, Canadian Center for Architecture, Montreal. (hereafter CCA GMC) 002:004.

16
Kenneth Frampton, "Notes on American Architectural Education from the End of the Nineteenth Century until the 1970s," Lotus International 27, no. 3 (1981): 27.

17
Alexander Caragonne, The Texas Rangers: Notes from an Architectural Underground (Cambridge, MA: MIT Press, 1995), 10–11.

18
Colin Rowe, Texas, Pre-Texas, Cambridge, vol. 1 of As I Was Saying: Recollections and Miscellaneous Essays, ed. Alexander Caragonne (Cambridge, MA: MIT Press, 1996), 37.

Bay Area–émigré Harwell Hamilton Harris in the previous decade to help "stir up" UT's long-established methods. Which they did. The pedagogical program developed by the Rangers between 1954 and 1958 was as ultimately successful as it was initially ruinous to their UT employment; a senior-faculty revolt over the program led directly to Harris's resignation as director in 1956, and, absent his patronage, the young Rangers soon followed.[19]

Abandoning the social and political foundations of Bauhaus-inflected European modernism, the UT methodology appropriated Bauhaus precedents of formal analysis and "spatial" practice and applied them centrally to the precedents of Le Corbusier's concrete 1930s villas (particularly Garches and Savoye) as a generative tool for student work. This method was historical yet founded on manifold precedents, and was fundamentally shaped by Rowe's formalist outlook—an approach launched in his monumentally influential 1947 essay outlining formal and mathematical relationships between the canonical Corbusian villas and the work of Palladio. (The approach can be traced in turn to Rowe's own schooling in the Warburg institute of the 1930s and 1940s, where the influence of the Wölfflinian method—the comparison of two images with dual slide projectors being the most tangible effect on the classroom—was extended by Rowe's teachers, through a range of theoretical frameworks, including Gestalt psychology.) This influence was directly reflected in design teachings, and in exercises such as the "nine-square grid" problem developed by Hejduk and Slutzky together with Lee Hirsche.[20] Hejduk would also leave UT for Cornell before moving to the Cooper Union in 1960, where Slutzky would join him in 1968—and where the exercise is still taught. The *sine qua non* of the UT syllabus, the nine-square problem involved a small, gridded plateau on which students crafted and endlessly realigned primitives of Corbusian form: architecture literally without context, in conversation with itself.

While Rowe himself characterizes his influence on the Cornell undergraduate program as "inconsistent" during the time of Matta-Clark's BArch (his official title was director of the graduate program in urban design), his influence must have been palpable, first in Matta-Clark's own freshman Introduction to Design, taught jointly by Hogden and Seligman, and then directly, in the lecture course on Renaissance architecture he taught in the fall of Matta-Clark's second year,

19
Caragonne,
Texas Rangers, 64.

20
Ibid., 190–91.

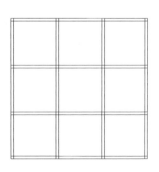 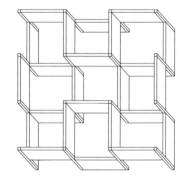

Fig. 3 — The Nine-Square Grid Problem. Adapted by the author from the exhibition catalog, Cooper Union for the Advancement of Science and Art, *Education of an Architect: A Point of View* (New York: Museum of Modern Art, 1971). Drawn by the author

21
Colin Rowe, Cornelliania,
vol. 2 of As I Was Saying,
6.

22
Anthony Vidler,
"'Architecture-to-be':
Notes on Architecture in
the Work of Matta and
Gordon Matta-Clark,"
in Briony Fer, Betti-Sue
Hertz, Matta, and
Gordon Matta-Clark,
Transmission: The Art
of Matta and Gordon
Matta-Clark (San Diego,
CA: San Diego Museum
of Art, 2006), 68.

23
Liza Béar, "Splitting: The
Humphrey Street Building,
Interview with Gordon
Matta-Clark," Avalanche
(December 1974): 36.
Anthony Vidler makes this
connection in his essay
noted above.

24
Museum of Modern Art
(New York, NY), Five
Architects: Eisenman,
Graves, Gwathmey,
Hejduk, Meier (New York:
Oxford University Press,
1975), 1.

25
Ibid.

26
See in particular Jennifer
S. Light, From Warfare
to Welfare: Defense
Intellectuals and Urban
Problems in Cold War
America (Baltimore:
Johns Hopkins University
Press, 2003), 139–42.

after his return from Paris.[21] In the memory of Anthony Vidler, Rowe's student from an identical course he taught at Cambridge a year prior, the survey dwelt almost entirely on formal studies of layered Renaissance facades.[22] (The course was given in the year before Cornell switched to using letter grades, and so Matta-Clark earned a 72.)

We can easily imagine that it was precisely this endless overlay of facade studies that produced the following exchange in a 1974 interview with Liza Béar in *Avalanche*—the bible of the downtown art scene—on the occasion of Matta-Clark's *Splitting*:

> Béar: You studied architecture at Cornell, didn't you.
> Matta-Clark: Yeah, that was my first trap. But the things we studied always involved such surface formalism that I had never a sense of the ambiguity of a structure, the ambiguity of a place, and that's the quality I'm interested in generating in what I do.[23]

WHITE ON WHITE

Rowe's formally precise, para-historical approach to time, mass, and surface played a central role in the UT curriculum, as well as its later development at Cornell. It also became central to the second UT-and-Cornell-connected group of architects of which Rowe was an "honorary member" and critical figurehead: Peter Eisenman, Michael Graves, Charles Gwathmey, John Hejduk, and Richard Meier—the New York Five, or, as they came to be known, "the Whites." This was not a description of race (though, given the collection of Caucasians, it might as well have been) but rather the complexion of their Corbinflected buildings and the cover of the 1975 MoMA catalog *Five Architects*, which secured their lasting classification together as well as their rise to prominence.

The catalog's introduction, by curator Arthur Drexler, renders explicit the retreat from politics that accompanied the group's formal concerns; "architecture," it is declared, "is the least likely instrument with which to accomplish the revolution."[24] Rowe begins his second, longer introduction by excusing the apolitical nature of the work through an optimistic, alternative argument that in America, the revolution had already—in 1776—occurred. Rowe further presents the work as a necessary contrast to the "latent" politics of Miesian and Brutalist styles then in vogue, and goes on to establish another important contrast in the same paragraph, not to an architectural style, per se, but to the collision of what Rowe himself enquotes "'the computer' and 'the people.'"[25] More specifically, this is a nod not to fellow architects but to the technocratically inflected planners also inhabiting Cornell's Sibley Hall, educating Matta-Clark and many others on the data-driven model of city planning and urban design then in common currency.[26] Another undergraduate doggerel illustrates the ubiquity of urban calculation:

I walked uptown and down for a year
counting cars at intersections.
And I made a chart with Zipatone,
statistical perfections!
I then was ready to draw a plan,
but they said, "No forsooth, you are not ready.
You must first calculate, analyze and comprise
more nonsensical, irrelevant data!"[27]

Matta-Clark would have been exposed to this approach to urban design and planning not just in classes in Ithaca, but also in curricular visits to planning and government offices in New York City, where systems-based techniques would reach its apex under John Lindsay, who brought into the Mayor's office a dedicated suite of RAND consultants.[28] And it was (briefly but influentially) in this second milieu that Matta-Clark undertook his (only, unloved) professional appointment as an architect after college: drafting maps and charts for the redevelopment agency of Binghamton, New York.[29] This was a city where "redevelopment" comprised tearing down much of the city's historic fabric in favor of well-analyzed government centers, arenas, and highways.[30] It was the same year, after all, that Hubert Humphrey, then the nation's vice president, had declared that "the techniques that are going to put a man on the Moon are going to be exactly the techniques that we are going to need to clean up our cities."[31] That is to say, numerical, systematic, and, even as Humphrey spoke, already in large part underway, especially in New York.[32]

The young Matta-Clark was, as a result, flanked by two distinct abstract frameworks claiming authority over the city. On one hand lay the black-and-white, solid yet immaterial abstractions of Cornell's architectural curriculum. And on the other, the equally technocratic abstractions of late-1960s sociological and "scientific" planning. (Urban citizens were thus described in the rest of the doggerel above: "All had a number but never a name...Perfection of standardization."[33])

For Matta-Clark, though, staying in Ithaca provided a huge, deeply influential bonus: a role as assistant and hanger-on to the pathbreaking exhibition Earth Art, staged at Cornell in 1969, in which the campus became a temporary center for the nascent movement and featured a series of commissioned installations adorning the glacial landscape. To enact the actual art on Cornell's earth, Matta-Clark served as an assistant to the artist Dennis Oppenheim, cutting a long, dogleg trench into frozen Cayuga Lake with a chainsaw, and, perhaps even more influentially, loaned the earthwork artist Robert Smithson his truck. Seizing the latter opportunity (Smithson was an idol), he cultivated a steady, ongoing friendship with the pathbreaking artist, spending days at the artist's studio and loft and finding himself the recipient of long lectures—particularly, as remembered by Smithson's wife, on the theme of entropy as a creative practice.[34] Oppenheim remained a close friend and confidante as well, easing Matta-Clark's transition to the downtown scene.

27
The song continues, "In the basement I stayed for another year, / Filling up the calculator. / There were jobless and homeless and dogless and boneless, / And some with no refrigerator. / They all had a number but never a name, / Not a face for identification. / But they all had a chicken in every pot, / Perfection of standardization. Rowe, Cornelliania, 3.

28
Light, From Warfare to Welfare, 64–65.

29
CCA GMC 001:071. Matta-Clark would write in an early biographical statement, "I was born in New York, 1945. I studied French literature at the Sorbonne, 1963–1964 then returned to Cornell Univ. To major in architectural and urban design 1964–1968, after which I worked a year for the Binghamton, NY Urban Renewal...."

30
Gerald Smith, Partners All: A History of Broome County, New York (Virginia Beach, VA: Donning, 2006).

31
"HHH on the Space Program," Aerospace Technology 21, no. 24 (May 20, 1968): 19.

32
See Light, From Warfare to Welfare, 65–75.

33
Rowe, Cornelliania, 3.

34
Lee and Matta-Clark, Object to Be Destroyed, 36.

Matta-Clark's final attitude toward his architectural education, not to mention the Cornell crowd's movement (parallel and alongside his own downstate trajectory) into the city's avant-garde, was never so violently and publicly illustrated as when he shot out the windows of Peter Eisenman's Institute for Architecture and Urban Studies (IAUS) with an air rifle. "He once borrowed my air-gun to do a piece at the Institute for Architecture and Urban Studies," remembers Oppenheim. "I was extremely excited about that."[35]

According to Andrew MacNair, curator of the exhibition Idea as Model, which precipitated the act, Matta-Clark's contribution was supposed to be something quite different: the partial, artful demolition of the windowless, sheetrocked cube of a conference room in the center of the IAUS space. (Also included were Graves, Gwathmey, Hejduk, and Meier, as well as more up-and-coming designers such as Tod Williams, Rodolfo Machado, and Jorge Silvetti.[36]) But in the predawn hours of the long night of gallery installation, Matta-Clark arrived with a very different contribution from the imagined conference-room cutting. He entered the gallery bearing sheaves of photographs of shard-shrouded, defenestrated housing projects mounted on matboard—and a gun. After asking permission to break a few, already-cracked panes in the lofty Chelsea studio, Matta-Clark

35
Dennis Oppenheim, interview in Diserens, Gordon Matta-Clark, 192.

36
Kenneth Frampton and Silvia Kolbowski, Idea as Model: 22 Architects 1976–1980, IAUS exhibition catalogs 1, cat. 3 (New York: Institute for Architecture and Urban Studies and Rizzoli International, 1981), exhibition catalog.

68
69

Fig. 4 — Gordon Matta-Clark, *Window Blow Out*, for the Institute for Architecture and Urban Studies, 1976. **Black-and-white photograph.** © The Estate of Gordon Matta-Clark/ARS. Courtesy of David Zwirner Gallery.

shattered every one.[37] And if the critical and historical position was implied, the emotion was not. "These were the guys I studied with at Cornell," he reportedly explained; "these were my teachers. I hate what they stand for."[38] The windows were just as quickly replaced by an appalled Eisenman, though in the catalog to the exhibition, emerging four years later, he allowed only that the installation made the gallery "too chilly."[39]

ANTI-ARCHITECT ARCHIT'ETRE

"Keep writing me, I'm very interested in your anti-architect Archit'etre," Matta wrote to Matta-Clark in an archived and undated letter, the cross-language pun meaning "how to be an architect" and "against architects" at once.[40]

"Work with abandoned spaces," Matta-Clark was to write in 1974, "began with my concern for the life of the city of which a major side effect is the metabolization of old buildings. [In New York] as in many urban centers the availability of empty and neglected structures was a prime textual reminder of the ongoing fallacy of renewal through modernization."[41] His arrival in New York in 1970 marked not just a moment of reinvention of his own self (a new name, a new resolve toward artistic practice), but also of the reinvention and repurposing of much of the city itself that he encountered. *Metabolization* is a word well chosen here. From the Greek μεταβολή, *metabole*, or "change," it acquired the specific meaning in the nineteenth century of the complex network of interactions characteristic of life.[42] And it was at the living fabric of New York that Matta-Clark threw himself most robustly: sessions with Smithson, a circle of friends in the new artistic neighborhood of SoHo, and the circumstances of renovating and physical crafting of a home in it all. His architectural training was here directly applied, not as a theoretical position, but as practical experience and understanding of studs, pipes, and sheetrock. He became an invaluable resource in the circle of pioneers transforming the ironclad industrial spaces of SoHo into that eventual paradigm of gentrification: the downtown loft.

In April 1972 Matta-Clark sent a long letter to his father, responding to a postcard ("a bautiful [*sic*] architectural treat and the 1st postcard you have ever sent a real surprise"). A marked-up and multiply revised draft survives in the Matta-Clark archive. It describes Matta-Clark's recent move to his first loft, which had "space for my sculpture-photography," with then partner Carol Goodden, a welcome move "from a studio where we were constantly fighting with our landlord."[43] The letter also touches at length on the difficulties experienced by his twin brother, Batan. "He has been in and out of hospital now finally committed himself to Belview [*sic*] where I visit him from time to time." The brothers' financial security was each, Matta-Clark explains, tied up in real estate. Batan, beset by depression and delusion, would tragically end his life with a fall from his twin's own window in 1976, just before, and no doubt contributing emotionally to, Matta-Clark's attack on IAUS. But four years earlier, in the letter, the focus of Matta and Matta-Clark's shared attention was the renovation

37
Andrew MacNair, interview in Gordon Matta-Clark: A Retrospective, ed. Mary Jane Jacob (Chicago: Museum of Contemporary Art, 1985), 96.

38
Ibid.

39
Who, in MacNair's recollection, compared the broken glass to Kristallnacht. (Ibid.); Frampton and Kolbowski, Idea as Model.

40
Matta to Matta-Clark, undated, CCA GMC PHCON2002:0016.

41
Gordon Matta-Clark, undated and unaddressed proposal, ca. 1974, CCA GMC 001:073 1/5.

42
Oxford English Dictionary, s.v. "metabolism," OED Online, accessed January 1, 2015, http://www.oed.com/view/Entry/117160.

43
CCA GMC 002:038.

of a loft on Twelfth Street, south of Union Square, providing a place for Batan to live and work, or, should he so decide, a rental income instead. It was this concern for Batan, as well as architecture—and so in particular the architecture of this concern—that brought father and son together. Matta *père* underwrote the work, which was undertaken in turn by Matta-Clark. "I am now some what of a contractor," he concludes, reassuring Matta, "The rising value of the loft and equity (money payed [*sic*] back on mortgage) increas maesk [*sic*] it an ok [*sic*] the securest of investments."[44] In the end, a twin hope of remaking through renovation—one physical, the body of the apartment, the other psychological and physiological, in the person of Matta-Clark's own troubled double.

REALITY PROPERTIES

And here, then, some observations:

First, Matta-Clark's pathbreaking cuttings, transformations, and excisions of built fabric, dated curatorially to several transgressive, small actions on abandoned housing in the Bronx, followed by quickly public, and curatorially popular actions on masonry buildings in Matta-Clark's visit to Europe in 1974, are in point of fact extensions and alterations to operations begun several years earlier on the built fabric of New York City.

The work Matta-Clark himself identified as beginning this thread of production—the moving of a single pipe to the interior of a gallery, along with photography of its further travel in the building in 1971—is as unimaginable without the artist's experience in loft construction as it is (in retrospect) inevitable as a result. Even the separate inspirations cited by other contemporaries for Matta-Clark's building cuts all emerge from Matta-Clark's renovation, such as Carol Goodden's citation of a "wall sandwich" Matta-Clark cut from an unneeded partition while renovating the restaurant/art space FOOD in 1972, or Manfred Hecht's description of the cutting works "as an extension of" Matta-Clark's Fourth Street loft renovation in 1971.[45]

Second, the strange realities of land, value, ownership, and use on which *Fake Estates* rests were not idle, artistic abstractions, but the lifeblood reality of 1970s New York: near bankrupt, falling apart, but also being held together and rebuilt by the artists of Matta-Clark's *milieu*. The investment of $17,000—and the equity of Matta-Clark's own toil—in Batan's Twelfth Street loft transformed an abandoned industrial space into something that generated $5,000 per year in 1972 (let alone today).[46] Matta-Clark's own career as a renovator and speculator (by 1976 he, Carol Goodden, and Dennis Oppenheim owned a whole building at 39 Walker Street) would also literally have exposed him to the exercise of cataloging and acquiring property—abandoned and cheaply auctioned above all—long before he attended the auction in October 1973 at which the first *Fake Estates* were purchased. Alana Heiss, whose work identifying and acquiring abandoned property for artistic purposes would become the contemporary gallery P.S.1, has a specific memory of

44
Ibid.

45
Carol Goodden, interview in Jacob, Gordon Matta-Clark, 39; Manfred Hecht, interview in ibid., 73.

46
In 2014 an apartment in the building sold for $2.95 million. See "42 E 12th St Apt 2," Zillow, accessed January 8, 2014, http://www.zillow.com/homes/for_sale/31498514_zpid/days_sort/40.735429,-73.989261,40.731361,-73.995168_rect/17_zm/1_fr/.

introducing Matta-Clark to the world of abandoned property auctions. She would recall, as well, "He wasn't a self-less entrepreneur. He loved making investments, funding spaces, buying properties."[47] And so, even if he had never become famous for his own, more creative use of the Sawzall and building jack, Matta-Clark, as contractor to himself and his contemporaries, would have remained an essential actor in one of the city's great remakings: the transformation of an abandoned, industrial SoHo into a landscape of creative practice, in which the renovated urban landscape itself (as in the case of FOOD, but also for example Matta-Clark's contemporary Donald Judd's workshop and studio) became a work of art.

Gordon Matta-Clark at work on *Splitting*, 1974
© The Estate of Gordon Matta-Clark/ARS.
Courtesy SFMOMA.

Here, Matta-Clark's conception of his own architectural work begins to take shape: concerned not so much with the physical shape or statistical outlines of the city but with its processes and operations (just as his own drawings and sketchbooks would abandon fixed outlines to become filled with circling cascades of arrows). In this light, the famously extended, tool-inflected building cuts can be seen not just as they have come to us—in precise, documented moments of staged, entropic intervention—but also as a deliberate framing, staging, and figural delineation of the perpetual process of deconstructing and remaking urban fabric. All of this, with an attentiveness to the documentation that combined the exhaustive practices of mundane site documentation with the alchemical creation of curatorial artifact: an amplification and annealing of the hard edge of renovation. Take, as an example, the house at 322 Humphrey Street.

The top-to-toe *Splitting* of the Englewood, New Jersey, house in 1974 cemented Matta-Clark's New York reputation; Matta-Clark only had access to the house (already slated for demolition) because the land underneath was the investment property of Horace Solomon, his gallerist. Matta-Clark had already renovated and built two gallery spaces for the Solomons; while the splitting of Humphrey Street was even more deliberate and delineated, the tools—string, level, Sawzall, and chisel—were precisely the same, as well as, in many ways, the increase in value. (The four attic corners of the house, preserved as the work *Splitting: Four Corners*, rest in the collection of San Francisco's SFMOMA, their value countless times that of their structure of origin.)

47
Richard et al., in Kastner, Najafi, and Richard, Odd Lots, 40.

Fig. 5 — Gordon Matta-Clark, *Splitting* (322 Humphrey Street, Englewood, New Jersey), 1974. Gelatin silver photograph.
© The Estate of Gordon Matta-Clark/ARS. Courtesy SFMOMA.

"COMB YOUR HEIR RIGHTS"

A 1971 journal entry:

> The piece is to buy a small piece of New York. Real.
> Sell the Air Right—Mineral and water to your truck.
> Exercise your air rights
> Comb your heir rights.
> A comfortable place to live between the bricks.
> Ash-Track
> An Abstract A (the History of property.)
> Wills!![48]

The development of this process-focused legacy of architecture, city, and the arbitrary nature of property flows clearly through Matta-Clark's creative collaboration with a group of contemporaries, centered around the 112 Greene Street gallery. They called themselves the "Anarchitecture Group," and consisted of Carol Goodden, Laurie Anderson, Tina Girouard, Suzanne Harris, Richard Nonas, and

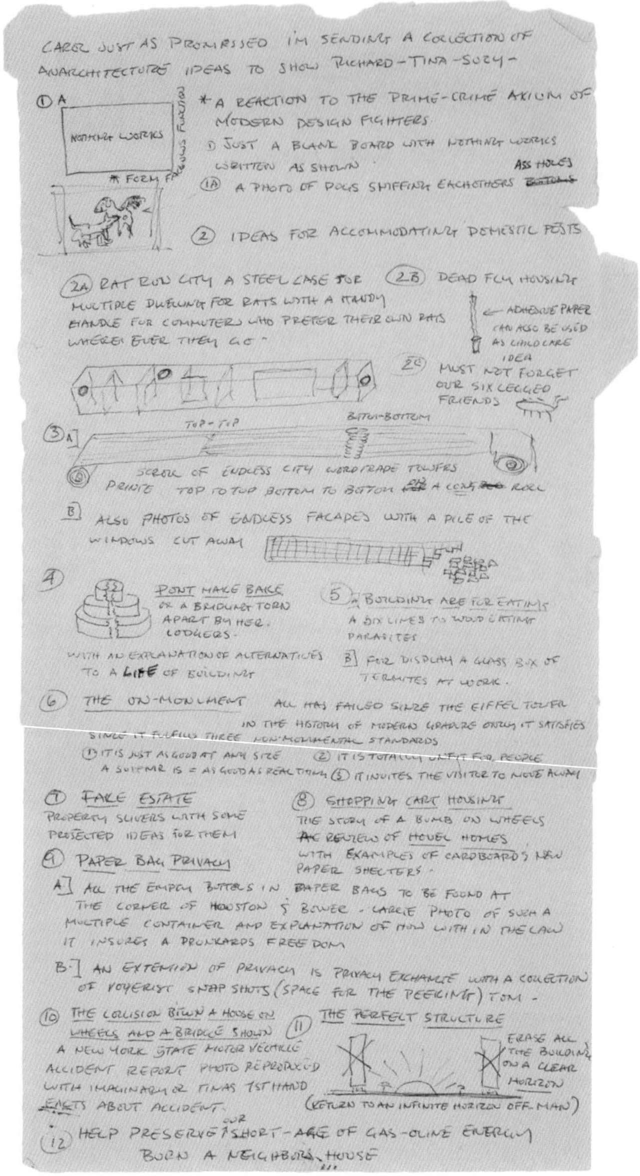

CAROL JUST AS PROMISSED I'M SENDING A COLLECTION OF
ANARCHITECTURE IDEAS TO SHOW RICHARD-TINA-SUZY-
① A
NOTHING WORKS
FOLLOWS FUNCTION
* FORM F
* A REACTION TO THE PRIME-CRIME AXIUM OF MODERN DESIGN FIGHTERS
① JUST A BLANK BOARD WITH NOTHING WORKS WRITTEN AS SHOWN
(1A) A PHOTO OF DOGS SNIFFING EACHOTHERS ~~BOTTOMS~~ ASS HOLES
② IDEAS FOR ACCOMMODATING DOMESTIC PESTS
(2A) RAT RUN CITY A STEEL CASE FOR MULTIPLE DWELLING FOR RATS WITH A HANDY HANDLE FOR COMMUTERS WHO PREFER THEIR OWN RATS WHERE EVER THEY GO"
(2B) DEAD FLY HOUSING
← ADHESIVE PAPER CAN ALSO BE USED AS CHILD CARE IDEA
(2C) MUST NOT FORGET OUR SIX LEGGED FRIENDS
③ A] TOP-TOP
BOTTOM-BOTTOM
SCROLL OF ENDLESS CITY WORLD TRADE TOWERS PRINTS TOP TO TOP BOTTOM TO BOTTOM ON A LONG ROLL
B] ALSO PHOTOS OF ENDLESS FACADES WITH A PILE OF THE WINDOWS CUT AWAY
④ DONT MAKE BAKE OR A BUILDING TORN APART BY HER LODGERS.
WITH AN EXPLANATION OF ALTERNATIVES TO A LIFE OF BUILDING
⑤ BUILDING ARE FOR EATING
A DIX LINES TO WOOD EATING PARASITES
B] FOR DISPLAY A GLASS BOX OF TERMITES AT WORK.
⑥ THE ON-MONUMENT ALL HAS FAILED SINCE THE EIFFEL TOWER IN THE HISTORY OF MODERN GRANDURE ONLY IT SATISFIES SINCE IT FULFILLS THREE NON-MONUMENTAL STANDARDS
① IT IS JUST AS GOOD AT ANY SIZE A SOUVENIR IS = AS GOOD AS REAL THING
② IT IS TOTALLY UNFIT FOR PEOPLE
③ IT INVITES THE VISITOR TO MOVE AWAY
⑦ FAKE ESTATE
PROPERTY SLIVERS WITH SOME PROJECTED IDEAS FOR THEM
⑧ SHOPPING CART HOUSING
THE STORY OF A BUMB ON WHEELS ~~AK~~ REVIEW OF HOVEL HOMES WITH EXAMPLES OF CARDBOARD'S NEW PAPER SHELTERS.
⑨ PAPER BAG PRIVACY
A] ALL THE EMPTY BOTTLES IN PAPER BAGS TO BE FOUND AT THE CORNER OF HOUSTON & BOWER. LARGE PHOTO OF SUCH A MULTIPLE CONTAINER AND EXPLANATION OF HOW WITH IN THE LAW IT INSURES A DRUNKARDS FREEDOM
B] AN EXTENTION OF PRIVACY IS PRIVACY EXCHANGE WITH A COLLECTION OF VOYERIST SNAP SHOTS (SPACE FOR THE PEEKING) TOM -
⑩ THE COLLISION B'TWN A HOUSE ON WHEELS AND A BRIDGE SHOWN
A NEW YORK STATE MOTOR VECHILE ACCIDENT REPORT PHOTO REPRODUCED WITH IMAGINARY OR TINAS 1ST HAND FACTS ABOUT ACCIDENT.
⑪ THE PERFECT STRUCTURE
ERASE ALL THE BUILDINGS ON A CLEAR HORIZON
(RETURN TO AN INFINITE HORIZON OFF-MAN)
⑫ HELP PRESERVE OUR SHORT-AGE OF GAS-OLINE ENERGY
BURN A NEIGHBORS HOUSE

Fig. 6 — Gordon Matta-Clark, aerogramme to the Anarchitecture Group, 1973 © The Estate of Gordon Matta-Clark. Courtesy of the CCA.

others, all of them musicians, performance artists, and sculptors; Matta-Clark was the only one with formal architectural training. The name, a typical Matta-Clark neologism, could mean at least two things. First, "An-architecture": *an*, the Greek ἀν, meaning "without," or "wanting" (the implied extra word, *an-archy*, meaning "without a leader"; the *archi-tect* the leader of τέκτων, builders, or craftsmen). Then, "ana-(a)rchitecture": *ana*, the greek ἀνά; "back, again"; literally, "architecture anew."

"Our thinking about anarchitecture," Matta-Clark explained to journalist and interviewer Liza Béar in 1974, "was more elusive than doing pieces that would demonstrate an alternate attitude to buildings, or, rather to the attitudes that determine containerization of usable space. Those attitudes are very deepset....Architecture is environment too. When you're living in a city the whole fabric is architectural in some sense. We were thinking more about metaphoric voids, gaps, leftover spaces, places that were not developed...."[49] Even the name of the group was not allowed to be fixed: it changed with each mention, from "Anarchy Torture," to "An Arctic Lecture," to "An Art Collector."[50]

In 1974 the group showed a collection of anonymous photographs at the Greene Street space, many of which were assembled from archival expeditions by Matta-Clark. They showed, above all, architecture and city in flux; a train that had become a bridge, a house on a trailer on a boat, graveyards and skyscrapers, parts of Penn Station in the Meadowlands. The year prior, Matta-Clark sent an aerogramme—a single, folded page, the postage inexpensive—to the group. Twenty small sketches and proposals coat every surface.

49
Béar, "Splitting," 34.

50
Lee and Matta-Clark, Object to Be Destroyed, 105.

Along with "A Machine for not living (extract from Corbusier's verso un archit showing the virgin machine he wants us all to live in)," "a third generation of the formal international stool," and "buildings are for eating (termites in the gallery)," there is mentioned for the first time, "Fake Estates: Property slivers with some projected ideas for them."[51]

51
CCA GMC 001:043 V.

PROJECTED IDEAS (1)

Death brings unasked-for certainty. And the current view of *Fake Estates* more often than not declares them finished, or abandoned—much like the buildings that vexed and transfixed the artist. But even if these slivers and their records were never to have been disinterred, the threads they connect to in Matta-Clark's documented, unfinished intentions are palpable. These threads also weave a more complex, unfinished image of the work than often, today, appears.

One thing that becomes clear is that by 1977 Matta-Clark was tired of cutting buildings. He had wanted his last such work, 1978's *Circus, or Caribbean Orange*, at the Museum of Contemporary Art in Chicago, to take the form of a combination of balloons and cables, amplifying his "net-work" installation for Documenta 6 in Kassel (a long ladder of netting raised up to an industrial chimney). But, as remembered by Jane Crawford, "they wanted another cutting...and he felt he was being corralled into being the cutting artist when he wanted to branch out."[52] Matta-Clark admitted to his friend Les Levine at the time "that he was tired of doing works—the building actions—that required so much physical dexterity. He was physically exhausted by them," Levine recalls, "and he wanted to make art that required less physical strength."[53]

52
Jane Crawford, interview by Crow, "Gordon Matta-Clark," in Diserens, Gordon Matta-Clark, 126.

53
Les Levine, interview in Jacob, Gordon Matta-Clark, 95.

54
CCA GMC 004:124.

At least one attempt at a more ephemeral medium is marked extensively in correspondence, appearing in a November 1977 letter to Don Piccard (the son of pioneering aeronauts Jean Felix Piccard and Jeannette Piccard, and proprietor of the world's first hot-air balloon company): "I am an architect and sculptor who has received some support in recent years from private and government funds," Matta-Clark writes, "for my work in experimental, environmental design. At present I am researching a project that will attempt to combine 'net-work enclosures'" with the structural lift of a series of tethered balloons...."[54]

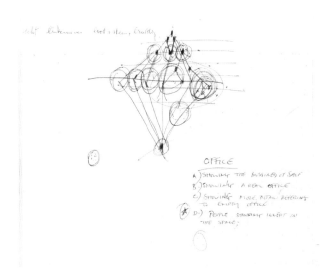

Fig. 7 — Gordon Matta-Clark, undated sketch (from a sketchbook for Office Baroque) © The Estate of Gordon Matta-Clark. Courtesy of the CCA.

The balloon net above the city—incompletely sketched by Matta-Clark at the time—also presents a certain conceptual incompleteness: a shape that hovers, abstractly, above architecture and the city, even as it traces an aerial analogy to of that most urbane of mathematical concepts, the network as a functional mechanism. On a sketchbook devoted to the contemporaneous cuttings of Office Baroque, a Belgian art gallery, the circles of the incisions are doodled over by a new kind of figure, implying the edges and nodes of infrastructure, circulation, and social engagement. In the end, these are the materials from which the city is, most fundamentally, made.

"OPTICS AS MUCH AS COMPUTER GRAPHICS SEEM TO BE PART OF MY SEARCH TO CHART AND REOCCUPY SPACE..."

Other threads emerge as well. When Matta-Clark spent two weeks in September 1975 cutting *Conical Intersect* into two masonry townhouses, set for demolition, adjoining the then rising Centre Pompidou in Paris, he asked his friend Gerald Hovagimyan to join him from New York and share the difficult physical labor; Hovagimyan had performed similar service on the trespass-laden masterpiece *Day's End*—a series of immaculate illegal cuts into the abandoned Pier 52 in New York—earlier that year.

Recalling their plaster-shrouded discussions on site, Hovagimyan credits *Conical Intersect's* inspiration to an influential media-piece by Anthony McCall first shown two years prior: *Line Describing a Cone*, which consists of a dark room, where a white circle slowly appears on a black background, projected on film; the room is also filled with smoke.

McCall describes the effect in a 2004 catalog: "The base of the cone, an emerging circle of light projected onto the wall, is tall enough, at between eight and eleven feet, to fully incorporate several spectators, and the length of the beam may be anything from thirty to sixty feet. This three-dimensional object, like sculpture, calls for a mobile, participating spectator, and, like film, it takes time."[55] Participative, time-based, and spatial, it is also, fundamentally virtual: a word that means, literally, something that exists only through its power to effect. Here we might attend to a March 23, 1976 letter from Matta-Clark to Bill Mitchell, then at the University of California, Los Angeles's (UCLA) School of Architecture & Planning (later to become dean at the Massachusetts Institute of Technology [MIT] and director of its Media Lab).

55
Helen Legg, ed., Anthony McCall: Film Installations (Coventry: Mead Gallery, 2004), 219, exhibition catalog.

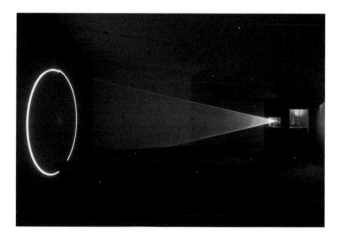

Fig. 8 — Anthony McCall, *Line Describing a Cone*, 1973. **16mm film projection.** © Anthony McCall. Courtesy of Tate Modern, London.

Fig. 9 — Gordon Matta-Clark, *Conical Intersect*, 1975.
Gelatin silver print, 10 ⁵⁄₈ x 15 ⁵⁄₈ in. (27 cm x 40 cm).
© Estate of Gordon Matta-Clark/ARS. Courtesy SFMOMA.

> Dear Bill Mitchel [*sic*]
> ...As I explained over the phone, I am an artist who has been
> working sculpturally with buildings slated for demolition,
> by cutting them to alter their internal space. Since there
> are immense economical and physical barriers to overcome
> in producing a full scale work I have wanted to catalog a set
> of more idealized spacial [*sic*] variations by using computer
> graphic techniques.[56]

56
Ending, "I am sorry we
never got a chance to
speak in person. It would
have been a far more
fruitful exchange."
CCA GMC 004:016.

A new direction, possibly, but also, at least in tool and technique, a
return to the calculated urbanism of late-1960s Cornell. The UCLA
computer laboratory was famous at the time in computer-graphics
circles for producing the first computer-created film of urban space, a
simulation of modernist proposals for downtown Los Angeles accomplished using General Electric's Apollo lunar landing simulator in
1966 (literalizing the text of Hubert Humphrey's 1968 "same techniques" speech). Earlier that year, Matta-Clark had also approached
the Center for Advanced Visual Studies at MIT, which again was
deliberately reappropriating the military-industrial oeuvre of the
research university to creative and artistic ends. Matta-Clark wrote
to the director, Otto Piene, as well as a friend-in-residence at the Lab,
pioneering video artist Peter Campus. But MIT's financial anxieties

became evident: "I don't know how much computer time we can get for your plans," Piene wrote back to Matta-Clark, "Could you get your own other-than-MIT [funding]?"[57]

Matta-Clark remained optimistic. "I also have a group of spacial-structural [sic] project 'drawings'—that involve working with a computer," he writes to Paula Hutchings at UCLA in January 1976. And in March, to Munich gallerist Wolfgang Becker: "This spring I have been getting back to making films, which, although very different, owe some sm[a]ll adherence to Anthony McCall...optics as much as computer graphics seems to be part of my search to chart and reoccupy space."[58] "For most of this technical entertainment," Matta-Clark adds, "I will rely on those treasurehouses of Pentagon resourcefullness [sic, note pun], the American scientific community."

NASCENT NETWORKS

In the same interview in which he reflects on Matta-Clark's "exhaustion" with the solitary, physical reality of his building cuts to date, Les Levine also reflects on Matta-Clark's "desire to help people," for example, on the Lower East Side—to "work with them." Levine concludes, pessimistically, that "he was never able to surrender to that space or idea."[59] Yet history argues otherwise. An artist's statement from 1974 or 1975 imagines that "[a] specific project might be to work with an existing neighborhood youth group and to involve them in converting the all too plentiful abandoned buildings into a social space. Thus the young could get both practical information about how buildings are made and, more essentially, some first-hand experience with one aspect of the very real possibility of transforming their space." "In this way," Matta-Clark continues, "I would adapt my work to still another level of the given situation. It would no longer be concerned with just personal or metaphoric treatment of the site, but finally responsive to the express will of its occupants."[60] Then, a letter in 1976: "At the moment I am making good on a long standing promise to myself involving a move from my past sculptural exercises to a direct collaboration with the people and their problems in a lower east side community of New York."[61] Over multiple drafts in the summer of 1976, Matta-Clark worked out a detailed proposal for the scheme: *A Resource Center and Environmental Youth Program for Loisaida.* Submitted to the John Simon Guggenheim Foundation in late 1976, it resulted in a grant and fellowship awarded to Matta-Clark in March 1977.[62]

A RESOURCE CENTER AND ENVIRONMENTAL
YOUTH PROGRAM FOR LOISAIDA

The proposal itself begins discussing "network of community groups and individuals engaged in open space and rehab projects, sweat equity, community gardens, playlist, cultural events, alternative living structures etc."[63] The imagined enterprise would make use of one or more vacant lots and buildings, then "effect theoretical-experimental innovations" toward the rehabilitation of

57
CCA GMC 003:114; for more on Piene's work at MIT, as well as an extended recounting of MIT's funding-focused efforts in cultural production, see Arindam Dutta, ed., **A Second Modernism: MIT, Architecture, and the "Techno-Social" Moment** (Cambridge, MA: MIT Press, 2013).

58
The latter turn of phrase is especially interesting in light of Rowe's intellectual heritage in the Warburg of the 1930s, where Ernst Gombrich and Erwin Panofsky brought the science of optics into art historical practice through works such as **Perspective as Symbolic Form** (written by Panofsky in 1924), letter to Wolfgang Becker, June 10, 1976, CCA GMC 004:008.

59
Jacob, Gordon Matta-Clark: A Retrospective, 95.

60
CCA GMC 001:085.

61
Matta-Clark to Guy Baldwin, CCA GMC 004:057.

62
Gordon Ray, President of the John Simon Guggenheim Foundation, to Matta-Clark, March 16, 1977, CCA GMC PHCON2002: 0016:004:062:001.

63
"A Resource Center and Environmental Youth Program for Loisaida," proposal draft, August 18, 1976, CCA 001:086.

64
"A Resource Center and Environmental Youth Program for Loisaida," CCA GMC 001:085.

65
A Resource Center and Environmental Youth Program for Loisaida," proposal draft, August, 18, 1976, CCA GMC 001:086.

66
CCA GMC.

further structures, "derived through the studio design process."[64] The work, it is proposed, would rely on the fact that "[t]hroughout the Lower East Side, large amounts of reusable materials have become available because of the increasing rate of abandonment and demolition of building."[65]

Let's note once more the word *network*. It was at the time part of the vernacular of city planning, as well as, of course, of Matta-Clark's nascent sculptural interest in floating, immaterial assemblages. The word would have formed part of his own scientifically inflected planning education. (Norbert Wiener's *Cybernetics*, the system planner's bible, remained a heavily marked-up volume in Matta-Clark's own library.[66]) But the term also formed an essential part of its developing opposition; across much of Matta-Clark's childhood and education at Cornell, activist and intellectual Jane Jacobs was continuing to develop a countertheory, grounded in the city's social reality, but also on further ideas in the science of networks and living systems (see "The Map and the Territory").

It is hard to imagine that Matta-Clark would not have been exposed to Jacobs's work, especially given her notoriety in architecture and planning circles during his undergraduate years—which immediately followed the 1961 appearance of *Death and Life of Great American Cities*. This in addition to the fact that Jacobs lived only two blocks away throughout his childhood, and the fact (likely not lost on any remotely architecturally aware resident of the West Village and SoHo) that the neighborhoods Jacobs helped save from

Fig. 10 — Gordon Matta-Clark, *A Resource Center for Loisaida*, as published in the monograph *Gordon Matta-Clark* (Chicago: Museum of Contemporary Art Chicago, 1992) © The Estate of Gordon Matta-Clark. Courtesy of the Museum of Contemporary Art, Chicago.

scorched-earth urban renewal in general, and the Lower Manhattan Expressway in particular, were very much Matta-Clark's own—both as a child and as an adult. The celebrations following the final defeat of the expressway proposal in 1961 thronged the streets in front of his childhood home, and culminated in the burning of cars in Washington Square Park. (This latter spectacle was unlikely to have been lost on a young neighbor with latent anarchic tendencies.)

Whatever its origin, however, Matta-Clark's vision, like Jacobs's, was of the city as a living body, present in his deliberate use, for example, of words like *metabolization* to describe the process of undoing and remaking built fabric.[67] Such a vision emerges in the Loisaida proposal itself, which proposes "an emphasis on environmental awareness, that is, attention not only to the internal needs of a building," but also its inherent connections to "surrounding areas and neighborhood interests."

67
Gordon Matta-Clark, undated and unaddressed proposal, ca. 1974, Estate of Gordon Matta-Clark, CCA GMC 001:073 1/5.

A CONCRETE PROPOSAL

The educational project framed in the Loisaida proposal—"the environmental-structural design program"—is further explained as follows: "In order to demonstrate new approaches to solving the housing crisis, substantially deteriorated structures, weakened either by fire or age would be used...with attention paid to providing more flexible floor space. One such alternative is to introduce concrete construction...." The proposed addition of concrete-framed insertions into the fabric of abandoned structures is then assessed at length. Matta-Clark justifies this most unusual of proposals initially due to cost concerns (a savings would be unlikely, given the expense of steel reinforcement and formwork compared to wood structure), fire-proofing (certainly true, though less relevant in the hybrid wood-brick-concrete structures that would result), the ability to recycle that portion of the replaced wood that could be reused, and then, "finally from the design aspect, it would allow cadets to experiment with more advanced structural problems yielding greater spatial freedom."

These last points—the benefit of concrete structure to spatial flexibility, and the resulting favorability of a "free" plan—being none other than the most important of the five points proposed by Corbusier in 1926 as the basis for modern architecture. First published in Corbusier's journal *L'Esprit Nouveau* in 1926, they were, by the time they appeared in the book-length manifesto *Vers une Architecture*, illustrated chiefly by those structures—the Villa Stein-de Monzie at Garches, the Villa Savoye at Poissy—the concrete texts that formed the bible of the Texas-born, Cornell-bred formalism that Matta-Clark so violently professed to despise. Which is a surprise.

With a return or reversion to the idea of a social program shaping an architectural environment, and a return or reversion to the Corbusian free plan, there is in this narrow sense a circle of return (even to his father's legacy) in Matta-Clark's work, even as it was abruptly interrupted by his sudden illness and death in 1978.

FAKE ESTATES AND REALITY PROPERTIES

Several months after his last cutting was completed, with explorations in computer graphics and urban education just begun, Matta-Clark's wrote to Belgian curator Florent Bex: "I am sorry to be the bearer of bad news but...since I last wrote the doctors opened me up and looked inside with horror (they are such moral and spiritual cowards) closed me up with an advanced cancer of the pancreas and liver." [68] Matta-Clark eschewed chemotherapy in favor of natural medicine; the summer brought the marriage to Crawford, with Matta in attendance; the death came on August 26, in a Nyack hospital, surrounded by friends.

There was much in Matta-Clark's life and work that—tacitly or explicitly—appropriated and destabilized the very ideas of inheritance, legacy, and the rituals of documentation surrounding those events. The geographical territory—the definitive family inheritance of land and real estate—that featured in *Fake Estates* still exists, returned to the city for nonpayment of taxes after Matta-Clark's death, where they remain in the survey of New York vacant land included in this book. But as with that of his Land Art peers, the essential presence of that artwork would appear to have settled onto the papers, deeds, and drawings that they required, whether saved in a banker's box or briefly affixed to a gallerist's wall. Conversely, the architectural objects on which he practiced his most celebrated cuts were explicitly already enroute to oblivion as ruins or demolition sites. So again we are left with drawings and photos as evidence for, or perhaps displacing, the work itself.

Matta-Clark's own interest in data and documentation—his assiduous experiments in film and photography, schooled by his father in the value of the artifact to the artist—means that his work, which was in the built environment so often a vanishing and a removal—thrives in the archive. It has become an essential citation for critics and architects interested in any condition of destabilization or any operation of incision—even at the expense of understanding of Matta-Clark's complementary concern for connectivity, process, and net-works of every kind. This steady, constant citation has (in a measure of success and perhaps also of failure) not even escaped appropriation by the very architects of whose work it was an acute critique.

"A SOVEREIGN CONTEMPT"

Rosalind Krauss begins her 1996 essay-collaboration with Yves-Alain Bois, "A User's Guide to Entropy," with a discussion of entropy that must have mirrored, in many ways, Matta-Clark's introduction to the concept under the tutelage of Robert Smithson: a child in a sandbox, or the way of all flesh. [69]

In the subsequent text, several sections (contributed by Bois) consider the work of Gordon Matta-Clark as exemplary of "entropic" practice. Ordering Matta-Clark's works' collective disorder in successive scales, Bois considers first the artist's experiments in molding, layering, and burning physical objects (such as the scorched,

68
Jacob, Gordon Matta-Clark, 97; Matta-Clark to Florent Bex, May 26, 1978, CCA GMC.

69
Yve-Alain Bois and Rosalind Krauss, "A User's Guide to Entropy," October 78 (Autumn 1996): 38–88.

gold-leafed Polaroid prints of *Photo-Fry*), moving on to the cutting and dismembering of buildings, and concluding with an extended consideration of *Fake Estates*. Bois emphasizes throughout the "sovereign contempt in Matta-Clark's attitude toward architects." At the time the essay was written, the question was far from academic. In the 1980s, the personal computer combined with new kinds of computer modeling software (of the sort that Matta-Clark was no doubt dreaming) allowed a sudden, unexpectedly facile modeling of objects through deletion, staged subtraction, and

Fig. 11 — Peter Eisenman's Wexner Center for the Arts, The Ohio State University, 1983–1989 © Wikimedia Commons

addition—what are known mathematically and geometrically as Boolean operations.[70] And the tendency of this software toward an appearance (however virtual) of the systematically partial, the subtractive, and the deleted led to its swift adoption by architects still advancing a project of formalism. Which all explains—at least partially—why by as early as five years after his death, Matta-Clark's career had become for formalism's latest incarnation—so-called deconstructivism—a method.

Self-consciously articulating this school, Peter Eisenman's first public building, the Wexner Center for the Arts at the Ohio State University (opened in 1989), consists of a reconstructed brick form of a formerly demolished armory on the building site, in turn cut into and apparently "de-constructed," flanked by a large, functionless white grid of a pergola; the goal, according to the contemporaneous *New York Times* review, was "to recall scaffolding."[71]

As with the New York Five, this latest grouping was cemented by a show at MoMA. The catalog includes Eisenman, as well as others who had moved in the Cornell and IAUS orbit—Rem Koolhaas, Bernard Tschumi, Daniel Libeskind, and Frank Gehry (the latter having discovered and attempted to purchase Matta-Clark's work in 1977).[72] Matta-Clark's 1974 *Splitting* is illustration number three in Mark Wigley's introductory essay. And soon enough, Eisenman himself was to explicitly write, for example, of Matta-Clark's "cutting of a building *in half*...and so denying its function" (mathematic emphasis added) as part of a recounting of the lineage of his own architectural ideas. Eisenman's House VI, for example, the third built, involved having his mathematical manipulations of a gridded cube just happen to cut the marital bed in half. (The resulting 1950s-sitcom standard twin beds emasculated the client to the architect's will even more so than when Corbusier himself took the part of husband to his client's wife in the 1932 film *Vers une Architecture*.)

70
These had been developed as an architectural modeling tool since the late 1960s. While form•Z, the first commercial 3-D modeling software for desktop computers to popularize Boolean operations, was not released until 1989, Peter Eisenman had been collaborating with form•Z's author, Chris Yessios, since at least 1984, and used the mainframe-based form•Z predecessor, Archimodos, in studios taught at Yessios's Ohio State University from 1987 onwards. Mark Wigley, author of the 1989 MoMA deconstruction catalog's opening essay (see below), was an assistant for the 1987 studio. See Pierluigi Serraino, History of Form•Z (Basel: Birkhäuser, 2002), 36–38.

71
Paul Goldberger, "The Museum that Theory Built," New York Times, November 5, 1989.

72
Crow, "Gordon Matta-Clark," in Diserens, Gordon Matta-Clark, 120.

73
Bois and Krauss, "User's Guide," 38–88. (The particular irony being that Eisenman's visually deconstructed buildings proved particularly vulnerable to entropic deconstruction as well. Falling victim to "staggering maintenance costs," House II was abandoned by its original clients, falling over the course of three decades into extended disrepair. And even the $43 million Wexner Center was soon subject to a $16 million refit. See Gwenda Blair, "House Proud: A White Elephant Reincarnated," New York Times, October 10, 2002; and Robin Pobegrin, "Extreme Makeover: Museum Edition," New York Times, September 18, 2005.

74
CCA GMC 001:061.

In Bois and Krauss's text, one can sense the outrage at this turn of events, and the particular contempt of a conventionally architectural—and therefore self-consciously "permanent"—evocation of a building in transformation. Bois adopts Matta-Clark's voice for the purpose: "What I do, you could never achieve, since that presupposes accepting ephemerality...architecture has only one destiny, and that is, sooner or later, to go down the chute...."[73]

BEEN-GONE BY NINE SQUARES

Yet if the formal adoption of Matta-Clark's aesthetic of transformation into the heart of the architectural culture of the 1980s and 1990s—into the aesthetic of self-consciously "permanent" structures—would have likely been anathema to the artist, how in particular should we understand the reverse? In particular, the unexpected inclusion of archetypically Corbusian architecture, column, slab, and free-plan, into the renovated heart of the Loisaida proposal?

Here, another example may serve; in 1974, following *Splitting*, the architect undertook another house-transformation. "'BINGO,'" Matta-Clark explains in an artist's statement, "is the finalized title for a work that, in progress, was called 'Been-Gone by Ninth.' The piece involved the use of a 'typical' American small-town home," he explains, "that was to be demolished for urban-renewal."[74] During the project, "a major part of the exterior was to be sectioned into nine

82
83

Fig. 12 — Gordon Matta-Clark, *Bingo*, 1974, Niagara Falls, New York © The Estate of Gordon Matta-Clark/ARS. Courtesy of David Zwirner Gallery.

equal parts, measuring five feet by nine feet. Eight of these facade segments were cut free, lowered intact and crated for transport... leaving the center of the nine-part grid undisturbed." The completion of the project, interrupted by the scheduled demolition of the house by the city, was to have entailed the same grid, with only the center missing, on the reverse of the house. The nine-square grid problem, of course, was the fundamental unit of Matta-Clark's first undergraduate studio, but here subject to an emphatic *detournement*. Instead of an enduring utopian Cartesian plane, it is the adaptive and opportunistic edge of the house's unmaking (and remaking, as well). The Texas-Cornell grid remains as an instrument, but its purpose is, fundamentally, reversed.

CUT WITH THE KITCHEN KNIFE

Colin Rowe's later years involved both a softening of dogma and an opening to the particular possibilities of form in the urban context. In the late 1960s and 1970s, Rowe would turn to a renewed interest in the less dogmatic figure-ground of as-built cities, the subject of a seminal thesis under Rowe by Wayne Copper in 1966.[75] Ultimately, the notion of addition and adjustment in urban fabric would lead to 1979's *Collage City*. In the book, Rowe and his coauthor, Fred Koetter, lament in this context architecture's failure in the 1920s to embrace the conceptual and formal properties of collage, illustrating the point with several works of Picasso.[76]

Yet a more apt counterexample to formal modernisms would replace the polite Picasso with the more violent and radical roots of Dada collage. Hannah Höch's *Cut with the Kitchen Knife through the Last Weimar Beer-Belly Cultural Epoch in Germany* would figure prominently in such a story, not only for it's political content, but for how its action—the cut with the kitchen knife—is set against the (alcoholic, rotund, masculine) power structure of the day. The kitchen knife, of course, is a tool ready-to-hand—first as the instrument of an oppressive hierarchy (the woman relegated to service), but then precisely the instrument of rebellion, remaking, and creation at the same time.

It is in light of this lineage that we might regard the Loisaida proposal's uncanny introduction of a collage of Corbusier's five points into the interior fabric of wasted buildings. Here, with the same logic as the demolition chisel became a creative implement in Matta-Clark's building cuts, the very same instrument of the midcentury city's unmaking—the tower-in-the-park visions that were of a piece with *Vers une Architecture*'s five points—are unmoored from their origins and rearranged into the reverse. Like an oyster's unwelcome irritation, they are metabolized, coated, and incorporated into the urban fabric, the resulting pearl providing structure and value.

From today's distance, we truly cannot imagine the shapes that would have emerged from Loisaida's studio exercises, the excisions, remakings, repurposings, and reinventions, whether they would have

75
See Wayne W. Copper, "The Figure/Grounds," *Cornell Journal of Architecture* 2 (Fall 1983): 42–53.

76
See in particular Colin Rowe and Fred Koetter, *Collage City* (Cambridge, MA: MIT Press, 1978), 138–39.

Fig. 13 — Hannah Höch, *Cut with the Kitchen Knife through the Last Weimar Beer-Belly Cultural Epoch in Germany (Schnitt mit dem Küchenmesser durch die letzte Weimarer Bierbauchkulturepoche Deutschlands)*, 1919–1920. Photomontage and collage with watercolor, 44 ⁷⁄₈ x 35 ⁷⁄₁₆ in. (114 x 90 cm) © Hannah Höch/ARS. Staatliche Museen zu Berlin, Nationalgalerie

been real or virtual, concrete or conceptual, or all at once. But we can imagine their precision, and precise framing of something distinctly, and quintessentially urbane, representing not the inevitable failure of architecture to cheat death but the city's enduring ability to frame, and reframe, life. For it is, truly, the destiny of architecture to "go down the chute." But it is in the nature of the city, in its shifting networks and networked metabolisms, to endure.

Los Angeles
Case Study 2010–2011

Throughout the Los Angeles River basin, the presence of freeways along historic watersheds coincides with both at-risk neighborhoods and the presence of lots leased by outdoor advertising companies purely for their proximity to automotive vision. A partnership with the Pasadena nonprofit Amigos de los Rios brought our focus to these sites in 2010.

Disguised through a range of land ownership and leasing arrangements, the presence of billboards on underutilized lots was confirmed via Google Earth using crowdsourced labor. (Requests to Clearchannel and CBS Outdoor for specific information on billboard locations and ownership were refused.)

For each site, a set of water-focused retention landscapes are proposed, which would serve both ecological and community purposes, providing open space and amenities to park-poor communities, retaining water and its ecological influence during times of drought, and mediating flooding during infrequent times of plenty.

These proposals remain compatible with the presence of outdoor advertising, but add a variety of new and old media, ecological and physical, to the sites' potential and promise.

1625879 2100 FIGUEROA ST / ARROYO SECO

345002 21701 DEVONSHIRE ST /
BROWNS CANYON WASH

162380 13035 VICTORY BLVD /
TUJUNGA WASH, LOS ANGELES RIVER

2076519 5016 RIVERGRADE RD / SANTA FE
FLOOD CONTROL BASIN, SAN GABRIEL RIVER

1088248 16035 PIUMA AVE / COYOTE
CREEK, SAN GABRIEL RIVER

741680 3501 SEPULVEDA BLVD /
BALLONA CREEK

**BILLBOARDS AND
UNDERUTILIZED PARCELS**
located with Google Earth &
Amazon Mechanical Turk

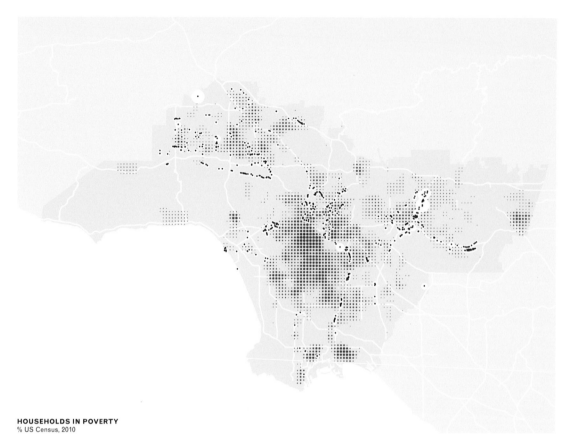

HOUSEHOLDS IN POVERTY
% US Census, 2010

**RESPIRATORY
ILLNESS** INCIDENCE,
% US Census, 2010

REPORTED CRIME
INCIDENT COUNT, LAPD, 2012

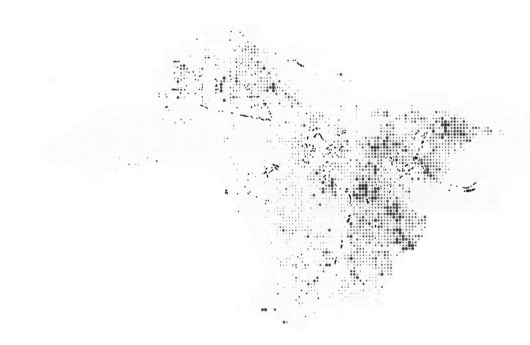

URBAN HEAT ISLANDS
Landsat Infrared Image Analysis, 2012

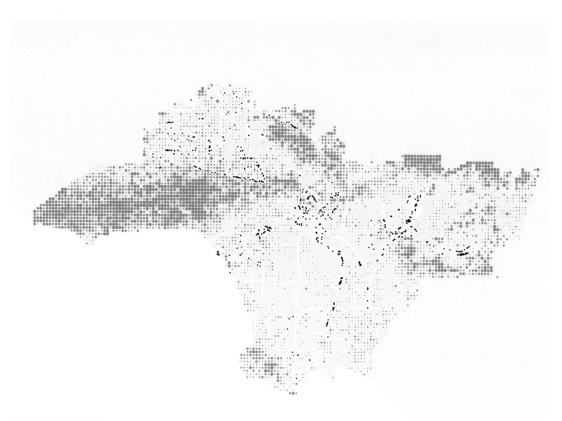

URBAN GROUND COVER
ASTER image analysis, 2012

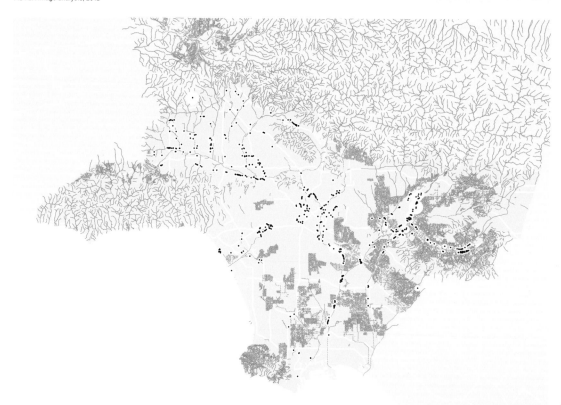

HYDROLOGY SHOWING NATURAL CHANNELS (BLUE)
AND ARTIFICIAL CHANNELS (GRAY)
LA County Department of Public Works, 2013

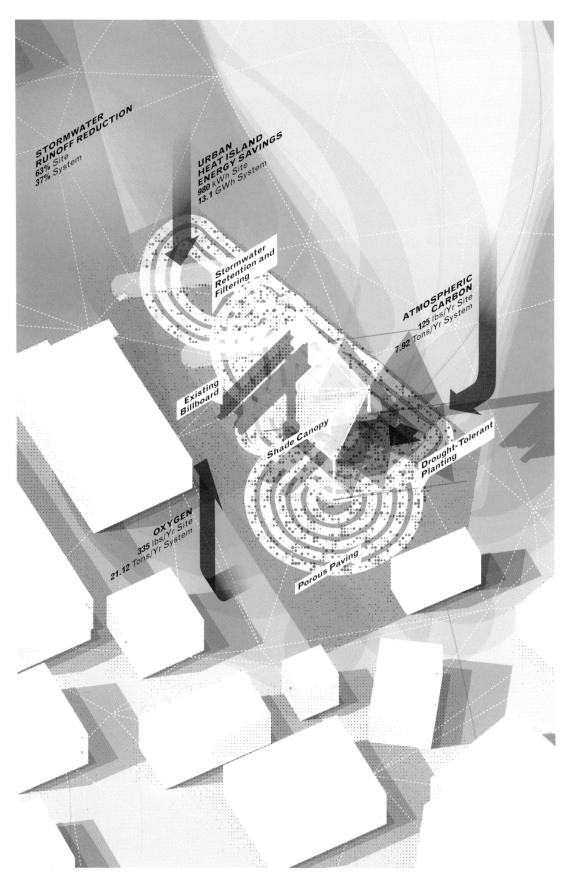

STORMWATER
RUNOFF REDUCTION
63% Site
37% System

URBAN
HEAT ISLAND
ENERGY SAVINGS
980 kWh Site
13.1 GWh System

ATMOSPHERIC
CARBON
125 lbs/Yr Site
7.92 Tons/Yr System

Stormwater
Retention and
Filtering

Existing
Billboard

Shade Canopy

Drought-Tolerant
Planting

OXYGEN
335 lbs/Yr Site
21.12 Tons/Yr System

Porous Paving

186630 4100
GREENBUSH AVE

1648986 500
AVENUE 64

21711

21722 5200
RIGOLETTO ST

1615249

1062391 I-5

2263723 22829
VENTURA BLVD

332819 17601 CHATSWORTH ST /
TUJUNGA WASH, LOS ANGELES RIVER

167765 5632
TUJUNGA AVE

2095924 400
CLOVERLEAF DR

335696

20770

1705288

768559

2256509

9365

56716

56725 21801
SHERMAN WAY

2076516

1604872 2201 SUNSET BLVD /
BALLONA CREEK

56777

2114174

1635740

1422967

1649107

2261946

233410 14101 FOOTHILL BLVD /
LOWER PACOIMA WASH

2370804

74980 6800
INDEPENDENCE AVE / TUJUNGA
WASH, LOS ANGELES RIVER

69558

2077540 100
LONGDEN AVE

114759

1630271

262861 7501
FOOTHILL BLVD

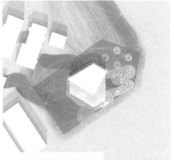

1422662 8501 VENICE BLVD /
BALLONA CREEK

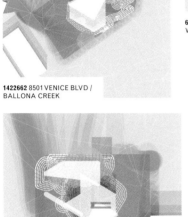

73500 7124 MASON AVE / TUJUNGA
WASH, LOS ANGELES RIVER

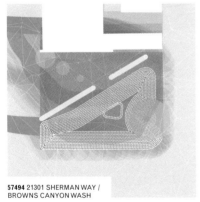

57494 21301 SHERMAN WAY /
BROWNS CANYON WASH

1604951

2234985

69540 19231 VANOWEN ST / TUJUNGA
WASH, LOS ANGELES RIVER

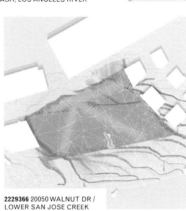

2229366 20050 WALNUT DR /
LOWER SAN JOSE CREEK

84178

1625452

56724 21801
SHERMAN WAY

84665 18001 VENTURA BLVD /
TUJUNGA WASH, LOS ANGELES RIVER

1483488

97735 5100
ZELZAH AVE

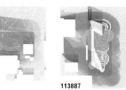

172548

1621863

717495 11801
MAJOR ST

729781

1675265

1236856

186188

101532 7528
BALBOA BLVD

1884976

114757 7076
BALBOA BLVD

113886

113887

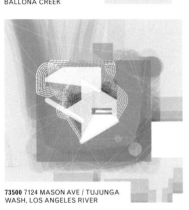

2078075

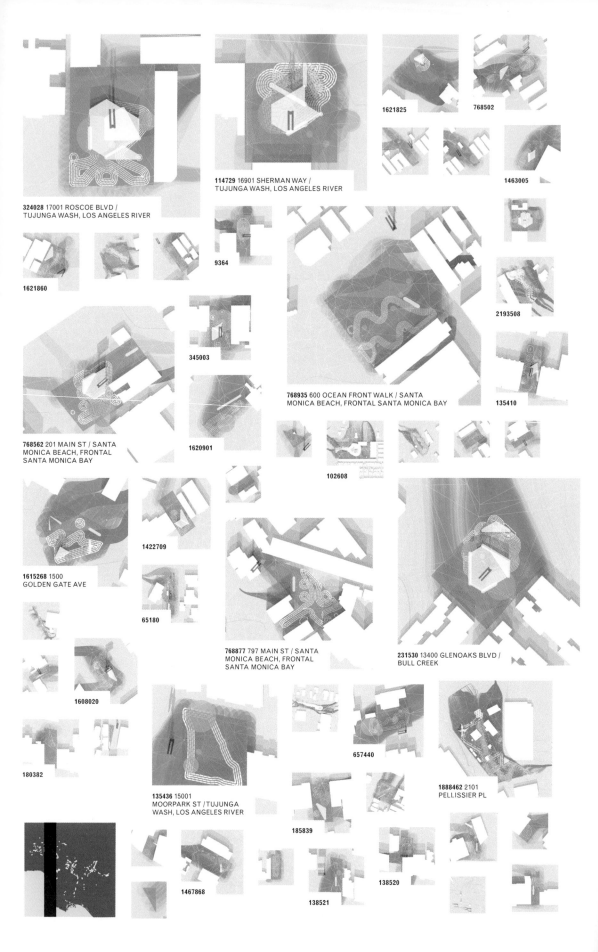

324028 17001 ROSCOE BLVD /
TUJUNGA WASH, LOS ANGELES RIVER

114729 16901 SHERMAN WAY /
TUJUNGA WASH, LOS ANGELES RIVER

1621825

768502

1463005

9364

1621860

345003

768935 600 OCEAN FRONT WALK / SANTA
MONICA BEACH, FRONTAL SANTA MONICA BAY

2193508

135410

768562 201 MAIN ST / SANTA
MONICA BEACH, FRONTAL
SANTA MONICA BAY

1620901

102608

1422709

1615268 1500
GOLDEN GATE AVE

65180

768877 797 MAIN ST / SANTA
MONICA BEACH, FRONTAL
SANTA MONICA BAY

231530 13400 GLENOAKS BLVD /
BULL CREEK

1608020

657440

180382

1888462 2101
PELLISSIER PL

135436 15001
MOORPARK ST / TUJUNGA
WASH, LOS ANGELES RIVER

185839

138520

1467868

138521

779890 1901 LA CIENEGA BLVD /
BALLONA CREEK

299678

1463186

1609868

1486364

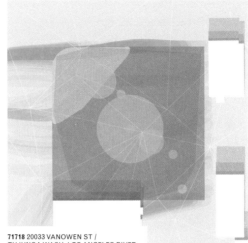
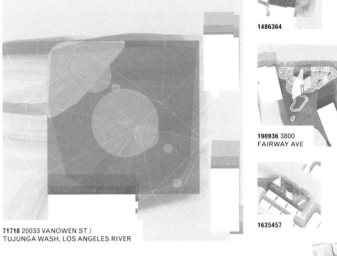

190936 3800
FAIRWAY AVE

1635457

167413 5936 LANKERSHIM BLVD /
TUJUNGA WASH, LOS ANGELES RIVER

71718 20033 VANOWEN ST /
TUJUNGA WASH, LOS ANGELES RIVER

261388

1914172

728088
VENICE BLVD

1001609

1887023 I-605 / COYOTE
CREEK, SAN GABRIEL RIVER

1630264

57497 7100 DEERING AVE /
TUJUNGA WASH,
LOS ANGELES RIVER

741680 3501 SEPULVEDA BLVD /
BALLONA CREEK

358779 18701 PARTHENIA ST /
TUJUNGA WASH, LOS ANGELES RIVER

161805 6400 FULTON AVE /
TUJUNGA WASH,
LOS ANGELES RIVER

1423534 6051 SAWYER ST /
BALLONA CREEK

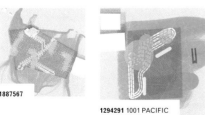

1887567

1294291 1001 PACIFIC
COAST HWY

742429 2901 WESTWOOD
BLVD / BALLONA CREEK

1470981

355324 8300
DE SOTO AVE

2347494

2095566 13140
VALLEY BLVD

172555

97733

163247

171897

164444

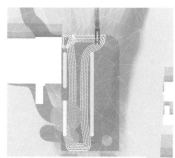

163253 6330 GOODLAND AVE /
TUJUNGA WASH, LOS ANGELES RIVER

2241853

2096097 ON-RAMP
(GARVEY AVE)

1923599 15500 VALLEY BLVD /
LOWER SAN JOSE CREEK

184940

1431259

1431156
2801 7TH ST

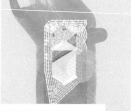

56767 7100 TOPANGA
CANYON BLVD / BELL
CREEK, LOS ANGELES RIVER

148299 13231 SATICOY ST / TUJUNGA
WASH, LOS ANGELES RIVER

1611758

253940

1625587 3400
FIGUEROA ST

173846 11301
BURBANK BLVD

157865 6400 BEN AVE /
TUJUNGA WASH,
LOS ANGELES RIVER

185840

184506

186146

785312

186033 11701
VENTURA BLVD / TUJUNGA
WASH, LOS ANGELES RIVER

186065

1470982 101
GAREY ST

1921465 101 4TH AVE /
SANTA FE FLOOD CONTROL
BASIN, SAN GABRIEL RIVER

189011

188871

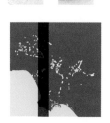

2625813 2400 14TH ST /
CHAVEZ RAVINE,
LOS ANGELES RIVER

1002254

1423622

2079543 11600
MCBEAN DR

1300128

648346 6701 ALVERN ST /
BALLONA CREEK

1120152

1088246 16035
PIUMA AVE

785343

136677

1264913

61564

202548 4700
LANKERSHIM BLVD

785295

358596 8300 SYLVIA AVE /
ALISO CANYON WASH

1409978

265095 7401
FOOTHILL BLVD

188877

1048318

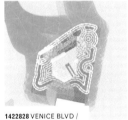

1422828 VENICE BLVD /
BALLONA CREEK

65179 18441 VICTORY BLVD /
TUJUNGA WASH, LOS ANGELES RIVER

202496 10723
BLIX ST

1421530

167195 11301
BURBANK BLVD

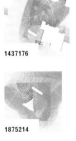

1437176

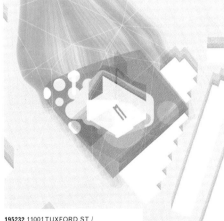

1875214

2641819 8940 LAUREL CANYON BLVD /
TUJUNGA WASH, LOS ANGELES RIVER

195232 11001 TUXFORD ST /
TUJUNGA WASH, LOS ANGELES RIVER

262940

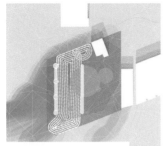

20774 5300 FALLBROOK AVE /
BELL CREEK, LOS ANGELES RIVER

2095565 13100 VALLEY BLVD /
SANTA FE FLOOD CONTROL
BASIN, SAN GABRIEL RIVER

172565 12401 CHANDLER BLVD /
TUJUNGA WASH, LOS ANGELES RIVER

202965 10801
RIVERSIDE DR / TUJUNGA
WASH, LOS ANGELES RIVER

84276 5338
OTIS AVE

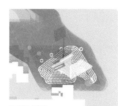

203452 4142
LANKERSHIM BLVD

2223556

268384

1421378 5443 WASHINGTON
BLVD / BALLONA CREEK

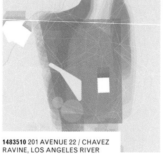

1483510 201 AVENUE 22 / CHAVEZ
RAVINE, LOS ANGELES RIVER

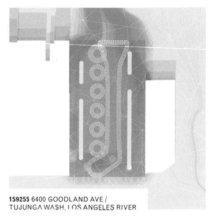

159255 6400 GOODLAND AVE /
TUJUNGA WASH, LOS ANGELES RIVER

335701 10300 OWENSMOUTH AVE /
BROWNS CANYON WASH

158603 12801 VANOWEN ST /
TUJUNGA WASH,
LOS ANGELES RIVER

1424406 1801
ALSACE AVE

1426638

1431258

162381

306449 8700 SEPULVEDA BLVD /
TUJUNGA WASH, LOS ANGELES RIVER

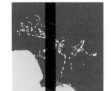

84324

2076460   **1119810**

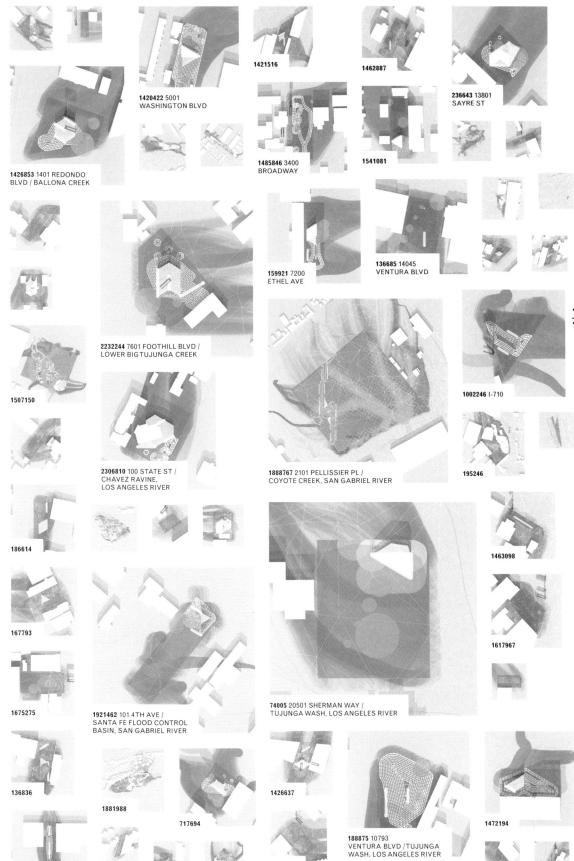

1420422 5001
WASHINGTON BLVD

1421516

1462887

236643 13801
SAYRE ST

1485846 3400
BROADWAY

1541081

1426853 1401 REDONDO
BLVD / BALLONA CREEK

159921 7200
ETHEL AVE

136685 14045
VENTURA BLVD

2232244 7601 FOOTHILL BLVD /
LOWER BIG TUJUNGA CREEK

1507150

2306810 100 STATE ST /
CHAVEZ RAVINE,
LOS ANGELES RIVER

1888767 2101 PELLISSIER PL /
COYOTE CREEK, SAN GABRIEL RIVER

1002246 I-710

195246

186614

1463098

167793

1617967

1675275

1921462 101 4TH AVE /
SANTA FE FLOOD CONTROL
BASIN, SAN GABRIEL RIVER

74005 20501 SHERMAN WAY /
TUJUNGA WASH, LOS ANGELES RIVER

136836

1881988

717694

1426637

188875 10793
VENTURA BLVD / TUJUNGA
WASH, LOS ANGELES RIVER

1472194

1611613

163248

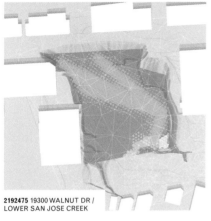

2192475 19300 WALNUT DR /
LOWER SAN JOSE CREEK

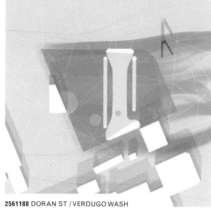

2561188 DORAN ST / VERDUGO WASH

1613029 1600
OCCIDENTAL BLVD /
BALLONA CREEK

1478437 2100
WHITTIER BLVD

301576 9600 VESPER AVE /
LOWER PACOIMA WASH

1613471 3123 SUNSET BLVD /
BALLONA CREEK

1923624 15500 VALLEY BLVD /
LOWER SAN JOSE CREEK

1486279
SOTO ST

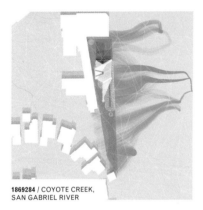

1869284 / COYOTE CREEK,
SAN GABRIEL RIVER

1613440 3201
SUNSET BLVD

188872

1294323 1001 PACIFIC COAST HWY /
LONG BEACH HARBOR,
FRONTAL SAN PEDRO BAY

186185

1611600

135409

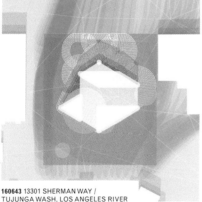

160643 13301 SHERMAN WAY /
TUJUNGA WASH, LOS ANGELES RIVER

335695 21729 DEVONSHIRE ST /
BROWNS CANYON WASH

1426636

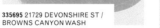

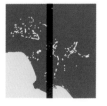

2640312

1882316 2120
DURFEE AVE / ALHAMBRA
WASH, RIO HONDO

1610877 1500
MORTON AVE

19274 22801 VICTORY BLVD /
BELL CREEK, LOS ANGELES RIVER

1001428 10001 MILLER WAY /
ALHAMBRA WASH, RIO HONDO

1236871 19801
SUSANA RD

167194 5600
BAKMAN AVE

1421505

239584 12420
BROMONT AVE

159256

1620862 2750
FLETCHER DR

1611741

162379

1617099

2640309 1700 GLENDALE BLVD /
BALLONA CREEK

1620905

1300126

1609965

2256973 2801 SAN
FERNANDO RD

2077543 100
LONGDEN AVE

57496 7100 DEERING AVE /
TUJUNGA WASH,
LOS ANGELES RIVER

1471286 1200 6TH ST /
CHAVEZ RAVINE,
LOS ANGELES RIVER

1621824

2193497

1879319 12300 FINEVIEW ST /
ALHAMBRA WASH,
RIO HONDO

1621583 FLETCHER DR / SCHOLL
CANYON, LOS ANGELES RIVER

1437132 1301 CURSON AVE /
BALLONA CREEK

138519

2256987 2900
EAGLE ROCK BLVD

265115

1471327 601 MATEO ST /
CHAVEZ RAVINE,
LOS ANGELES RIVER

1608017 215 ANN ST / CHAVEZ RAVINE, LOS ANGELES RIVER

1883103

1463068

1486384

1609274

1462888

188858 3976 EUREKA DR / TUJUNGA WASH, LOS ANGELES RIVER

1615216

1608388 500 MISSION RD

2078066

1472620 CHAVEZ RAVINE, LOS ANGELES RIVER

1143483 3750 PACIFIC PL

1626045 1772 SPRING ST / CHAVEZ RAVINE, LOS ANGELES RIVER

1625861

1608408 1000 VILLA ST

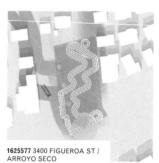

1625577 3400 FIGUEROA ST / ARROYO SECO

180379

9349 22201 SHERMAN WAY / BELL CREEK, LOS ANGELES RIVER

1483474

268382

183475

1483511

1477587

1425498

1477591

1887624 I-605

1236819

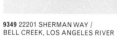

1635462 4400 FIGUEROA ST / ARROYO SECO

1635733 5516 FIGUEROA ST

330330 21101 DEVONSHIRE ST

1070691

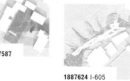

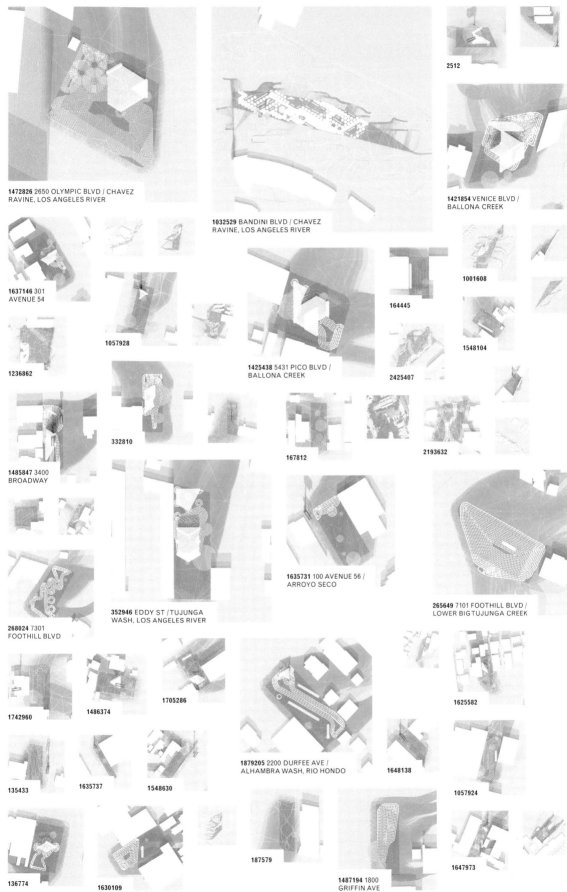

1472826 2650 OLYMPIC BLVD / CHAVEZ
RAVINE, LOS ANGELES RIVER

1032529 BANDINI BLVD / CHAVEZ
RAVINE, LOS ANGELES RIVER

1421854 VENICE BLVD /
BALLONA CREEK

2512

1637146 301
AVENUE 54

1057928

1236862

1001608

164445

1548104

1485847 3400
BROADWAY

332810

1425438 5431 PICO BLVD /
BALLONA CREEK

167812

2425407

2193632

268024 7301
FOOTHILL BLVD

352946 EDDY ST / TUJUNGA
WASH, LOS ANGELES RIVER

1635731 100 AVENUE 56 /
ARROYO SECO

265649 7101 FOOTHILL BLVD /
LOWER BIG TUJUNGA CREEK

1742960

1486374

1705286

1625582

135433

1635737

1548630

1879205 2200 DURFEE AVE /
ALHAMBRA WASH, RIO HONDO

1648138

1057924

136774

1630109

187579

1487194 1800
GRIFFIN AVE

1647973

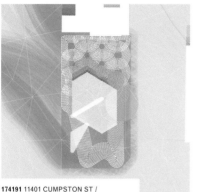

174191 11401 CUMPSTON ST /
TUJUNGA WASH, LOS ANGELES RIVER

1884738 STATE HIGHWAY 60 /
ALHAMBRA WASH, RIO HONDO

1422892
VENICE BLVD

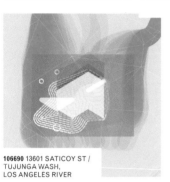

106690 13601 SATICOY ST /
TUJUNGA WASH,
LOS ANGELES RIVER

1647995

1001488 10198
BURTIS ST

1462699

268141 9936 COMMERCE AVE /
LOWER BIG TUJUNGA CREEK

1630262

159902

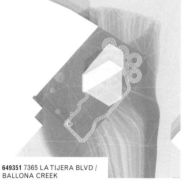

649351 7365 LA TIJERA BLVD /
BALLONA CREEK

2612493

1001200 9501
FRONTAGE RD

1426626 5151 PICO BLVD /
BALLONA CREEK

1046762

1942319

2223557

1000838

2095522

56775

1048455

1061967

1486314

1625859

1879306 12300
FINEVIEW ST / ALHAMBRA
WASH, RIO HONDO

707079

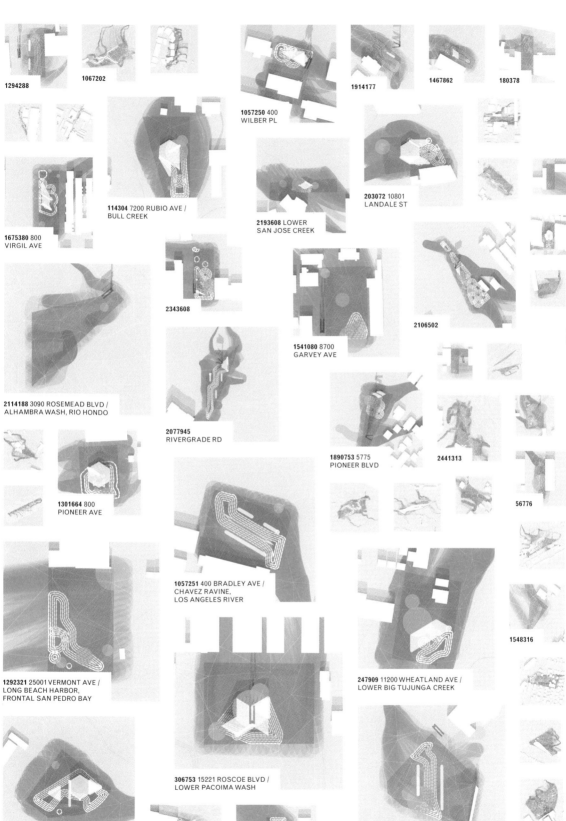

1294288

1067202

1914177

1467862

180378

1057250 400
WILBER PL

114304 7200 RUBIO AVE /
BULL CREEK

2193608 LOWER
SAN JOSE CREEK

203072 10801
LANDALE ST

1675380 800
VIRGIL AVE

2343608

2106502

1541080 8700
GARVEY AVE

2114188 3090 ROSEMEAD BLVD /
ALHAMBRA WASH, RIO HONDO

2077945
RIVERGRADE RD

1890753 5775
PIONEER BLVD

2441313

56776

1301664 800
PIONEER AVE

1057251 400 BRADLEY AVE /
CHAVEZ RAVINE,
LOS ANGELES RIVER

247909 11200 WHEATLAND AVE /
LOWER BIG TUJUNGA CREEK

1548316

1292321 25001 VERMONT AVE /
LONG BEACH HARBOR,
FRONTAL SAN PEDRO BAY

306753 15221 ROSCOE BLVD /
LOWER PACOIMA WASH

2244347 AVENUE 61 /
ARROYO SECO

1835508 COYOTE CREEK,
SAN GABRIEL RIVER

136841

332811

58364 7600 OSO AVE / TUJUNGA
WASH, LOS ANGELES RIVER

717452 11801 MAJOR ST /
BALLONA CREEK

1630101

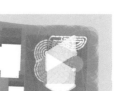

1423800 1601
LA BREA AVE

136690

9363

1548091

265650

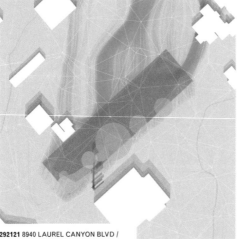

292121 8940 LAUREL CANYON BLVD /
TUJUNGA WASH, LOS ANGELES RIVER

186628

1882363 2100
DURFEE AVE / ALHAMBRA
WASH, RIO HONDO

1883184 I-605

1483485 2100
BROADWAY

16476 23701 VANOWEN ST /
BELL CREEK,
LOS ANGELES RIVER

728086
VENICE BLVD

728090
VENICE BLVD

1882371 2000 DURFEE AVE /
ALHAMBRA WASH, RIO HONDO

1882325 2120 DURFEE AVE /
ALHAMBRA WASH, RIO HONDO

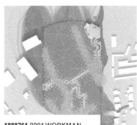

1888761 2201 WORKMAN
MILL RD / COYOTE CREEK,
SAN GABRIEL RIVER

1609439

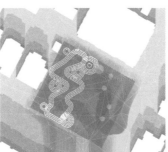

1462891 2301 JAMES M WOOD BLVD /
BALLONA CREEK

2096132

2252207 I-605 / SANTA FE
FLOOD CONTROL BASIN,
SAN GABRIEL RIVER

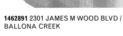

176270 5140
COLFAX AVE

1609875

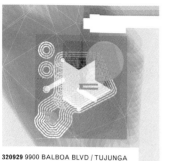

320929 9900 BALBOA BLVD / TUJUNGA
WASH, LOS ANGELES RIVER

1635703 101 AVENUE 56 /
ARROYO SECO

718971 4525
CENTINELA AVE

2084922 I-605

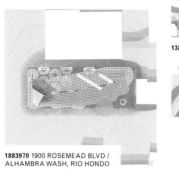

138504

188832 11201
VENTURA BLVD / TUJUNGA
WASH, LOS ANGELES RIVER

1507141 4500
26TH ST

1236827

1883970 1900 ROSEMEAD BLVD /
ALHAMBRA WASH, RIO HONDO

968696 I-710 / COMPTON
CREEK, LOS ANGELES RIVER

2099260 LIVE OAK AVE / SANTA
ANITA WASH, RIO HONDO

186280 11501 VENTURA BLVD /
TUJUNGA WASH, LOS ANGELES RIVER

2095848 BIG
DALTON WASH

1236725 18401 SUSANA RD /
COMPTON CREEK,
LOS ANGELES RIVER

1467840 2701
3RD ST

138502 4300 MATILIJA AVE /
TUJUNGA WASH,
LOS ANGELES RIVER

1742962

61565

306475 15301
PARTHENIA ST

2192510 STATE HIGHWAY 60 /
LOWER SAN JOSE CREEK

1472195

257582 11200 WHEATLAND AVE /
LOWER BIG TUJUNGA CREEK

1294290

1835443 10500
FIRESTONE BLVD / COYOTE
CREEK, SAN GABRIEL RIVER

2078170 RIVERGRADE RD /
SANTA FE FLOOD CONTROL
BASIN, SAN GABRIEL RIVER

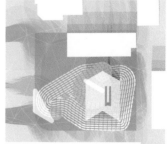

2239927

56761 7200 TOPANGA CANYON BLVD /
BELL CREEK, LOS ANGELES RIVER

163249 12801
VICTORY BLVD / TUJUNGA
WASH, LOS ANGELES RIVER

2354448 2301 CRYSTAL ST /
SCHOLL CANYON,
LOS ANGELES RIVER

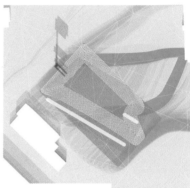

648610 6801 LA TIJERA BLVD /
BALLONA CREEK

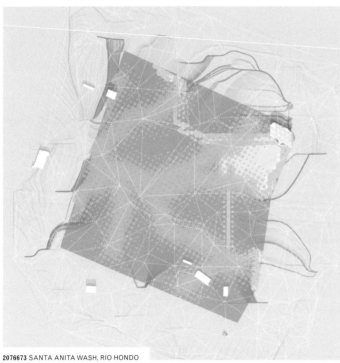

2076673 SANTA ANITA WASH, RIO HONDO

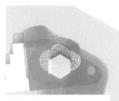

1618098

184927 12001
VENTURA BLVD / TUJUNGA
WASH, LOS ANGELES RIVER

74982 20901
VANOWEN ST

1649103

1617089

1002253

1472621 2600
8TH ST

2077542 100
LONGDEN AVE

2101974

742396

330327 21101
DEVONSHIRE ST /
ALISO CANYON WASH

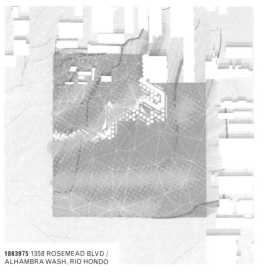

1883975 1358 ROSEMEAD BLVD /
ALHAMBRA WASH, RIO HONDO

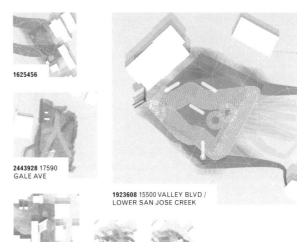

1625456

2443928 17590
GALE AVE

1923608 15500 VALLEY BLVD /
LOWER SAN JOSE CREEK

167813

1471777 2200 OLYMPIC BLVD / CHAVEZ
RAVINE, LOS ANGELES RIVER

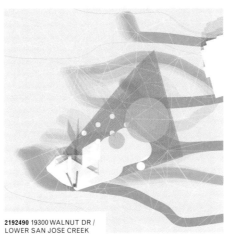
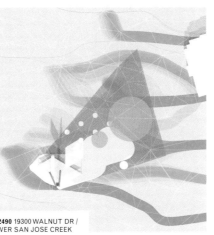

2192490 19300 WALNUT DR /
LOWER SAN JOSE CREEK

1483467 2200
BROADWAY

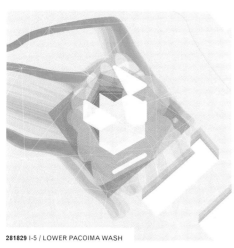

281829 I-5 / LOWER PACOIMA WASH

344463 10200 TOPANGA
CANYON BLVD /
BROWNS CANYON WASH

49822 18981
ROSCOE BLVD

2248805

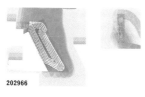

202966

Life Attracts Life

"Life attracts life"—a description, on page 348 of Jane Jacobs's *The Death and Life of Great American Cities,* in the context, as it happens, of the inadvisability of separating pedestrian traffic from the rest of the street's manifold, overlapping functions. But the phrase just as easily serves as an epigram—not only to the seminal book, but to the life that provided its foundation.

"PEOPLE LOOKED THE WAY I FELT"

1
Jane Jacobs, biographical statement, 1961, Jane Jacobs Papers, Boston College, Boston (hereafter JJP).

"I came to New York," Jane Jacobs would write in 1961, "to seek my fortune, Depression or no."[1] She had been born Jane Butzner in 1916 in Scranton, Pennsylvania, the independent daughter of an independent-thinking doctor. She attended two years of secretarial school in Pennsylvania before coming to Manhattan in 1932. The move was a revelation. Depression-era job hunting meant many hours on the street; uptown to midtown and back again. And all too often, in between brief stints of work (a clock company, a drapery hardware company, a candy manufacturer, a steel distributor), job hunting was the order of the day. Mornings were spent inquiring at offices; afternoons, wandering the city. The former was endured; the latter, embraced.

To fill her unemployed time, Jacobs began to combine her sidewalk observations with the narrative craft she had honed during a year at one of Scranton's newspapers—where, amid other duties, she composed agony-aunt letters as well as their responses, finding her own voice among imagined others. She wrote a series of articles on spec describing several of Manhattan's working neighborhoods, and sold her first, a set of reflections on the fur district, to *Vogue.* (Who else, she professed to think, would be interested in coats?) Other publications followed, supplementing a meager income. When times were especially tight, she and her sister, Betty, subsisted on bananas and the mealy children's cereal Pablum—"It was not good."[2] Jacobs first settled at her sister's apartment near Brooklyn Heights, but an impulsive jaunt from the Christopher Street subway led her to move to Greenwich Village in 1935. "In Midtown, I remember, I always felt so depressed. Everyone looked so well-dressed and with-it. But down on Christopher Street, people looked the way I felt."[3]

2
Jane Jacobs, interview by James Howard Kunstler, "Godmother of the American City," Metropolis (March 2001): 130.

3
Jane Jacobs, 2004 speech, quoted in Alice Sparberg Alexiou, Jane Jacobs: Urban Visionary (New Brunswick, NJ: Rutgers University Press, 2006), 21.

Fig. 1 — Jane Jacobs in the White Horse Tavern, 1961 © Cervin Robinson

Fig. 2 — Ernst Haeckel, "Phaeodora," Plate 61
from *Kunstformen der Natur*, 1904

4
Jane Jacobs, quoted in Jonathan Karp, "Jane Jacobs Doesn't Live Here Anymore," At Random (Winter 1993): 48.

5
Jane Jacobs, biographical statement, 1961, JJP.

6
Henry Edward Crampton, The Department of Zoology of Columbia University, 1892–1942 (New York: Columbia University, Department of Zoology, 1942), 7.

7
From, for example Edmund B. Wilson, The Cell in Development and Inheritance (New York: Macmillan Company, 1900), up to Theodosius Dobzhansky, Genetics and the Origin of Species (New York: Columbia University Press, 1951).

8
Crampton, Department of Zoology.

9
Jane Butzner, ed., Constitutional Chaff: Rejected Suggestions of the Constitutional Convention of 1787 with Explanatory Argument (New York: Columbia University Press, 1941).

10
Jane Jacobs, biographical statement, 1961, JJP.

11
See, as but the first example, Lewis Mumford's review of Death and Life, "Mother Jacobs Home Remedies," The Sky Line, New Yorker, December 1, 1962, 148.

In the morning twilight, from the rooftop of her apartment building, Jacobs would survey garbage trucks making their slow way through the rivers of tightly set streets, thinking, "What a complicated, great place this is, and all these pieces of it that make it work."[4] Then in 1937, Jacobs's father, her intellectual and emotional hero, suddenly died. Jacobs finally took the money her parents had saved (and never spent) for her college education, enrolling as a special student, far uptown, in the Columbia University School of General Studies.

By her own account, the younger Jane had slid without note through her primary education, distracted as often as not by a book hidden underneath her desk.[5] But she thrived in the intellectual freedom afforded by the nontraditional program at Columbia. Taking whichever courses she chose, she followed her interests in law, public policy, geology, and, most particularly, zoology. The latter subject, modeled on the department established by Louis Agassiz at Harvard University in 1848, and influenced heavily by the later teachings of Charles Darwin, was established, after a petition from Columbia College juniors and seniors, in 1892.[6] Founded only a few decades after Ernst Haeckel coined the word *ecology* in his *Generelle Morphologie* of 1866, the department was indebted to Haeckel's pioneering study of the systematic connections in nature through the study of particular specimens.

Zoology, as Jacobs would have encountered it, combined embryology, morphology, genetics, and evolution. The department was home to fundamental work in the developing modern sciences of cell biology, embryology, and genetics, and their relationship to evolution.[7] Its most influential member at the time would have been the recently retired Edmund B. Wilson, known for his detailed, empirical work in observing the structure, evolution, and complexities of the cell through careful microscope study, at the time when cell structure and function was just beginning to be understood.[8]

Jacobs did extraordinarily well at Columbia; a manuscript inspired by her 1938–39 law coursework became an edited Columbia University Press volume.[9] With this success came the prospect of transferring to a degree-granting program at Barnard, Columbia's women's college. But to do so would mean taking required courses, from which, especially given her mediocre high-school grades, Jacobs was not exempt. (Whether she was finally admitted to Barnard or not is itself a matter of dispute.) Exasperated, she departed, "and therefore," in her own telling, "was allowed to continue getting an education" in the streets of New York.[10]

THE BIRTH OF DEATH AND LIFE

There is an oft-told tale of the origin of *Death and Life* that casts Jacobs as an "activist housewife."[11] Of all the stories one could tell of the book's birth, this is the least true—by a wide margin. Not only did Jacobs's primary career as an activist (most notably opposing the urban renewal of West Greenwich Village and the revival of the Lower Manhattan Expressway) actually postdate the completion of

Death and Life, but she was a full-time professional—as should already be clear—from her teenage years onward.

REDEVELOPMENT AND "RENEWAL"

Another, truer story would involve the literal continuation of Jacobs's uptown education, not in Columbia's Morningside Heights, but a few blocks and a world away in the emerging housing projects and disappearing social fabric of East Harlem. William Kirk, the executive director (he preferred the title "head worker") of Union Settlement, a charity arm of Union Theological Seminary, brought her there in April 1955. Kirk had only met Jacobs a few days earlier, at the offices of *Architectural Forum*, her employer since 1952. A tall, well-connected WASP, Kirk was visiting friends at the *Forum* offices in search of someone to talk to about the insidious and catastrophic effects of what was still called, without irony, urban renewal. Jacobs herself sat in the gracious *Time* Inc. headquarters building because by 1952 she had long left behind the life of a freelancer for that of a professional journalist—and, more so, a critic.

Years earlier, Jacobs had begun her rise from the typing pool at the trade journal *Iron Age*. ("They hired me," she explained, "because I could spell molybdenum." [12]) In 1941 wartime and a chauvinist *Iron Age* supervisor sent her into the arms of the US government, where by the postwar years she was producing articles for *Amerika, illyustrirovannyy zhurnal*, a *Life* magazine–like State Department glossy sent to Soviet newsstands. The photo-heavy pages covered American habits, cities, and, increasingly, given their prominence in postwar life, architecture and urbanism. [13]

In the case of the latter, Jacobs's interest became more than professional: in 1942 she married the young architect Robert Hyde Jacobs Jr., a rakish, old-religion convert to the power of building for good. The two moved to 555 Hudson Street, and there, although it was Mr. Jacobs who subscribed to *Architectural Forum*, Mrs. Jacobs soon became the first one to seize the magazine when it arrived. After the State Department operation went to Washington, D.C., this growing interest in building led her to abandon plans to apply to *Natural History* magazine in favor of *Architectural Forum*, where a probationary period soon gave way to a staff position.

Jacobs's general role at *Architectural Forum* was precisely the part in which Kirk, fatefully, sought to cast her: a critic. From the Greek κριτικός, *critic* means, most essentially, "one who judges." Douglas Haskell, Jacobs's equally autodictatic, Yugoslavian-born editor at *Forum*, was determined that the magazine be a literal forum: a shared, public place (from the Latin for "out of doors") for substantial criticism of the already-apparent excesses of postwar American architecture and urbanism. In a memo written to his staff just a month before Jacobs appeared on the masthead, Haskell enjoined "genuine architectural criticism—not the wrist slapping kind, but the kind where you first consult your lawyers about possible action." [14]

12
Jane Jacobs, quoted in Mark Feeney, "City Sage," *Boston Globe Magazine*, November 14, 1993, 10.

13
For example, a 1950 article titled "Planned Reconstruction of Lagging City Areas," published in *Amerika, illyustrirovannyy zhurnal* (America Illustrated), 43.

14
Haskell to staff, memorandum July 23, 1952, box 57, folder 3, Douglas Putnam Haskell Papers, Avery Architectural & Fine Arts Library, Columbia University (hereafter DPHP).

15
Unsigned review, "An Articulate School of Glass," *Architectural Forum* (February 1955): 134. *Forum* carried no bylines at the time, but Jacobs's prose style is evident, and her responsibilities at *Forum* were explicitly the coverage of hospitals and schools. See Anthony Flint, *Wrestling with Moses: How Jane Jacobs Took on New York's Master Builder and Transformed the American City* (New York: Random House, 2009), 18.

Fig. 3 — Jane Jacobs walking in the streets of New York in 1963 © Bob Gomel/Time Life Pictures/Getty Images

16
Unsigned review,
"The Big City School,"
Architectural Forum
(November 1954):
136; unsigned article,
"Schools and Daylight"
Architectural Forum
(April 1955): 140.

17
Unsigned article, "News,"
Architectural Forum
(October 1952): 103.

18
The other five contained
minor revisions to existing
housing legislation,
budget provisions, and
funding for farm housing
and research.

19
Robert A. Caro,
The Power Broker:
Robert Moses and
the Fall of New York
(New York: Knopf, 1974),
12.

In 1955, for three work-filled years, Jacobs had already been a steady judge, praising "design that goes beyond mere organization of shelter" and critiquing that which did not.[15] Where one can discern her voice (*Forum* did not use bylines then), it applauds a relationship to nature—a school "welcomes Connecticut's soft and distant hills and turns inwards to create another kind of nature"—and commends resistance to authority, noting another school's "most radical departure to date from official preconceptions of what a school should look like."[16] Beyond this, the Jacobs-inflected articles are notable for their praise of pragmatism—in her words, "the consistent cleverness of double-duty economy"—and, quintessentially, for their heavy use of quotes on how the buildings actually work, which were far more likely sourced from the buildings' users than from their architects.[17] All of this, with William Kirk's encouragement, brought Jacobs to observe, describe, and judge the effects of the largest expenditure of public resources on architecture of the postwar years: the massive clearance and reinvention of neighborhoods through the legal and administrative vehicle known as Title I.

The name came from the first section of the Federal Housing Act of 1949, whose simple language belied sweeping provisions.[18] Under its outlines a local agency or government was encouraged to demarcate areas of urban fabric as "blighted"—a mostly numerical determination derived from population counts, surveys of building condition, and lot sizes. After review and approval (the almost universal result), the federal government would act as funder, banker, and guarantor for the acquisition and development of the land under eminent domain. And while prior to Title I the acquisition of land through such means had only been possible for public use—as in the construction of a railroad or courthouse—the 1949 law extended the reach of eminent domain to land for, as the legislation put it, any "public purpose," including government-promoted private development. The result: the coordinated demolition, repossessing, and reconstruction of large areas of American cities.

And by "American cities," we might as well say "New York." By 1957 $113 million of federal money had been spent on the rest of the continent, but west of the Hudson and north of 241 Street in the Bronx more than twice that amount was spent—$267 million.[19] As Robert Caro, the biographer of New York's Title I coordinator, Robert Moses, explains, "So far ahead was New York that when scores of huge buildings constructed under its urban renewal program were already erected and occupied, administrators from other cities were still borrowing New York's contract forms to learn how to draw up the initial legal agreements with interested developers."[20]

As Jacobs would write in the introduction to *Death and Life*, "The basic idea, to try to begin understanding the intricate social and economic order under the seeming disorder of cities, was not my idea at all, but that of William Kirk."[21] And even what Kirk showed her during those 1955 expeditions to East Harlem were not so much his own observations as those of his staff and colleagues (particularly Ellen Lurie), who were increasingly alarmed at the material effect of the large, Title I–funded housing projects on the society and its economy.

Kirk led Jacobs to regard, among other things, the corrosive effect of the lack of traditional street-and-stoop spaces in the Corbusian towers of the East Harlem Houses, the way even televisions were treated as community property along surviving street corridors—"Each machine, its extension cord run along the sidewalk from some store's electric outlet, is the informal headquarters spot of a dozen or so men who divide their attention among the machine, the children they are in charge of, their cans of beer, each other's comments and the greetings of passers-by...."[22]

From these Jacobs gathered, in her own words, "a basket of dry leaves" with which a fire would be set.[23] The match would come from elsewhere in the wide furnace of her imagination.

SCRAPS OF PAPER

"It won't do," Jacobs wrote Chadbourne Gilpatric, a program officer in the division of humanities at the distinguished Rockefeller Foundation, in July 1958, "to throw these intricacies at the reader like a basket of leaves. And it won't do, either, to begin with broad, simplified strokes and then embroider these with complications, because any valid simplifications and broad principles in this case can only be based on understanding of the underlying detail—not vice-versa."[24] So although *Death and Life* is a scathing critique of tower-in-the-park urban renewal—and thus at her bosses' request, given the delicacy of attacking the many builders, developers, and designers, and therefore also *Forum* advertisers, profiting from Title I, makes no mention of Jacobs's role at the magazine—it is also more than that.

In 1956, shortly after her uptown education, Jacobs was asked to fill in for Haskell (her editor) at the first Conference on Urban Design at Harvard, convened by Josep Lluís Sert in advance of the school's eventual program (begun in 1960) toward a master's degree in urban design. "If another woman besides Miss Tyrwhitt [a Graduate School of Design professor and co-organizer of the conference] would be not out of place," Haskell had written Sert, "might I suggest that my substitute be Mrs. Robert Jacobs—Jane Jacobs on our masthead. She has handled more of our redevelopment stories than anybody...."[25]

In the talk, Jacobs synthesized Kirk's observations about the diminishing fabric of East Harlem, concentrating for the sake of

20
Ibid.

21
Jane Jacobs, The Death and Life of Great American Cities (New York: Random House, 1961), 15–16.

22
Ibid., 95.

23
Alexiou, Jane Jacobs, 49.

24
Jacobs to Chadbourne Gilpatrick, July 1, 1958, JJP.

25
Haskell to Josep Lluís Sert, March 19, 1956, box 2, folder 5, DPHP, quoted in Peter L. Laurence, "Jane Jacobs (1916–2006): Jane Jacobs Before Death and Life," Journal of the Society of Architectural Historians 66, no. 1 (March 2007): 11–12.

26

The talk was reprinted as "The Missing Link in City Redevelopment," with a rare byline for Jacobs, in Architectural Forum (June 1956): 132–33.

27

Jane Jacobs, "Downtown Is for People," Fortune 57, April 1958, 133–40, 236, 238, 240–42.

28

Lawrence Lessig, memo to Haskell, Hazen and Frotz, January 24, 1958, box 60, folder 1, DPHP, quoted in Laurence, "Jane Jacobs (1916–2006)," 5–15; Jane Jacobs, "Downtown is for People."

29

Ruth Kammler, "Selections from Letters Received During April," Fortune Letters Department, with handwritten note from "HW" to "Doug Haskell and company," JJP.

30

See Laurence, "Jane Jacobs (1916–2006)," 5–15.

illustration on the multiple, irreplaceable functions of the neighborhood grocery. Of all the manifold roles that such establishments serve, she argued, the retail supply of food was only a small portion, and their replacement in a new, systematic plan was all but impossible as "the physical provisions for this kind of process cannot conceivably be formalized. [T]he least we can do," Jacobs continued, "is to respect—in the deepest sense—strips of chaos that have a weird wisdom of their own not yet encompassed in our concept of urban order."[26]

The ten-minute talk (Jacobs was so nervous throughout that afterward she had "no memory of giving it") was instrumental. Practically, it served as an introduction to the established figures of urban theory and practice: professors at MIT and Harvard, *New Yorker* critic Lewis Mumford, and, perhaps most importantly, William H. "Holly" Whyte (who, although they had never met, was actually her colleague at *Time* Inc., where he had written on social, economic, and, increasingly, urban issues for the marquee brand *Fortune* since 1946). Whyte was taken by Jacobs's critical voice, and with the article she ultimately produced synthesizing her developing views on redevelopment: "Downtown Is for People."[27]

What her *Forum* friends termed "Jane's blockbuster on the superblock" was a piece of criticism ultimately deemed too controversial for the magazine's trade-funded pages, and too potentially popular not to appear in *Fortune*, the thoroughbred of the Luce stable, where in April 1958 it served as the capstone of a compilation edited by Whyte, *The Exploding Metropolis*.[28] The article's trenchant critique of urban renewal produced a popular response beyond all expectation. "Just look what your girl has done for us," Whyte wrote to Haskell, over a memo-compendium of popular response to the piece. "This is one of the best responses we've ever had!"[29]

One response in particular would prove instrumental. Chadbourne Gilpatric of the Rockefeller Foundation received from Haskell a copy of Whyte's memo, as well as (some months previously) an early manuscript of the article; this led to an invitation. As part of its expanding interest in urban affairs, the foundation had already commissioned new work in urban theory (giving a grant to György Kepes and Kevin Lynch, which ultimately resulted in Lynch's 1960 *Image of the City*) and urban history (resulting in the eight-volume *International History of City Development* by the UPenn professor E. A. Gutkind), and sought to balance these by commissioning a major work in criticism of current urban design practice—an intellectual space theretofore commanded by Lewis Mumford and few others. Impressed by "Downtown Is for People," and assuming (incorrectly, as it happened) that Jacobs was already working from an understanding of Lynch's foundation-funded work, the invitation came: Would Jacobs, asked Gilpatric, be interested in expanding the architectural critique she had started in *Fortune*, and was continuing in presentations and talks?[30]

But a more expansive critique would need a robust foundation. One "scientific" approach to Jacobs's work had been recommended to her by Martin Myerson and James Q. Wilson of the Harvard-MIT Joint Center for Urban Studies. Her specific response to their advice (to perform a sociological survey of six hundred public housing residents, and so scientifically grounding her empirical observations) is not recorded. But her later response to the inclusion of "Downtown Is for People" in an ostensibly critical volume edited by the center (1966's *Urban Renewal: The Record and the Controversy*) was: "NO. I do not care to appear in this book. Indeed, the idea dismays me greatly. To include *that* piece, in *this* context, quite falsifies my position and ideas concerning urban renewal."[31] In Jacobs's view, the problem with the discourse around urban renewal was that it accepted the fundamental premise of what Gordon Matta-Clark would later term "renewal through modernization," and simply questioned the means and tools of clearance and wholesale rebuilding, with the fact of it as given. Jacobs did not accept the premise, but sought her own effective tools for reframing it.

ORGANIZED COMPLEXITY

As she outlined to Gilpatric in 1958, Jacobs's primary tool in *Death and Life* was to be a far more specific form of empirical observation. Again, she describes her trips to Harlem with William Kirk: "I hardly knew what he was driving at, at first, but the accumulation of detail and incident soon began to make pretty exciting sense, and opened my eyes to other things in other places. This is the process I will have to try to duplicate in the reader's mind...."[32]

Jacobs was, of course, no stranger to urban observation. It was her own ability to wring representative detail from the sidewalk's bustle that had led to her very first commissioned pieces for *Vogue* and other publications. However, what the examples in *Death and Life* represent, from the "daily ballet" of Hudson Street (described on pages 53 and 54) to the sidewalk televisions of East Harlem (dutifully recorded on page 95), was an enfolding of the urban metabolism with the larger instincts of Jacobs's intellectual habit. By 1958, it had long been the practice of Jacobs's independent, inquisitive mind to acquire facts and observations, far in advance of any assumed usefulness, as an inventor hoards steel and spring, or a child shiny stones.[33] Or, for that matter, as her instructors at Columbia collected and structured biological specimens—Thomas McGregor, Jacobs's professor for two introductory zoology courses, spent much of his years prior to teaching her class in the jungles of Tanganyika, Cameroon, and the Belgian Congo (all while in his sixties) for the purpose of collecting gorilla specimens. Her subsequent embryology professor, Edmund B. Wilson, was famous for his cytological specimens, examples of particularly remarkable and exemplary cells preserved between glass slides.

Jacobs's own specimens, scissor-cut slips of paper, appear today in the archive, enveloped in acid-free manila, among the notes for the

31
James Q. Wilson, Urban Renewal: The Record and the Controversy (Cambridge, MA: MIT Press, 1966); Jane Jacobs, handwritten response to letter from James Q. Wilson, original letter dated July 8, 1965, JJP.

32
Jacobs to Chadbourne Gilpatrick, 1958, JJP.

33
Lucia Jacobs, conversation with the author, 2010.

manuscripts in which they eventually came to rest. While the notes that constituted *Death and Life* were not saved, those complied for subsequent works survive—for example, from 1968's *Cities and the Wealth of Nations*:[34]

34
From a folder, "Notes, Cities and the Wealth of Nations," JJP.

— "Not houses finely roofed or the stones of walls well-builded, nay nor canals and dockyards, make the city, but men able to use their opportunity."—A quote from the Greek poet Alcaeus, clipped from a 1962 *Christian Science Monitor*

— "Penn brought to Philadelphia craftsmen and workers by advertising for 'Ingenious Spirits that, being low in the world, are much clogg'd and opressed about a livelihood.'"— A quote from William Penn, the page dated June 1936

— "All things have two handles, beware the wrong one."— "Old saying invoked by Ralph Waldo Emerson, August 31, 1937"

In the text of *Death and Life*, such seemingly extraneous ideas and metaphors are threaded together with detailed empirical observations on urban life. The combination of the two served more often than not to arrange the fabric of urban observation on the living body of the ideas from biology and the natural sciences with which Jacobs had made her acquaintance decades before, and which were to prove an essential scaffolding for her own, emerging edifice. In example:

35
Jacobs, <u>Death and Life</u>, 68.

— "The street grapevine news systems that have their ganglia in the stores...."[35]

36
Ibid., 91.

— "The science-fiction nonsense that parks are 'the lungs of the city.' It takes about three acres of woods to absorb as much carbon dioxide as four people exude in breathing, cooking and heating."[36]

37
Ibid., 172.

— "This tiresome muddle arises not in the least from contradictions between demands by the city as an organism and demands by various specific uses...."[37]

Or, at even greater length, on the issue of gentrification:

38
Ibid., 251–52.

— "Here is a process, then, that operates for a time as a healthy and salutary function, but by failing to modify itself at a critical point becomes a malfunction. The analogy that comes to mind is faulty feedback. The conception of electronic feedback has become familiar with the development of computers....A similar feedback process, regulated chemically rather than electronically, is now believed to modify some of the behavior of cells...."[38]

This is especially provocative given Jacobs's own stated antipathy to the use of scientific metaphor to discuss the city: "[Medical and biological] analogies, applied to social organisms, are apt to be far-fetched, and there is no point in mistaking mammalian chemistry for what goes on in a city." Where such language appeared in the text, it was therefore in service of a more subtle and radical assertion, the deep spark of Jacobs's first book: that cities themselves were a particular form of life.[39]

THE NATURE OF CITIES

When Jacobs received the first of three grants from the Rockefeller Foundation in 1958, her award was announced in the foundation's flecked-cardstock, Smyth-sewn Annual Report. That year, it was elaborately produced to mark the retirement of Dr. Warren Weaver, the foundation's director of natural sciences since 1932. In the report, Weaver had revised an article he first published in 1948, freshly titled "A Quarter-Century in the Natural Sciences."[40] The original title had been "Science and Complexity."[41] The article does not mention cities, or the foundation's urban efforts at all. (Neither do Weaver's 728-page reflections on this Rockefeller tenure, nor his 1970 autobiography.[42]) But to Jacobs it became an essential artifact to be repurposed and extended into a set of essential speculations—grounded in the convergence of biology, information theory, and network science—on, as she was to put it, "The Kind of Problem a City Is."

WARREN WEAVER

While Warren Weaver's initial career was as a mathematician—first at the California Institute of Technology, then at his native University of Wisconsin—he was recruited to the Rockefeller Foundation by a Caltech mentor, Max Moran, in 1932. In his first interview at Rockefeller, he presented an argument that the foundation should expand its program in the "Natural Sciences" (theretofore a catchall for all nonmedical grants) beyond the physical sciences (where it had, for example, recently funded the two-hundred-inch telescope at the Palomar Mountain observatory). Weaver particularly proposed forays into the realm of biology.[43]

Presciently, Weaver had already come to believe that the advances pioneered in the instrumentation, mathematics, and observations of physics and chemistry during the late nineteenth and early twentieth centuries would subsequently allow life to be examined and investigated as never before. Which proved to be the case—of the eighteen Nobel prizes awarded between 1953 and 1965 for fundamental discoveries in genetics and cell biology, seventeen were recipients of grants approved by Weaver, most some decades prior.[44] Throughout the first half of the 1940s, however, Weaver balanced such grant giving with a separate, equally influential posting.

By 1940 Weaver's regular contact with European scientists convinced him "that the world was in for a mess."[45] When the widely admired Vannevar Bush, then President of the Carnegie Institution,

39
Ibid., 13.

40
Warren Weaver, The President's Review: Including "A Quarter Century in the Natural Sciences," The Rockefeller Foundation Annual Report" (New York: Rockefeller Foundation, 1958).

41
Warren Weaver, "Science and Complexity," American Scientist 36, no. 4 (October 1948): 536–44.

42
Warren Weaver, interview by Barbara Land, "The Reminiscences of Warren Weaver," New York Times Oral History Program, and Columbia University Oral History Collection 4, no. 210 (New York: Columbia University Oral History Collection, 1962); Warren Weaver, Scene of Change: A Lifetime in American Science (New York: Scribner, 1970).

43
Ibid., 58.

44
George W. Beadle, foreword to Warren Weaver, Science and Imagination: Selected Papers of Warren Weaver (New York: Basic Books, 1967), xi.

45
Weaver, Reminiscences, 559.

46
Ibid., 561.

47
Harold Hazen, "Fire Control Activities of Division 7, NDRC," in Summary Technical Report of Division 7, NDRC, vol. 1: Gunfire Control, by Summary Reports Group of the Columbia University Division of War Research (New York: Columbia University Press, 1946), 4, as quoted in David Mindell, "Automation's Finest Hour: Radar and System Integration in World War II," in Systems, Experts, and Computers: The Systems Approach in Management and Engineering, World War II and After, ed. Agatha C. Hughes, and Thomas P. Hughes (Cambridge, MA: MIT Press, 2000).

48
Weaver, Reminiscences, 563.

was asked by Franklin Roosevelt to head a new National Defense Research Committee (NDRC; later renamed the Office of Scientific Research and Development, or OSRD), Weaver offered to take up a full-time appointment with the group, which he did. (He was able to retain the support of his Rockefeller salary, relieving him of much of the government-inflicted administrative burdens of his colleagues.[46])

FIRE CONTROL

At OSRD, Weaver's wartime work was instrumental most of all in this: the transformation of military weapons from objects—manipulated things—into systems. That is to say, collections of interconnected things, human beings among them, whose operation depended less on each individual component (including the human), and far more on the number and nature of their connections. As they expanded in complexity and scope, it was also true that the margins of these systems were often hard to define. "It is an integrated whole with interrelated functioning of all its parts and one is safe in considering parts separately only if one always keeps in mind their relation to the whole"—so Weaver's colleague Harold Hazen described the work they each in turn supervised at the OSRD, the division of Fire Control.[47] Weaver himself explained the subject with more humor: "This not relating to the dangers of forestry but to the aiming and controlling of guns."[48]

The most important product of the fire control division during this time, the combined SCR-584 radar system and M9 artillery

Fig. 4 — The combined SCR-584 radar system and M9 artillery control under postwar testing at Edwards Air Force Base, 1947 National Archives at College Park, Still Pictures and Film Collection

control, is exemplary of the origins of systems-based thinking in the military-industrial realm—even prior to the discipline's formal origins. Even beyond its function, the sudden tendency of system-designed military artifacts toward acronyms of numbers and letters, so radically exemplified by the SCR-584/M9 assemblage, was to be theorized decades later by Don DeLillo: the language, he asserts in *Underworld,* comes "from remote levels of development, from technicians and bombheads in their computer universe-storky bespectacled men who deal with systems so layered and many-connected that the ensuing arrays of words must be atomized and redesigned, made spare and letter-sleek."[49]

This early, exemplary system, the SCR-584/M9, only came into being as the product of Warren Weaver's institutional abilities. While Weaver's fire control division (in charge of aiming at the target) had been set up as Division 2 of the OSRD, and MIT's Radiation Laboratory (in charge of finding targets) was organized under Division 1, Weaver saw the need to both define and integrate the two projects, leading to the creation of a special committee, "D 1.5," to integrate the two. In a memo to the head of his corresponding division, Weaver suggested the systematic form of this collaboration, concluding to his colleagues that "your output...was our input."[50] The importance of integrating the automated detection of targets and artillery guidance was further underscored by the director of Sperry Gyroscope's fire control division, Earl Chafee, in his brief assertion that "the emphasis is to be place on the over-all aspects of the *system.*" (The latter emphasis original to Weaver's diary.[51]) Eight years later, imagining a vast, anti-Soviet expansion of automated targeting systems, wartime fire control alumnus George E. Valley Jr. would consider the word *system* still so uncommon in English usage that a definition was provided for the readers of his instrumental October 1950 report to the Defense Department: "The word itself is very general...[as for instance] the "solar system" and "the nervous system"...the isolated systems of thermodynamics, the New York Central [Railroad] System, and the various zoological systems."[52]

The combined SCR-584 radar system and M9 artillery can again serve as an apt illustration of a shift from objects to their systematic array. In purely physical terms, the system combined a radar dish, electronics, and trailer-housed control room (the SCR-584), together with a Bell Labs M3 gun data computer and M9 fire control director (both produced under Weaver's direct supervision). All of these guided and fired a servo-driven 90mm M2 artillery gun, lofting twenty-four-pound explosive shells beyond the speed of sound. The control room of the combined system was hidden in a windowless trailer, which in itself is deeply revealing. Instead of (as in all prior artillery aiming devices) being seated outside in noisy, dirty, direct engagement with the gun and the enemy it was firing at, the operators of the SCR-584 were for the first time seated inside, in a darkened room, seeing targets as illuminated "blips" on a cathode-ray tube, which were in turn selected for targeting by moving a real-time

49

Don DeLillo, Underworld (New York: Scribner's, 1997), 142.

50

Warren Weaver, diary, meeting with Loomis, December 5, 1940; Warren Weaver to Loomis, December 10, 1940; Warren Weaver, diary, December 14, 1940, ORSD7 general project files, box 70, collected diaries, vol. 1., quoted in Mindell, "Automation's Finest Hour," 33.

51

Warren Weaver, diary, November 12, 1942, ORSD7 General Project Files, box 72, collected diaries, vol 5., quoted in Mindell, "Automation's Finest Hour," 33.

52

Air Defense Systems Engineering Committee, Air Defense System: ADSEC Final Report (Bedford, MA: MITRE Corporation Archives, October 24, 1950), 2–3.

53
Mindell, "Automation's Finest Hour," 33.

interface—a targeting "pip." In the words of historian David Mindell, the operators were suddenly "technicians more than soldiers, reading and manipulating representations of the world," lodged not in the field of battle, but removed, in "a control room, a laboratory."[53] A further section of Valley's 1950 Air Defense Systems Engineering Committee report points further: "The Air Defense System...is also a member of a particular category of systems: the category of organisms, a structure composed of distinct parts so constituted that the functioning of the parts and their relations to one another is governed by their relation to the whole....All...organisms possess in common: sensory components, communication facilities, data analysing devices, centers of judgement, directors of action and effectors, or executing agencies." "It is the function of an organism," the section concludes, "to achieve some defined purpose."[54]

54
Air Defense Systems Engineering Committee, ADSEC Final Report, 3.

New systems of objects required new systems of thought. This is especially true of Weaver's post-1943 role as head of the NRDC's newly formed Applied Mathematics Panel. Officially, the panel was responsible for bringing academic mathematicians into the war effort to do applied work. (The nation's original supply of applied mathematicians was already fully engaged in the conflict). One of the most difficult and brilliant mathematicians recruited by Weaver was MIT professor and ex-prodigy Norbert Wiener. "It seemed to me that one of the things that I could do, as a service during the war," Weaver later reflected, "was to maintain my temper and patience and keep Norbert [Wiener] working."[55]

55
Weaver, Reminiscences, 627.

Weaver asked Wiener to work on the same problem of prediction that Weaver's work in fire control attempted to address. "In broad terms," Weaver had himself explained at the time, the problem represented "a *signal* which is immersed in and confused by a very large amount of *noise*."[56] Typical of his own genius, however, Wiener elected not to solve the problem in question, but to instead produce a general theory of signaling and information that could cover the problem as a special case. "He wrote a book for us," Weaver explained, "a report which was bound in yellow covers and which was promptly dubbed the 'Yellow Peril,' which was so abstruse and difficult that practically nobody could understand any of it."[57]

56
Weaver, Reminiscences, 625–26.

57
Weaver, Reminiscences, 626.

A more popular edition of the work, however, revised and expanded after the war, would become an unlikely bestseller: 1948's *Cybernetics: Or Control and Communication in the Animal and the Machine.* As reflected heavily in George Valley's influential 1950 air defense proposal, *Cybernetics* proposed a mathematical and conceptual equivalence between signals, feedback, and control across natural and man-made systems, tied to the provision and manipulation of information.[58]

58
See Thomas Parke Hughes, "MIT as System Builder," in Rescuing Prometheus (New York: Pantheon Books, 1998), 21.

SCIENCE AND COMPLEXITY

In the same year of 1948, Weaver would produce his own set of reflections on his wartime discoveries. The first was an introduction to Claude Shannon's *The Mathematical Theory of Communication* (published in 1949). Shannon had been seconded to Bell Labs and worked alongside Weaver on fire control; his own abstraction of the problem of signal and noise contained therein, along with related work in cryptanalysis, would become, alongside *Cybernetics*, one of the foundational texts of twentieth-century computing and information theory.

The second text was "Science and Complexity." In the essay (as elucidated in turn by Jacobs), Weaver used his wartime experience to divide scientific problems in into thirds. The first, so-called problems of simplicity, involved a few variables that changed according to each other in predictable ways, such as the motion of planets or the dispersal of electric charge. At the other extreme lay problems of "disorganized complexity," which could be made legible by the statistical techniques of the eighteenth and nineteenth centuries—the movement of a gas, or characteristics of a population. In the middle, Weaver identified a third class of problem, those presenting "organized complexity," consisting of multiple, interrelated variables. In her concluding chapter to *Death and Life*, Jacobs uses Weaver's text to argue against the immediate computability or comprehensibility of urban systems—even a simple prediction as to the success of an urban park becomes, in her words, "as slippery as an eel."[59]

Yet what becomes clear upon a contextual reading of Weaver's argument is that he was arguing, in many ways, precisely the reverse. Far from expressing reservations about the definability of such problems, Weaver was pointing toward attempts at their systematic and cybernetic solution—an ambition that was to have disastrous effects on the fabric of American cities.

MODEL METROPOLIS

"It is within the range of conjecture," Weaver himself later explained of the essay, "that modern computers, with their speeds, their logical flexibility, their capacity of storage, can be adapted to [problems of organized complexity]." "In fact," he concludes, "some substantial evidence for this is already before us."[60] By 1967, in a final revision of the essay that appeared in his collected papers, he would go even further: "The solution of a system of say one hundred interlocked nonlinear differential equations...became a wholly practical possibility. Input-output analysis of the economy of a nation, involving as many as 450 interdependent commodities, can successfully be handled...."[61] As Weaver mentioned, by the late 1960s cybernetically inflected models of multivariable systems were entering popular use by academics and policymakers. And, almost immediately, this conversation was closely related to urban administration and design.

"A city is primarily a communication center, serving the same purpose as a nerve center in the body. It is a place where railroads, telephone and telegraph centers come together, where ideas, information and goods can be exchanged"—so Norbert Wiener had written in 1950, advocating the low-density dispersal of urban functions in order to better survive nuclear attack.[62] As the historians of

59
Jacobs, Death and Life, 433.

60
Weaver, Reminiscences, 652.

61
Warren Weaver, "Science and Complexity," in Weaver, Science and Imagination.

62
Norbert Wiener, Karl Deutsch, and Giorgio de Santillana, "The Planners Evaluate Their Plan," Life 29, no. 25 (December 18, 1950): 85. See also Jennifer S. Light, "Cybernetics and Urban Renewal," chap. 3 in From Warfare to Welfare: Defense Intellectuals and urban Problems in Cold War America (Baltimore: Johns Hopkins University Press, 2003); Peter Galison, "War against the Center," in Architecture and the Sciences: Exchanging Metaphors, ed. Antoine Picon and Alessandra Ponte, Princeton Papers on Architecture 4 (New York: Princeton Architectural Press, 2003).

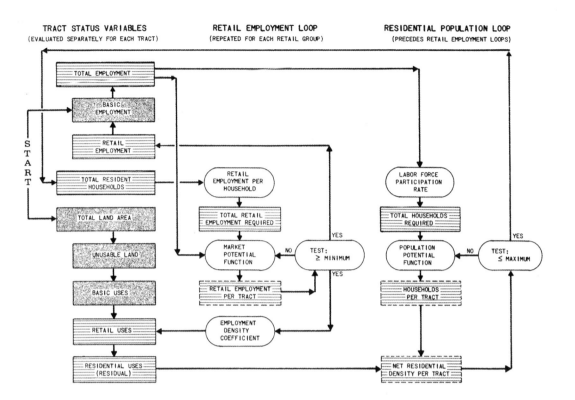

TRACT STATUS VARIABLES
(EVALUATED SEPARATELY FOR EACH TRACT)

RETAIL EMPLOYMENT LOOP
(REPEATED FOR EACH RETAIL GROUP)

RESIDENTIAL POPULATION LOOP
(PRECEDES RETAIL EMPLOYMENT LOOPS)

Fig. 1 — Information Flows in the Pittsburgh Model

Fig. 5 — A page from "Model of Metropolis," 1962 © The Rand Corporation

technology Thomas and Agatha Hughes have written, a range of organizations cultivated and spread the cybernetically studied systems approach from their origins "in the communities of engineers and scientists who dealt with problems of gunfire control."[63] These included in particular the RAND (Research ANd Development) and MITRE corporations (funded by the air force in 1948 and 1958, respectively, the latter as an offshoot of MIT), and the Ramo-Wooldridge Corporation (in collaboration with Bernard Schriever's intercontinental ballistic missile, or ICBM, project in the air force). And so it was Ira Lowry of the RAND Corporation who produced the influential 1964 study "A Model of Metropolis," which modeled the city of Pittsburgh as a "system of equations."

"The potential advantage of a computer model," Lowry wrote, "over *ad hoc* planning procedures derives mainly from the computer's ability to deal simultaneously with the large numbers of variables intrinsic to comprehensive planning."[64] Lowry's RAND colleague Paul Baran was to write three years later, advocating for a cybernetic, communications-based dispersed city, that "unwholesome mélanges have resulted from the haphazard development of urban concentrations."[65] The computer pioneer Jay Forrester, whose work on the Whirlwind computer transformed into the direct product of the 1950 Valley air defense report—the SAGE Air Defense System, designed and built by IBM and MITRE, and discussed at length in "The Map

63
Hughes and Hughes, Systems, Experts and Computers, 3.

64
Ira S. Lowry, A Model of Metropolis (Santa Monica, CA: RAND Corporation, 1964), 1.

65
Paul Baran and Martin Greenberg, Urban Node in the Information Network (Santa Monica, CA: RAND Corporation, 1967).

and the Territory"—had by the mid-1960s devoted himself to the study of multivariable urban models, culminating in 1969's *Urban Dynamics*.[66] That same year, ICBM system engineer Simon Ramo would write that "the biggest example we can cite of threatened complete disintegration, resulting from inadequate consideration and handling of the major parameters of what is a systems problem, is the typical large American city."[67]

This view was mirrored, throughout the 1960s, in the professions of planning and design. The same Harvard-MIT Joint Center for Urban Studies with which Jacobs violently resisted association in 1962 published Richard Meier's *Communications Theory of Urban Growth*, which was explicitly indebted to Shannon's *Mathematical Theory of Communication*. This center would influentially house a range of scholars, including Carl Steinitz, and help orchestrate instrumental efforts around information flow models and maps in urban planning and design (explored at further length in "The Map and the Territory"). The City of Los Angeles invested heavily and collaboratively with RAND on the Mathematical Model and Simulation Section of the Department of City Planning. A preparatory study prepared at the University of Southern California, *The Cybernetic Approach to Urban Analysis*, advocated a "total systems approach...[to] the exceedingly complex...system of subsystems" composing the city.[68]

Yet what is abundantly clear—especially in retrospect—is that such multivariable urban models, far from usefully enhancing the previous, statistical methods dismissed by Jacobs as "a collection of file drawers," in fact led to the same oversimplification, abstraction, and calamitous results as the methods they replaced.[69] From the disastrous, data-justified closing of firehouses in the Bronx recommended by RAND consultants (resulting indirectly in the scale and severity of the 1974 fires), to the more everyday difficulties of reconciling digital models with unpredictable urban realities in Los Angeles, San Francisco, and Pittsburgh, multivariable urban simulation was to prove almost exactly as limited, and limiting, in its outcomes throughout the 1960s and 1970s as more simplistic models had through the previous decades.[70]

MORE IS DIFFERENT

Why, precisely, was this the case?

An attempt to characterize such difficulties in a scientific context came in a 1972 paper by the physicist P. W. Anderson (who had arrived at Bell Labs at the dawn of postwar cybernetic enthusiasm in 1949). It was titled "More Is Different."[71]

Reflecting, among other influences, Anderson's own experience implementing the tenets of cybernetic thought at Bell Labs, the paper asserted the fundamental difference between the knowledge of essential principles in a complex system and any ability to predict or understand the behavior of such a system in aggregate. "The ability to reduce everything to simple fundamental laws," Anderson argued,

66
Jay W. Forrester, Urban Dynamics (Cambridge, MA: MIT Press, 1969).

67
Simon Ramo, Cure for Chaos: Fresh Solutions to Social Problems through the Systems Approach (New York: D. McKay, 1969), 36.

68
Leland M. Swanson and Glenn O. Johnson, eds., The Cybernetic Approach to Urban Analysis (Los Angeles: University of Southern California, 1964), iii.

69
Jacobs, Death and Life, 436.

70
See Joe Flood, The Fires: How a Computer Formula Burned Down New York City—and Determined the Future of American Cities (New York: Riverhead Books, 2010); see also Light, "Cybernetics."

71
P. W. Anderson, "More Is Different: Broken Symmetry and the Nature of the Hierarchical Structure of Science," Science 177, no. 4047 (August 4, 1972): 393–96.

"does not imply the ability to start from those laws and reconstruct the universe." In the case of complex systems in particular, he continues, "the whole becomes not only more than but very different from the sum of its parts." Anderson concludes the paper by reflecting that "there may well be no useful parallel to be drawn between the way in which complexity appears in the simplest cases of many-body theory and chemistry and the way it appears in the truly complex cultural and biological ones, except perhaps to say that...the relationship between the system and its parts is intellectually a one-way street. Synthesis is expected to be all but impossible; analysis, on the other hand, may be not only possible but fruitful in all kinds of ways."

ROBOT BOMBS

In his postwar reflections, Warren Weaver presents the success of his own administrative efforts in fire control as a cause for optimism in the technical solution of complex problems. He notes in particular the astonishing success of the SCR-584/M9 in the battle against the 1944 threat of the V1 guided missile, or "buzz bomb." "Our 90mm batteries, with radar range and our predictor," Weaver would later boast, "just knocked those buzz bombs out of the sky like nobody's business. There was battery after battery that had killing ratios of 90 percent."[72] A moment later, Weaver reflects: "During this experience on the fire control problem I became very deeply interested in computers and what they were going to mean, and this led to some thinking after the war...." The latter leads directly to "Science and Complexity."[73]

Yet the real reason for the targeting effectiveness lauded by Weaver (which would actually have to wait for the addition of an electromagnetic proximity fuse, added during the D-Day invasion, to achieve the kill rates remembered in the passage above) is perhaps best explained by General Sir Frederick Pile (G.C.B, D.S.O., M.C.!), commander of the British Anti-Aircraft Command: "It seemed to us that the obvious answer to the robot target of the flying bomb...was a robot defense...."[74] Because of the computational difficulty of allowing for curved airplane trajectories, and evasive maneuvers that pilots regularly engaged upon sighting the muzzle flash of antiaircraft guns (the attempts to mathematically formalize such man-machine interactions producing Norbert Wiener's "yellow peril"), even the sophisticated SCR-584/M9 fire control device assumed a level, constant speed and flat trajectory. With death the disincentive, German pilots quickly learned to avoid the predictable path it assumed through the sky. But the V-1, of course, had no pilot. Which is not to say it was not a deeply formidable weapon—driven by an innovative pulse-jet engine (whose audible 45hz resonant frequency endowed it's nickname, "buzz bomb"), the missile's 500-mph speed and low altitude made it exceedingly difficult for a ground-based human marksman to hit. However, its guidance system, built by the German watchmaker Askania, was only capable of directing the V-1 in a level, constant-speed trajectory. Thus, in a kind of cybernetic symmetry, it became the perfect target for the rapid-response SCR-584/M9,

72
Weaver, Reminiscences, 574.

73
Ibid., 579.

74
Mindell, "Automation's Finest Hour"; General Sir Fredrick Pile, Ack-Ack, Britain's Defence Against Air Attack During the Second World War (London: Harrap, 1949), 314.

predicting not the pilot's behavior but that of another automatic machine.

THE IMITATION GAME

Shortly after the end of the war, and its remarkable cultivation of computing devices in Britain and the United States, Alan Turing attempted to distinguish between the predictability of systems of computing and systems of reality in a paper more famous for its proposition of the so-called Turing test, or, as he himself termed it, the "imitation game."

> The system of the "universe as a whole" is such that quite small errors in the initial conditions can have an overwhelming effect at a later time. The displacement of a single electron by a billionth of a centimeter at one moment might make the difference between a man being killed by an avalanche a year later, or escaping. It is an essential property of the mechanical systems which we have called "discrete-state machines" [computers] that this phenomenon does not occur.[75]

Characterized contemporaneously with Anderson's 1972 paper as "the butterfly effect" by the mathematician Edward Lorenz, the inability to effectively predict the behavior of complex, self-organizing systems derives from the very connectivity and lack of hierarchy characterized by Jane Jacobs in her 1958 letter to Chadbourne Gilpatric. In the letter, Jacobs had asserted for the first time "that within the seeming chaos and jumble of the city is a remarkable degree of order, in the form of relationships of all kinds that people have evolved....Where it works at all well, this network of relationships is astonishingly intricate. It requires a staggering diversity of activities and people, very intimately interlocked (although often casually so), and able to make constant adjustments to needs and circumstances."[76] Underlining her own understanding of Weaver, and of complexity itself, Jacobs would reference his 1958 essay once more in 2000's *The Nature of Economies*, in a chapter titled "Unpredictability," immediately followed in the text by a presentation of Lorenz's work on the "butterfly effect." The phenomenon was first described by Lorenz in two 1963 papers, the second of which concludes that "if the theory were correct, one flap of a sea gull's wings would be enough to alter the course of the weather forever. The controversy has not yet been settled, but the most recent evidence seems to favor the sea gulls."[77] Lorenz presented the paper at the 139th meeting of the American Association for the Advancement of Science, where Lorenz's as "Predictability: Does the Flap of a Butterfly's Wings in Brazil Set Off a Tornado in Texas?"—which led to the name "Butterfly Effect."[78] As a result, especially in a system as complex and interconnected as a city, a true cybernetic planner would have to to treat all actions and interventions equally in such a calculation. Yet, recalling

75
A. M. Turing, "Computing Machinery and Intelligence," Mind 49 (1950): 433–60.

76
Jacobs to Chadbourne Gilpatrick, 1958, JJP.

77
Edward N. Lorenz, "Deterministic Nonperiodic Flow," Journal of the Atmospheric Science 20, no. 2 (March 1963): 130–41, and Edward N. Lorenz, "The Predictability of Hydrodynamic Flow," Transactions of The New York Academy of Sciences, 2nd ser. II, 25, no. 4 (February 1963): 409–32.

78
Edward N. Lorenz, "Predictability: Does the Flap of a Butterfly's Wings in Brazil Set Off a Tornado in Texas?" presented before the American Association for the Advancement of Science, December 29, 1972.

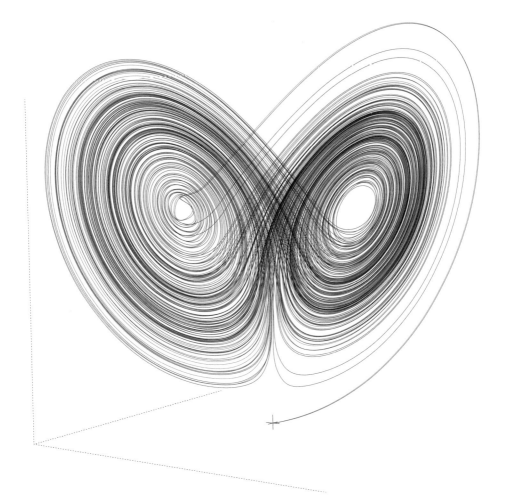

Fig. 6 — A mathematical model of the Lorenz attractor
showing divergent paths from near-identical initial
conditions, 2014 © Drawn by the author

Turing's displaced electron, the number of computational steps necessary to evaluate even a single intervention across a city (for example) of a million people turns out to be on the order of 106 × 106—a
number far larger than the number of atoms in the universe.[79]

79
See Luís Bettencourt,
"The Uses of Big Data
in Cities" (working
paper, Santa Fe Institute,
New Mexico, 2013),
accessed October 4, 2015,
http://www.santafe.edu/
media/workingpapers/
13-09-029.pdf.

IT HAS NO PURPOSE, IT IS ALIVE

After introducing the notion of "system" to its audience, and then
characterizing the air defense system proposed as an "organism," the
1950 Valley air defense report concludes, "It is the function of an
organism is to...achieve some defined purpose." When she was a girl,
Jacobs later reported, she once asked her father to explain to her the
purpose of life. "Look at that oak tree," she remembered her father
answering, "It's alive. What's its purpose?"

Stuart Kaufmann, whose own pioneering work with computer
simulation of genetic networks in the late 1960s established fundamental principles of the autocatalytic, large-order complexity fundamental to living systems, anchors a popular introduction to such

ideas with an image almost Jacobsian in its domestic ordering.[80] Imagine, Kaufmann asks, ten thousand buttons cast on a hardwood, living-room floor. As you connect them one by one, with thread, your labors are mostly unrewarded, until the ratio of buttons comes to an unexpected point, usually about one-half. Then the network will suddenly shift. All of a sudden, when you pick up a button, instead of a meager clump of one or two additional buttons arriving with it, you will suddenly find you have connected nearly all the buttons on the floor in one way or another. It is just on this knife-edge, between overdetermined connectivity and disordered disconnection—"the edge of chaos," as Jacobs would herself describe it in *The Nature of Economies*—that the unpredictable but remarkable organization of complex systems occur.

Kaufmann uses the image to illustrate in particular the complex, interrelated nature of metabolic networks in living systems, and how the very complexity of these networks is also their evolutionary strength and autocatalytic origin. "The analogue in the origin-of-life theory," Kaufmann explains, is that when enough connections come to exist, "a vast web of catalyzed reactions will suddenly crystallize. Such a web, it turns out, is almost certainly...alive."[81]

THE CITY NATURALIST

"Thinking has its strategies and tactics too," Jacobs opens "The Kind of Problem a City Is"; she continues, "Which avenues of thinking are apt to be useful and to help yield the truth depends not on how we might prefer to think about a subject, but rather on the inherent nature of the subject itself."[82] A decade before she argued to Chadbourne Gilpatric "that within the seeming chaos and jumble of the city is a remarkable degree of order," she had also written this: "The lights of New York are the city's jewels, but her buttons and hooks and eyes are the squares and circles of metal that dot asphalt and sidewalks." It was the opening sentence of one of her earliest freelance articles, for the entertainment magazine *CUE*, on the subject of manholes.[83] "Despite the almost hopeless variety," Jacobs explains, "the city naturalist, keeping an eye on the letters of the covers, can tell" what river, web, or network "he" (but really an autobiographical "she"), "is on the trail of."

From connected scraps of facts, to—as in the case of Warren Weaver's 1958 essay—appropriated and expanded theoretical edifice, what is in the end one of the most remarkable qualities of *The Death and Life of Great American Cities* is that just like the manifold maquettes and presentations that Jacobs was subject to in her formative role as an architecture critic, it was a model of what it proposed. Like her 1930s walks through the fabric and flesh of the city, as the original city naturalist herself, it follows the city as an intellectual network—thread and button, articulated fact and connective theory—all along the pathways of its own sustaining metabolism. And its discovery, more than anything else, is the complexity and interrelatedness of both urban idea and physical fact.

80
See, for example, Stuart A. Kaufmann, "Metabolic Stability and Epigenesis in Randomly Constructed Genetic Nets," Journal of Theoretical Biology 22 (1969): 437–67; Stuart A. Kauffman, At Home in the Universe: The Search for Laws of Self-Organization and Complexity (New York: Oxford University Press, 1995).

81
Ibid., 58.

82
Jacobs, Death and Life, 428.

83
Jane Jacobs (writing as Jane Butzner), "Caution: Men Working," Cue: The Weekly Magazine of Metropolitan Entertainment, May 1940, 24–25.

84

With the notable
exception of the
architectural historian
Peter Laurence, who
has written extensively
about this period in the
context of his dissertation,
"Jane Jacobs, American
architectural criticism
and urban design
theory, 1935–1965"
(PhD diss., University of
Pennsylvania, 2009) and
the articles noted above.
I am indebted particularly
to this research.

85

As, for example, in the
Lindsay-funded RAND
Institute. See Light,
"Cybernetics."

86

Roger C. Conant and
W. Ross Ashby, "Every
Good Regulator of a
System Must Be a
Model of that System,"
International Journal
of Systems Science 1,
no. 2 (1970): 89–97.

87

See Bettencourt,
"The Uses of Big Data
in Cities."

This is lastly also a reason (alongside *Forum*'s anxieties about advertisers and customers) why Jacobs's fourteen years as an architecture critic may be so absent from both her own books and popular discussion of her career.[84] *Death and Life* is a conceptual model of the city, echoing and aligning with the structure of urban life, even as it provides a description of it as well. But it is in the nature of such a model—diffuse, edgeless, interconnected, and in large part immaterial—to be fundamentally incompatible with the models that inhabit architectural culture. Despite the notoriety afforded *Death and Life* upon its publication, systems planning would continue to seek to create order out of the chaos of the city for decades to come—even in New York, where a RAND consulting team formed part of the mayor's office until 1972.[85]

In 1970 the systems scientists Roger Conant and Ross Ashby influentially would assert that "the living brain, so far as it is to be successful and efficient as a regulator for survival, must proceed, in learning, by the formation of a model (or models) of its environment."[86] The paper itself was titled "Every Good Regulator of a System Must Be a Model of That System." The irony being that the best model of the city we probably carry around with us is our brains themselves; our one hundred trillion synaptic connections roughly approximating the potential social connections in a city of ten million people. Given the potential—à la Lorenz—of each of these nodes proving potentially crucial, simulating these possible connections grows far faster than exponentially; for a city of a million people the connective possibilities number more than a one with six million zeros, a quantity far larger than the number of atoms in the universe, and far, far beyond our ability to accurately simulate.[87]

As a result, the city and the brain are both fundamentally resistant to prediction, including that implied in the conventional architectural model. Each is governed by a careful combination of serendipity and habit; each has the resulting capacity—exemplified in Jacobs's own text and patterns of thought—for opportunistic connections, unexpected alignments, and artful reimaginings. It was for their capacity to be repurposed in particular that Jacobs would advocate for a mixed stock of old buildings rather than new, purpose-built ones. (Gordon Matta-Clark's decade in the city as an adult, bent on the repurposing and reuse of such built fabric, ironically commenced just as Jacobs was leaving New York City for Toronto in 1969.)

In the end, trying to reimagine the city with a single, physical (or virtually physical) model is like trying to row a boat with a spiderweb. A city is not an artifact, or exhibit. Like Jacobs's text itself, urban structure cannot be understood in isolation, or even primarily through its literal form. And yet, we persist in envisioning buildings, and developments, as isolated things (and so more marketable), and uneasily resist their real nature as fleeting participants in manifold networks—social, ecological, physical, and temporal. Against such a realization, however, a single building, park, or plaza could not ever serve alone in imagining the architecture of the city. It would be as much use as a single specimen in imagining our earth as a whole.

Venice Case Study

Towards an Ecology of Strangers
(Verso una Ecologia di Forestieri)

An invited contribution to Spontaneous Interventions:
Design Actions for the Common Good, US Pavilion,
13th Venice Architecture Biennale, 2012

In the spectrum of cities, Venice is both singular and a *sine qua non*. In terms of both its urban and natural form, and of its contributions to historical continuity and artistic innovation, it is unique but indispensable. Yet for all the powerful continuities represented by Venice, the city-lagoon system is currently threatened by discontinuities and disparities of enormous scale: the twin tides of man and nature.

Once a city of hundreds of thousands, the lagoon now hosts only sixty-five thousand residents, who in turn mostly serve a tourist population of twelve million to twenty million annual visitors.[1] And the shallow lagoon, for thousands of years a cultivated balance between sea and silt, has also in the past forty years undergone ecological shifts—of level, composition, ecology, and salinity—that threaten not only its identity, but its very existence, and thus the city that depends on it.[2]

In Venice's historic context of subtlety, robustness, multiplicity, and celebration, current proposed physical and financial solutions to the city's problems appear singular, sudden, and even gargantuan.

1

See Robert C. Davis and Garry Marvin, Venice, the Tourist Maze: A Cultural Critique of the World's Most Touristed City (Berkeley: University of California Press, 2004), 211–37.

2

See John Keahey, Venice Against the Sea: A City Besieged (New York: T. Dunne Books/St. Martin's Press, 2002); Stefano Guerzoni and Davide Tagliapietra, Atlante della laguna: Venezia tra terra e mare (Venice: Marsilio, 2006), 57–74.

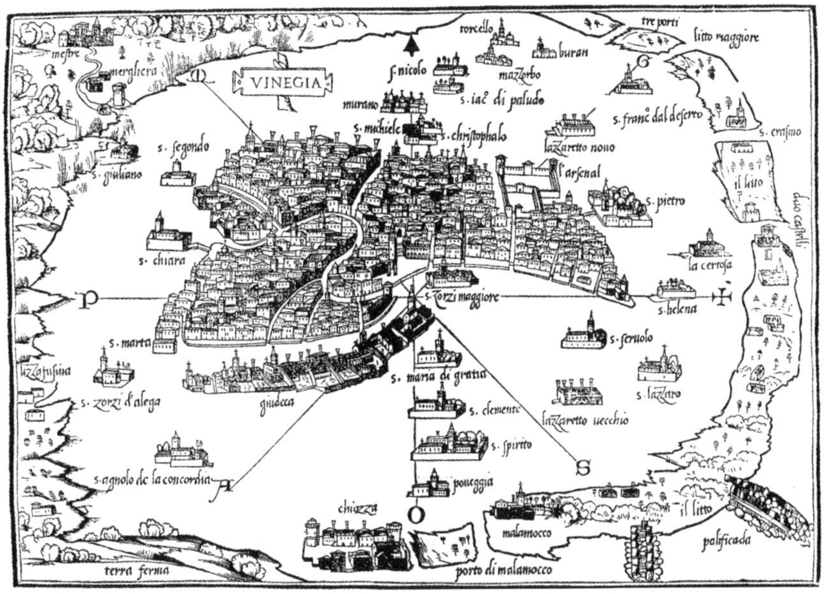

Fig. 1 — The Map of Venice prepared in the second decade of the 1500s by Benedetto Bordone and first published in 1528. Venice is already a city encompassing the whole lagoon, as a network of near and distant islands. Today's city is physically, as well as economically and socially, diminished.

Exemplary is the multibillion-euro MoSE floodgate project whose enormity lurks below the edges of the lagoon. On the streets of the city, however, one encounters such singular proposals not in the linear manner that they in turn seek to address Venice's problems, but rather through the labyrinthine arguments on facts and figures—causes and effects—that surround them. The nature of these debates reasserts the essential complexity and interconnectedness of any urban or natural system, and it is in a consideration of complexity and interconnectedness that Venice remains essential.

With these thoughts in mind, we imagine a new, networked future for the Venetian lagoon, in which ecological remediation and cultural residencies populate the diverse bodies of the islands, extending and buffering the city, and its ecosystem, to historic scales. The proposed urban interventions tackle the problem of Venice through the lens of both contemporary urban thinking and a deep understanding of its own influential history. Historically, the metropolis was not confined to what Venetians of today know as the "fish"—the dense network of *isolé*, formed out of sandbars and mudbanks in the early Middle Ages, cleaved by the Grand Canal and the Zattere. Rather, it was an interlinked archipelago, stretching the length and breadth of the lagoon, in which a variety of functions, incompatible or inconvenient to the city center, were spread throughout the lagoon's waterways.

From Napoleon's closure of monasteries and fortresses throughout the lagoon in the eighteenth century, to the current city's dependence on the ironically named (at least to native Venetians) causeway of the Ponte della Libertà, the city's shrinking material and cultural prospects have mirrored its physical circumscription into a single, shrinking island. Against this background, our proposal imagines a remaking and reinvention of the city through a systematic renovation of the lagoon's abandoned islands. Free from the pressures of historic preservation, and side-stepping the scenographic remediation of wetlands around the central *isolé* (in which sheet pilings substitute for a natural process), the outlying islands are here imagined as both cultural and ecological catalysts, our interventions shape and welcome processes whose disorder, and odor, have meant their excision from the contemporary city. Grounded in digital information about the current lagoon, these speculations are shaped by America's distinctive contribution to territorial studies—speculations on the entropic, informational, and infrastructural.

These proposals seek to imagine not the strict preservation that has frozen the city's core, but rather the robust embrace of history's possibilities.

LA CURA, 2008

LE SALINE, 2010

SAN GIACOMO IN PALUDE, 2010

SANTO SPIRITO, 2008

SANTO SPIRITO, 2008

SAN SECONDO, 2008

SAN GIORGIO IN ALGA, 2006

LOCAL CODE

VENETIAN LAGOON
SURVEY OF ABANDONED/
UNDERUTILIZED ISLANDS, 2012

DEPTH RANGE IN METERS
Magistrato alle Acque di Venezia -
Consorzio Venezia Nuova, 2002

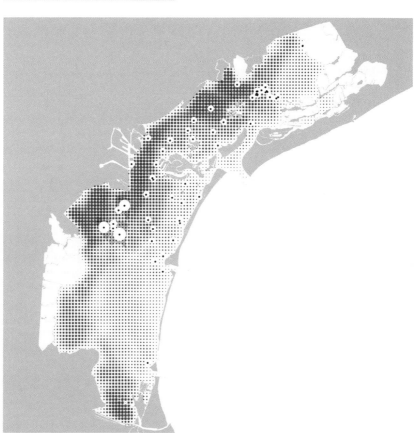

NITROGEN SEDIMENT
CONCENTRATIONS, 1995–2001
Magistrato alle Acque di
Venezia, Progetto ICSEL

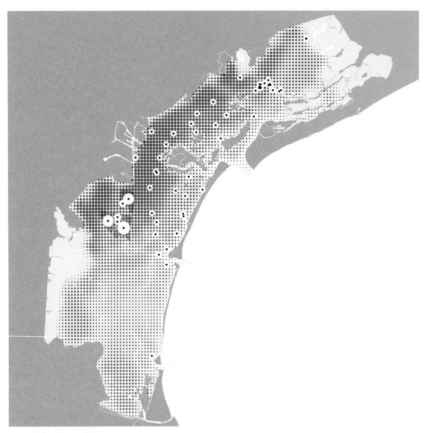

REACTIVE PHOSPHOROUS
IN WATER COLUMN UG/L,
AUTUMN & WINTER, 2001–2003
Magistrato alle Acque di Venezi

TYPICAL SALINITY
AUTUMN/SPRING, %
Magistrato alle Acque di Venezia

TIDAL AMPLIFICATION METERS
Institute of Marine Sciences of
the Italian National Research
Council (CNR-ISMAR), 2002

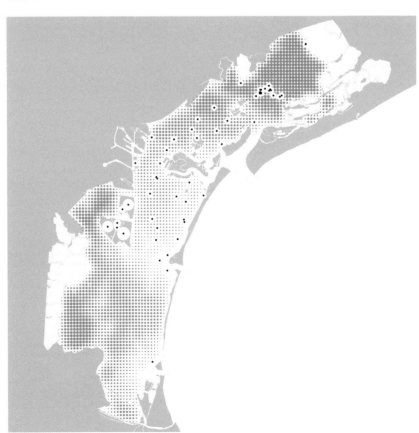

TIDAL PHASE TIDAL PHASE
SHIFT, MINUTES (MAX 120M)
CNR-ISMAR, 2002

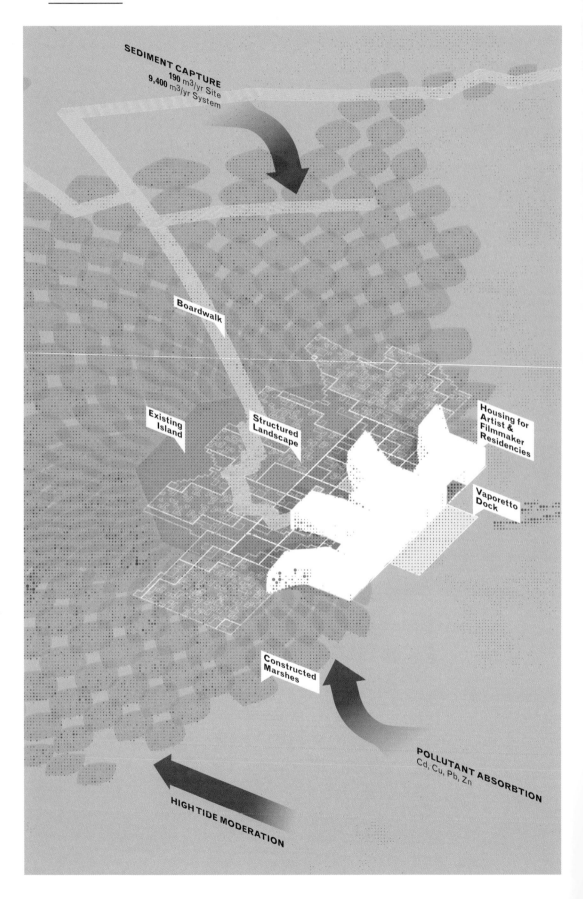

SEDIMENT CAPTURE
190 m3/yr Site
9,400 m3/yr System

Boardwalk

Existing Island

Structured Landscape

Housing for Artist & Filmmaker Residencies

Vaporetto Dock

Constructed Marshes

POLLUTANT ABSORBTION
Cd, Cu, Pb, Zn

HIGH TIDE MODERATION

SENZA NOME 450 m²
NEW WETLANDS

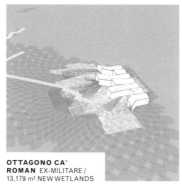

**OTTAGONO CA'
ROMAN** EX-MILITARE /
13,179 m² NEW WETLANDS

SENZA NOME 1,039 m²
NEW WETLANDS

SENZA NOME EX-NESSUNO /
55,132 m² NEW WETLANDS

**EX BATTERIA
FISOLO** EX-MILITARE /
880 m² NEW WETLANDS

**EX BATTERIA
POVEGLIA** EX-MILITARE /
5,284 m² NEW WETLANDS

**SENZA
NOME**

SAN GIULIANO EX-MONASTICA /
41,536 m² NEW WETLANDS

FARO SPIGNON EX-FARO
DI SEGNALAZIONE /
2,950 m² NEW WETLANDS

**SANT' ANGELO DELLA
POLVERE** 3,541 m²
NEW WETLANDS

**BATTERIA PODO O
CAMPANA** EX-MILITARE /
12,178 m² NEW WETLANDS

**SAN GIORGIO IN
ALGA** EX-MONASTICA /
9,687 m² NEW WETLANDS

**OTTAGONO SAN
PIETRO** EX-MILITARE /
5,653 m² NEW WETLANDS

TREZZE EX-MILITARE /
3,973 m² NEW WETLANDS

**OTTAGONO
ALBERONI** EX-MILITARE /
5,189 m² NEW WETLANDS

**OTTAGONO
ABBANDONATO**

S. SECONDO EX-MONASTICA /
8,812 m² NEW WETLANDS

**OTTAGONO
POVEGLIA** 1,508 m²
NEW WETLANDS

**SANTA MARIA DELLE
GRAZIE** 4,578 m²
NEW WETLANDS

CAMPALTO EX-MILITARE /
42,699 m² NEW WETLANDS

SACCA SESSOLA EX-DEPOSITO /
24,521 m² NEW WETLANDS

**POVEGLIA (ESCLUSO
OTTAGONO)** EX-RESIDENZIALE /
13,723 m² NEW WETLANDS

SENZA NOME EX-NESSUNO /
6,137 m² NEW WETLANDS

SANTO SPIRITO EX-MONASTICA /
21,577 m² NEW WETLANDS

TESSERA EX-MILITARE /
10,568 m² NEW WETLANDS

CARBONERA EX-MILITARE /
9,489 m² NEW WETLANDS

**LAZZARETTO
VECCHIO (COMPRESA
ORTALIA)** EX-MONASTICA /
14,200 m² NEW WETLANDS

BUEL DEL LOVO EX-MILITARE /
13,915 m² NEW WETLANDS

**MADONNA DEL
MONTE** EX-MONASTICA /
1,737 m² NEW WETLANDS

SAN GIACOMO IN PALUO EX-MONASTICA /
5,170 m² NEW WETLANDS

CREVAN EX-MILITARE /
2,300 m² NEW WETLANDS

MOTTA SAN LORENZO EX-RESIDENZIALE /
13,247 m² NEW WETLANDS

LAZZARETTO NUOVO EX-OSPIZIO /
10,334 m² NEW WETLANDS

LA CURA EX-RESIDENZIALE
E AGRICOLA / 10,267 m²
NEW WETLANDS

SENZA NOME EX-NESSUNO /
1,208 m² NEW WETLANDS

EX RIDOTTO MONTE DELL'ORO EX-MONASTICA /
5,785 m² NEW WETLANDS

SANTA CRISTINA EX-MONASTICA /
29,243 m² NEW WETLANDS

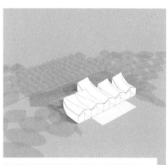

CASON MONTIRON EX-VALLICOLTURA /
3,936 m² NEW WETLANDS

SANT' ARIANO EX-MONASTICA /
7,677 m² NEW WETLANDS

MOTTA DEI CUNUCCI EX-RESIDENZIALE /
29,701 m² NEW WETLANDS

LA SALINA EX-MONASTICA /
12,457 m² NEW WETLANDS

The Map and the Territory

1
Howard T. Fisher to
Turpin C. Bannister,
March 2, 1954, Papers
of Howard T. Fisher,
Harvard University,
Cambridge, MA
(hereafter HTFP).

"A large part of an architect's life is spent beating his brains out trying to establish himself enough so that he can make a decent living—then when he arrives his career is about over...." So reflected the then fifty-one-year-old Howard T. Fisher in 1954. "While this may be good for building strong and moral fibre and advancing stamina," he concluded, "it is a pretty tough racket."[1] The irony was that Fisher, a patrician, well-mannered architect of shopping centers and prefabricated houses, and later a sought-after consultant, was to make the greatest impact of his long career in a field largely unknown to him until several years later—geographic information systems, or GIS.

Fisher's encounter with GIS, and in particular the way in which his architectural training caused him to deploy and demand from it more than had previously been accomplished, graphically and conceptually, would have a seminal (if underacknowledged) effect on the field. His insights, furthermore, came directly not from a background in geography or computing, but architecture. A decade after his pioneering work, Fisher himself would reflect that "my experience in design through architectural education and architectural practice is what made it possible for me to develop the original [GIS] program."[2]

2
Fisher to the Committee
to Review the Laboratory
for Computer Graphics
and Spatial Analysis,
memorandum response,
May 22, 1974, HTFP, 2–5.

Fisher's outlook and goals, moreover, offer an essential glimpse at a series of possible histories—and so also contemporary alternatives—for architecture's encounter with mapping and information. But such a history also demands that we understand that computing and mapping were already, from the beginning, bound together.

"THERE OUGHT TO BE A MACHINE"

"To all whom it may concern:" announced a submission to the US Patent Office in September 1884, "Be it known that I, Herman Hollerith, a citizen of the United States, residing at New York City, in the county and State of New York, have invented certain new and useful Improvements in Apparatus for Compiling Statistics."[3] The devices contained in the patent application, would, along with a third patent filed in 1889, form the basis for today's information processing machines.

3
Herman Hollerith to
US Patent Office, cover
letter, January 8, 1889
(US Patent 395,783, filed
September 23, 1884:
"Apparatus for Compiling
Statistics"; U.S. Patent
395,782, originally filed
September 23, 1884,
divided and filed October
27, 1885: "Art of Compiling
Statistics"; US Patent
395,781, filed June 8,
1887: "Art of Compiling
Statistics"), quoted
in Emerson W. Pugh,
Building IBM: Shaping
an Industry and Its
Technology (Cambridge,
MA: MIT Press, 1995),
1–13.

The US Census—required by Article I, Section 2, of the Constitution—mandates Congress to count the country's populace every ten years. And count not just their number but also their location, so as to ensure fair representation through congressional districts and fair taxation among the states. The first census of 1790 counted a population of just over four million souls (including, of course, African American slaves, whose disenfranchised numbers were reduced to three-fifths of free populations in apportioning representation). By 1870 the population was ten times as large. While the technology of the census—pen and ink—remained unchanged, what *had* changed alongside the nation's growing ranks was the more complex use of the census; it was by the late nineteenth century used not only to count heads but also gender, race, occupation, and origin. The census had become not just an instrument of apportionment, but also complex questions of policy.[4]

Hollerith knew this well. After graduating from the Columbia School of Mines (later the School of Engineering and Applied Science) at age nineteen in 1879, he worked as a statistician for the Census of 1880.[5] His original appointment was to collect and analyze information on the use of steam- and waterpower by iron and steel foundries. Ultimately, however (thanks to his developing friendship with John S. Billings, a doctor employed by the census in the Bureau of Vital Statistics), Hollerith became concerned with the Census' fundamental method of adding numbers. Which was not an immaterial issue—using hand-based methods, the 1870 census had been finished in eighteen months, and had counted over thirty million Americans. Thanks to an increase in population (to fifty million) as well as more complex social and spatial information requested by Congress, the 1880 census would take over seven years to count. If undertaken with the same methods, the 1890 census was forecast to take until 1904—long after the subsequent 1900 count had begun.

With these issues very much of concern, "one Sunday evening, at Dr. Billings' tea table," Hollerith was to recall, "he said to me there ought to be a machine for doing the purely mechanical work of tabulating population and similar statistics. We talked the matter over.... He thought of using cards with the description of the individual shown by notches punched in the edge of the card."[6] The trajectory of Hollerith's next decade (a decision to leave the Census Bureau, a year teaching at MIT, a year in the US Patent Office, even time spent devising better air brakes for trains) would be set by his goal of building, and patenting, such a device.

The first deployment of Hollerith's resulting machinery was at the unassuming Department of Health in Baltimore, where Billings arranged for a test in 1886. Information about the location, birthplace, and cause of death for thousands of Baltimoreans was recorded, one person to each $3\frac{1}{4} \times 8\frac{5}{8}$-inch card. Hollerith's plier-like hand punch reflected his inspiration for the method—the "punch photograph" used by Western train conductors to record the appearance of ticket-holders and so avoid fraud (with holes for dark or light hair, eye color, etc.).[7] It was also nearly his undoing: after a day spent continuously punching holes, Hollerith's hand and arm became temporarily paralyzed.[8] (Later improvements would include a pantograph-like device in which an operator could punch cards by pointing to a location with a stylus.)

The great innovation of Hollerith's machine was housed in a different device, which performed the electromechanical and spatial translation of statistical variables and spatial coordinates from the world into the easily digestible (if otherwise unrecognizable) field of the punched card. The device consumed these cards into a complex

4
Margo J. Anderson, The American Census: A Social History (New Haven, CT: Yale University Press, 1988), 85.

5
Geoffrey D. Austrian, Herman Hollerith: Forgotten Giant of Information Processing (New York: Columbia University Press, 1982), 1–4.

6
Hollerith to J. T. Wilson, August 7, 1919, in "Historical Development of IBM Products and Patents," prepared by J. Hayward for IBM (1957), 18–23, quoted in Pugh, Building IBM, 3.

7
Pugh, Building IBM, 6.

8
Austrian, Hermann Hollerith, 39–40.

Fig. 1 — Punch-card reader
attached to Hollerith Census Tabulator
Courtesy Marcin Wichary

assembly combining hundreds of pins in a grid, raised and lowered by a handle above a rubber surface, into which were set hundreds of corresponding tiny cups of mercury. Each time a pin passed through a hole in a card and into the electrified liquid—the cards positioned and guillotined singly by the operator—one of a series of clock-face counters facing the operator advanced. A further level of function was added by a row of boxes with electrically triggered lids: as the card was sandwiched into the electromechanical press, one of these lids opened based on the information it contained; the operator placed the card in the open box and closed the lid before the next card was counted. (This mechanism allowed sophisticated sorting procedures based on one or more variables punched into the cards.)

In 1889 Hollerith's former colleague on the 1880 census, Robert P. Porter, was named as superintendent of the 1890 census, and one of his first official acts was to commission a study of counting equipment. Headed by Dr. Billings, Hollerith's sometimes mentor, the commission studied Hollerith's device against two competing systems, using test data from St. Louis, Missouri. In the end, the device equipment made it easy for his friends to favor it against the others (both of which used color-coding to ease manual counting instead of electricity).[9] It counted the data 50 percent faster than the nearest competitor, and tabulated the results eight times as fast.[10] As was later reported by the newly founded journal *Electrical Engineer*, on the final 1890 count "it seems only possible to say one thing, namely, that the apparatus works as unerringly as the mills of the Gods, but beats them hollow as to speed."[11]

In the larger argument of this book—about adaptation and reappropriation in the space of cities and networks—the intellectual achievement of Hollerith's device is exemplary. Its subtlety is reflected in the time and care he took preparing his patent submission. First filed in September 1884, the application was divided, renewed, amended, and supplemented by a third filing in 1887, resulting in a series of patents issued together in January 1889. For as Hollerith was well aware, there was very little in his device—taken separately—that was new. Punched cards had stored information about fabric patterns since their original invention by Jacques Vaucanson in 1777 (later much improved by Joseph Marie Jacquard).[12] And the electromechanical components of Hollerith's device drew equally on other existing tabulating machines. Rather than claiming an original invention, he then elaborately prepared his patents on a lesser-used patenting premise—that his combination of existing mechanisms created a new device whose construction was not obvious to those already "skilled in the art."[13]

Of the further trajectory of Hollerith and his electromechanical tabulator, much could be said: The technology's adoption, then co-option by the Census Department (shielded at the time from patent claims by its status as a government entity). The extension of the census-based technology, through a more abstract series of numbered cards, to a wider range of accounting practices (begun through contracts with railroads, whose movements of goods through space and time proved particularly suitable for rapid addition and manipulation). The merger, arranged by financier Charles Ranlett Flint, with the International Time Recording, Computing Scale, and Bundy Manufacturing companies, to become in 1911 the Computing-Tabulating-Recording Company (CTR). And finally the name change arranged by CTR's fourth president, Thomas J. Watson (serving from

9
T. C. Martin, "Counting a Nation by Electricity," Electrical Engineer 12 (November 11, 1891): 1.

10
Pugh, Building IBM, 13.

11
Martin, "Counting a Nation," 2.

12
Herman Blum, The Loom Has a Brain: The Story of the Jacquard Weaver's Art (Philadelphia: Craftex Mills, 1959), 33.

13
Pugh, Building IBM, 8.

1915 until 1956), who rechristened the firm in 1924 as the International Business Machines Corporation, or IBM. The story of IBM leads directly to today's GIS as well.

WHIRLWIND AND SAGE

Here again we take up George E. Valley Jr.'s 1950 report to the Defense Department, in which the word *system* was newly deployed to describe an air-defense program—SAGE, the Semi-Autonomous Ground Environment—combining computation, mapping, and visual display. This in many ways derived from the SCR-584 radar system and M-9 artillery that Valley helped design during World War II under Warren Weaver's direction (and which proved so influential in Weaver's 1947 draft of "Science and Complexity," discussed above). But SAGE also profoundly advanced the ambition of its antecedents. For in the new system, Hollerith's brainchild, IBM, would for the first time compute not just a real-time electronic map of the world, but a framework for altering the world through the device's digital operation.

The system, designed to shoot Soviet bombers from the sky, had its origins in what one might imagine as the opposite pursuit—getting pilots off the ground. In 1943 US Navy Captain Luis de Flores proposed that, instead of investing in more of the then ubiquitous pneumatic airplane-training simulators (manufactured by a former pipe-organ company), the navy should attempt to create a single machine that could be quickly set to simulate many different aircraft. This rapid reconfigurability begat the project's name: Whirlwind. It was housed (not coincidentally) at de Flores's alma mater, MIT. Initially, the effort sought to build on the work of existing analog computers, such as the massive, IBM-built Harvard Mark 1, whose three thousand square feet of rotating metal drums were, at the time, computing firing tables for the army. By 1946, however, the attention of Project Whirlwind's director, Jay Forrester, turned to the army's very latest computers, such as the Electronic Numerical Integrator and Computer, or ENIAC, which stored its signals digitally, as discontinuous electromechanical states of "on" and "off," instead of the continuous curves of earlier devices.

By 1948 the airplane cockpit scheduled to be mated to a prototype Whirlwind simulator was moldering in a Cambridge scrap-metal yard, and Project Whirlwind had come to focus solely on the creation of a multifunction stored-program computer for the military.[14] Like the ENIAC's successor, the UNIVAC (UNIVersal Automatic Computer, built at the University of Pennsylvania), the Whirlwind computer would be able to perform calculations based not simply on the triggering of electrical or mechanical relays—the physical, "hard" reality of machinery—but rather on what "software," or stored program, it had been asked to perform. This was the so-called Von Neumann architecture described by the Princeton mathematician in 1945 (although the use of the word *architecture* to describe the configuration of computer parts would have to wait another two decades, as seen below).[15]

14
Kent C. Redmond and Thomas M. Smith, Project Whirlwind: The History of a Pioneer Computer (Bedford, MA: Digital Equipment Corporation, 1980), 60.

15
Paul Cerruzi, The History of Modern Computing (Cambridge, MA: MIT Press, 2003), 21.

The notion of Whirlwind as a mapmaker and analyzer was also present, almost from its creation. In 1947 a core argument was advanced to the navy to justify the newly digital strategy of the computer—the ability of a digital computer to more effectively map and chart submarine movements.[16] The final version of Whirlwind, though, deployed in 1954, would have been as unrecognizable to "computer" experts of the day as it is recognizable to modern eyes. (Indeed, as late as the 1940s, the word *computer* was used far more often in its prior meaning, to refer to a human being engaged in calculation work.) By then fully dubbed SAGE, the new system combined two things we often think of as fundamental to modern computing, and a third that we should add to the list. The first two were real-time computing and a screen-based interface (like the computer on which these words are being written, but unlike any before it). The third was a map of the world.

AN/FSQ-7

Mapping technique and technology has long been driven by the military's need to understand the lay of the land (as, for example, during the early nineteenth-century Napoleonic Wars, when the widespread adoption of topographical isolines, or contours, arrived part and parcel with the new reach and scope of artillery.[17]) In the case of SAGE, the revolution was the collapse of previously separate mapping technologies—the remote sensing of radar, the informational plotting of control and situation rooms, and the direction of military resources through orders and commands—into a single cathode ray–tube surface, shown to the operator who interacted with the world through its glass. As with the rest of SAGE's equipment, IBM crafted the device. The resulting enormous installation was officially known as the Army-Navy Fixed Special Equipment number seven, or—letter-sleek—the AN/FSQ-7.

The large round screen in SAGE's operating console did not (as had the wartime fire-control systems it emerged from) present radar sensor data directly. Rather, the computer driving the screen (itself occupying forty thousand square feet and using three million watts of power) interpreted the sensor's data and presented it to the operator as a series of abstracted symbols.[18] On the screen, the operator could target or dismiss the identified object/attacker using a light gun (complete with trigger),

Fig. 2 — A View of the SAGE Console, 1964 National Archives at College Park, Still Pictures and Film Collection

16
Redmond and Smith, Project Whirlwind, 58.

17
Norman J. W. Thrower, Maps and Civilization: Cartography in Culture and Society, rev. ed. (Chicago: University of Chicago Press, 1996), 97.

18
Thomas Parke Hughes, Rescuing Prometheus (New York: Pantheon Books, 1998), 51.

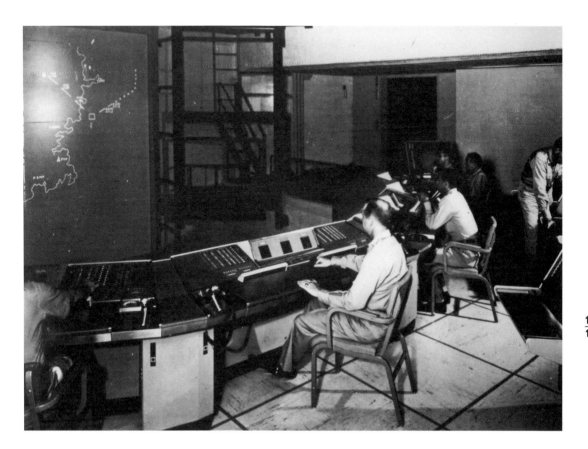

Fig. 3 — A view of the SAGE Installation, Hanscom
Field, Massachusetts, 1965 National Archives at
College Park, Still Pictures and Film Collection

whose position was sensed and reported by the console. This last ability, to assess and produce information in real-time, was the product of the AN/SFQ-7's most remarkable innovation: real-time magnetic memory, or RAM, 147,456 ferrite cores of which sat in a three-dimensional matrix at the computer's core. These replaced the slow and unreliable vacuum tubes and toxic heated mercury conduits of previous computers and allowed the devices to harness an unprecedented level of computing power. Much of this newfound power was used to draw and trace the outlines of the territory being defended; an electronically projected outline of Massachusetts's Cape Ann is visible in the graphic projection room of the first test SAGE installation at Hanscom Field.

It would be the mastery of electronic data processing that IBM gained from the SAGE project—as well as half a billion dollars of revenue from constructing SAGE equipment—that would allow IBM to achieve the enormous dominance in digital computing it held from the 1950s until the 1970s.[19] (In the realm of defense, by contrast, SAGE was seen as an expensive failure; imagined and conceived when bombers were the chief threat from the Soviet Union, it was rendered obsolete by intercontinental ballistic missiles soon after its inital deployment.)

19
Ibid.

The mapping functions of SAGE provided specific technical innovations in plotting and display: equally important to the origins of more widespread computer mapping were the vast improvements in calculation speed afforded by the real-time magnetic-core memory. From their post-SAGE introduction in the 1950s until the 1970s, the ubiquitous mainframe computers introduced by IBM would represent a hybrid of the punch card–based interface first invented by Hollerith, and the rapid processing of such cards afforded by the solid-state innovations developed during Whirlwind. (IBM's profits from the magnetic-core memory developed at MIT would see it the subject of lawsuits until 1964, ending with a multimillion-dollar payment to the university.)

"GRAPHICALLY TENTH-RATE"

Perhaps unsurprisingly, given the Hollerith punch card's origins, one of the first uses of IBM's computers by 1950s researchers was for the mapping of census data, a process pioneered by Edgar Horwood at the University of Washington. Horwood's process was only half-digital, however, adding a layer of computer-printed symbols to transparent, hand-drawn overlays, the two bound together in a final, photographic composite.[20] It was at a two-week workshop at Northwestern University in 1963, led by Edgar Horwood, that Howard Fisher was first introduced to the concept.

Almost immediately, Fisher thought he could do better. While he had closed his professional practice in 1957, retiring (or so he thought), he was moved by his own aesthetic outrage to begin a new career. "As I work on this whole problem," he would write in 1966, "I am impressed by how graphically tenth-rate a major portion of statistical maps are, regardless of the technique used."[21]

HOWARD T. FISHER

Fisher's own education in the built landscape and its representation began where his career ended—at Harvard. And it ended there as it began, with the drawing of ink onto the page.

Arriving in Cambridge in 1922 as the well-born son of President Taft's secretary of the interior, Fisher's skill in drawing drew him to the fine arts department, and thence to the nascent Faculty of Architecture (which had been formally organized only ten years prior). He graduated magna cum laude with a BS in architecture in 1926 from Harvard College, having won two summer scholarships to draw and study architecture in France. Until 1928 he taught classes in drawing and architectural history in the Faculty while taking graduate classes. But the opportunity to begin work on building his brother Walter's house in his native Chicago proved too tempting, and he left Cambridge without receiving a master's degree in the spring of 1928.[22]

Soon after, Fisher's first efforts to marshal systems in the service of design arrived. After six years of building in Chicago, and successfully completing his Architectural Registration Exam in the spring

20
Timothy W. Foresman, "GIS Early Years and the Threads of Evolution," in The History of Geographic Information Systems: Perspectives from the Pioneers, ed. Timothy W. Foresman (New York: Prentice Hall, 1998), 3. The use of overlaid layers to create complex maps itself became common in the nineteenth century, and found its roots even earlier; Louis Alexandre Berthier used hinged overlay maps at the 1781 siege of Yorktown to show troop movements to his own commander, Rochambeau, as well as General Washington.

21
Fisher to Phil Christiansen, memorandum, July 18, 1966, HTFP.

22
Howard T. Fisher, biographical sketch, dated "August 1930," HTFP.

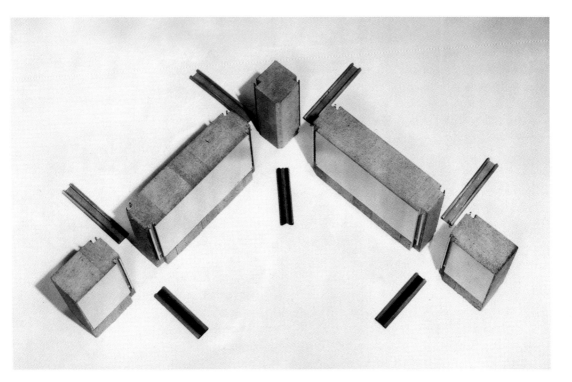

Fig. 4 — Parts to the General Houses Panel System, Howard Fisher, 1932 © The Estate of Howard Fisher. Courtesy of Harvard University Archives, Howard T. Fisher Papers.

23
Ibid.

24
General Houses Brochure, 1937, HTFP.

25
See Colin Davies, The Prefabricated Home (London: Reaktion Books, 2006).

26
Fisher to reunion committee, 1936, HTFP.

27
Fisher to Frederick Fisher, March 24, 1944, HTFP.

of 1931, he became a contributing editor of *Architectural Record* (a competitor, even then, to Jacobs's *Forum*), and turned himself to the problem, in his words, "of the low-cost factory fabricated house."[23] After detailing the history and prospects for prefabrication in the pages of *Record*, he leapt into the problem himself, organizing the General Houses Corporation in 1933 to produce his own models of panel-built, prefabricated dwellings. Beyond the claims of economy and speed, the emphasis in the houses' marketing materials, as well as Fisher's private correspondence, was in the their good design. After coverage in *Fortune*, and the display of a prototype at Chicago's Century of Progress exposition in 1933–34, General Houses would demand his full-time attention for much of the rest of the decade—but without providing him with a dependable income. For while the elegance and precision of the steel-framing and pressure-glued panel system he proposed was remarkable—"the last word in smartness, comfort, beauty, simplified living, efficient equipment," promised brochures—the challenges faced by the company were the same faced by a legion of other prefab firms throughout the twentieth century.[24] These included a lack of cooperation from local builders, conservatism in first-time homebuyers, difficulties securing mortgages.[25] And, of course, in the 1930s, challenged by the Depression as well: "If only the 'bottom' will stop 'dropping out' for long enough," Fisher was to write in 1936, "something may come of it."[26] It would take the demands and opportunities of wartime to alter his prefabricated fortunes; after limping through the 1930s, he was able to secure wartime contracts for prefabricated housing beginning in 1940.[27]

Having entered government service through the provision of "demountable" wartime housing, Fisher stayed in it through the post-war 1940s and early 1950s. First, he served as a consultant to the veteran's housing program; then, through 1953, he served as a consultant to the Inter-American Development Bank, the Organization of American States, and the United Nations, primarily in Honduras and Bogota, Colombia, where he became familiar with the machine-driven accounting and analytic procedures used in development work.[28] It was partially in recognition of this wide-ranging experience that Fisher was offered an adjunct position at Northwestern on his full-time return to Chicago in 1953, where, a decade later, he would first be exposed to computer mapping techniques.

DRAWING TOGETHER

While the techniques Fisher was exposed to in 1963 at Northwestern were highly original in their own way, they were also representative of the institutional origins and character of much of digital mapping. Even in the 1960s, computers were only owned by large institutions, and so the chief concerns in computer mapping were the interests of these institutions, who alone could fund the enormous costs associated with computer work. (The rental cost for a single IBM 7090, on which SYMAP first ran, was $63,500 a month, or more than $500,000 in 2015 dollars.) Edgar Horwood's work, for example, was funded largely from the enormous outlay of government funds associated with Title I urban redevelopment (see "Fake Estates and Reality Properties"), in particular from the Federal Department of Urban Redevelopment. The data-driven composite overlay maps produced from the University of Washington, the surveyed, for example, "census blocks with ten per cent or more deteriorating housing units" in Spokane, each offending hand-drawn block marked with a computer-plotted asterisk.[29]

Such a connection between resources and mapping was true—at a literal and continental level—of another pioneering computer mapping program of the time: the vast Canada Geographic Information System, which gave its name to the emerging field. The Canadian GIS emerged from a policy discussion of the continent's natural resources, and the fact, in the words of the system's founder, Roger Tomlinson, that "although these resources had long been regarded as limitless, there was now competition among the potential uses of land in the commercially accessible parts of the country."[30] Like Fisher's own efforts, the Canadian GIS was also influenced by the work of Edgar Horwood.[31] A 1968 film produced by the Canadian government, *Data for Decision*, highlights the sort of overlay-based map questions the system was intended to automate: "What resources can be developed?" "How fast?" "At what cost?"[32] In Canada, as in the vast expenditures of Title I that provided the context to Horwood's work, the chief questions were of resources and expenditure, and the chief role of the map was target blocks or regions that met specified conditions; much like the dynamics of the SAGE

28
And here, a moment of unexpected disclosure: as I learned only in 2012—partially through the surprising inclusion of a 1959 Christmas letter typed by my grandmother, the business-machine programmer Nell de Monchaux, in Fisher's Harvard archive—Fisher's housemate in Tegucigalpa was my grandfather, the French-Australian business-machine consultant Emile de Monchaux. And as a result his summertime assistant in housing work in Bogota, Colombia, in 1952 was my then sixteen-year-old father, Jean Pierre de Monchaux. My father's recollections were an unexpected asset in developing a full sense of Fisher's character, although the thesis and argument of this essay was crafted in the archives beforehand.

29
Edgar M. Horwood, Using Computer Graphics in Community Renewal; Computer Methods of Graphing, Data Positioning and Symbolic Mapping (Seattle: University of Washington, 1963), 5.0–1.

30
Roger Tomlinson, "The Canada Geographic Information System," in The History of Geographic Information Systems: Perspectives from the Pioneers, ed. Timothy W. Foresman (Upper Saddle River, NJ: Prentice Hall PTR, 1998), 21.

31
Nicholas R. Chrisman, Charting the Unknown: How Computer Mapping at Harvard Became GIS (Redlands, CA: Esri Press, 2006), 13.

32
Department of Forestry and Rural Development, Data for Decision, directed by David Millar (Ottawa: National Film Board of Canada, 1968).

system, the either-or logic of targeting was well suited to the core language of the digital computer. At its core (which, by virtue of the primitive nature of the hardware they used, the first mapping programs were not far from) the computer parsed the world through a series of yes/no statements, so-called Boolean operations, in a language of thresholds and absolutes—not shades of gray.

Fisher's interest, by contrast, was precisely in shades of gray—both literally and conceptually—as well as, in further contrast (as it were) to those who came before him, in making the tools for digital mapmaking as widely available as possible. In this he was guided by a vision of the process of shaping the physical environment—of design—that was as much intuitive as it was systematic. Fisher sought, in his own words, an "interaction of man and machines [that] emphasizes the power of each. The computer acts as a repository [*sic*] and processor of information, i.e., it deals with quantitative information, while the designer controls the design process and performs the final evaluation *which is not readily quantifiable* [emphasis added]."[33] The result of this approach, initially cemented during a year-long collaboration with programmer Betty Benson at Northwestern from 1963 to 1964, was what Fisher called the SYnagraphic MAPping program, or SYMAP. *Synagraphic*, a characteristic neologism of his, combined the Greek root συν, or *syn*, meaning "together," with γραφή, meaning "graphic" or "drawing." It emphasized the program's ability to not just envision the world as a separate set of layers, but to manipulate and encode multiple variables together, in the same graphic field; its goal was, literally, to draw together—visually, strategically, and creatively. In this, SYMAP emphasized the map less as method of optimally acting on the world and more as a method of seeing it anew.

As to the second point, Fisher's immediate predecessors viewed GIS either as a service provided by experts (Horwood did not distribute his software, but rather charged for its use in specific analyses), or as an expert-owned piece of governmental infrastructure (Tomlinson sought to set up a central, digital mapping bureau in the Canadian government). Fisher instead believed that "the computer at its very best is nothing more than a tool," to which he believed there should be as much access as possible.[34]

To help advance his work on SYMAP, he turned to the same foundations and public-interest groups he had been moving among since wartime. One of the people Fisher approached was Louis Winnick, a housing economist (known to Fisher from his own housing work) who had arrived at the Ford Foundation in 1962 to help direct its nascent program in public affairs. They discussed the idea of a large-scale grant to develop SYMAP further, but as of 1964 it was unclear who the institutional recipient of such a grant would be. Fisher's appointment at Northwestern was as an adjunct instructor only, and while demonstrations of SYMAP had roused interest at both MIT and the University of Chicago, very little credence was given to his academic qualifications (or, rather, his lack of them, with

33
"My basic approach to involvement with computers...," Howard T. Fisher, in an undated manuscript, HTFP.

34
Fisher to the Committee to Review the Laboratory for Computer Graphics and Spatial Analysis, memorandum response, May 22, 1974, HTFP, 1–5.

only a BS from Harvard and a long career in practice to his name).[35] The solution came in 1965 with an appointment as a lecturer at the Harvard Graduate School of Design (GSD), since 1936 its own professional school within the university. But the GSD, focused on professional training, needed to create a proper research-focused institutional setting to potentially receive the Ford funds.[36] And so, under Fisher's direction and with the cooperation of Dean Sert, the Laboratory for Computer Graphics was created. It was there, finally, that the Ford Foundation awarded $294,000 ($2 million today) in January 1966.[37] The grant's purpose was explicit: to develop and distribute SYMAP as widely as possible.[38]

THE SOFTWARE ITSELF

The first version of SYMAP, created in 1964, was later credited with establishing "the basic functions" of all subsequent cartographic display software, namely "separating the base geometric data from the thematic attribute, scaling the map to different sizes, and permitting distinct graphic treatment of the same source material."[39] Its instrument for doing so—the idea for which had occurred to Fisher upon observing Edgar Horwood's line-printed map layers in 1963—was a treatment of the entire thirteen-inch-wide surface of line-printed paper, output from the IBM 1403 electromagnetic chain printer, as a graphic "field." The technique literally coaxed scales of gray from a device otherwise incapable of providing it.

The 1403 printer was a device sufficiently iconic at the time that it featured in the set design and plot of Kubrick's *Dr. Strangelove* (where it fatefully hides the transistor radio that reveals that the remote-sensed Soviet attack is **not** real). Its more conventional purpose was to produce the text-based output from batch computing runs on IBM's mainframes. (First distributed with the 7090 mainframe in 1959, the printer was produced through 1971.) Instead of moving a type head to each position on the page—as in, for example, a contemporaneous electric typewriter—the iconic, computerized chain-printer moved a "chain" of raised letters behind an inked ribbon in front of the cog-driven paper. And, counterintuitively, it was an electromagnetically controlled hammer behind the vertically hanging paper, not above it, that jammed the sheet between the ink ribbon and the raised typography, marking the page. Within this mechanism, SYMAP could manipulate the printer's instructions so that, rather than printing recognizable strings of text, the device instead layered one character on top of the other to create a series of tones and lines, forming a recognizable image or map. Unlike standard IBM code, which was designed to allow overprinting of two characters only—to produce, for example, underlined text—SYMAP hacked the printer to overprint up to four characters on every point of the map's surface: the lightest texture could be given by a period; the heaviest by overprinting four characters such as "OXAV" or "MWI*."[40] From this humble misuse came an expressive range of tone and texture.

35
Fisher to Louis Winnick, January 14, 1965, HTFP.

36
Fisher, memorandum response, May 22, 1974, HTFP, I–2.

37
William A. Doebele Jr., Associate Dean for Development, memorandum to George Bennett, Treasurer, GSD, "Ford Foundation Grant of $294,000 to the Graduate School of Design for Training and Research in Computer Map-Making," April 1, 1966, HTFP.

38
Fisher, memorandum response, May 22, 1974, HTFP, I–2.

39
Chrisman, Charting the Unknown, 21.

40
Ibid., 26.

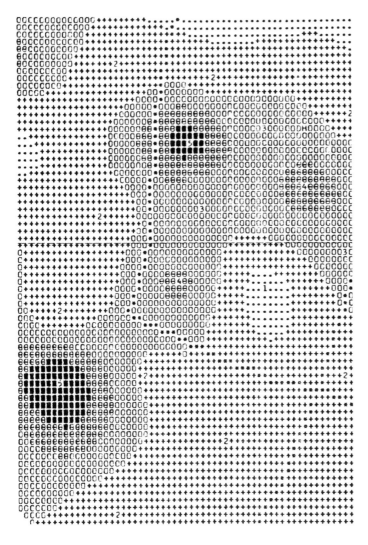

At Harvard, Fisher's Laboratory grew quickly to meet several goals: the further development of SYMAP and related tools, the support and training of those at other institutions eager to use the software, and, finally, the project of encouraging and experimenting with the use of the software by studios and programs within the GSD. And yet the Lab did not own or administer a single computer. Rather, it simply prepared punch card stacks, including those containing the source code of SYMAP in FORTRAN, for what was (at the Lab's founding) Harvard's only such device—an IBM 7090-series mainframe located in the raised-floor computing center several buildings away.[41]

Yet for all the singular success of Fisher's tenure as director of the Lab (which saw SYMAP become the most widely distributed software of its kind in the world), it was also singularly brief. He would reach Harvard's then mandatory retirement of sixty-six in 1969, the same year

Fig. 5 — A detail of a 1966 map prepared with SYMAP, showing a surface contour of car thefts in Boston Harvard University Archives, Howard T. Fisher Papers

as the Ford Foundation funds were depleted, and in the event chose to step down a year earlier in what would turn out to be an unsuccessful attempt to allow the Lab's new director, geographer William Warntz, to better establish his leadership.[42] "No man is indispensable," wrote William Doeble, acting dean after Josep Lluís Sert's 1968 retirement, "and retirement is an ultimate necessity of us all, but the Laboratory and its accomplishments are to a very special degree the personal achievement of Mr. Fisher."[43]

Nearly shuttered in 1974, when a sharply worded report judged its software-distribution activities ill-suited to Harvard's goals and culture, and its efforts reduced in scope until its eventual disbandment in 1991, the Harvard Laboratory would never again hold the central role in digital cartography that it did during Fisher's tenure. Yet, viewed from a half-century's distance, several essential

42
Fisher, memorandum response, May 22, 1974, HTFP, I–9.

43
Memorandum from William A. Doebele Jr., Acting Dean, Graduate School of Design, to William C. Pendleton, Program Officer, The Ford Foundation, May 1969, HTFP.

observations can be made about the contributions of this brief, mid-century moment, as well as to the alternative possibilities that might have (and might yet) emerge from its mold.

First, SYMAP established for the first time the nature of digital mapping as a visual tool, and not just an administrative technique. Unlike the more specific pieces of software prepared before and around it, SYMAP was not intended for a specific administrative purpose. And as a result, it had to define its own internal tools—of managing features, scale, data structures, and a variety of graphic representations—far more broadly, and in a way that continues to define digital mapping software to the present day. More often than not these functions were created out of a deliberate misuse, and reap-propriation, of the information technology of the time—most visible in the overprinting and layering of supposedly singular alphanu-meric outputs, but also visible throughout the software's economical source code.

Secondly, a result of his encounter with computing as a mature practitioner, Fisher made contributions toward an understanding of the precise limitations of digital mapping and practice. "It must be recognized," he wrote (in response to a 1974 GSD memorandum rec-ommending closure of the Laboratory), "that the computer at its very best is nothing more than a tool. It is a remarkable tool in terms of its accuracy, speed, and economy—and particularly in terms of its increasingly fabulous capability for storing information in memory ready for use. The computer must, however, be directed by human beings and thus can never be thought of as other than a tool." He then adds, for emphasis, "It is particularly important that this fact be rec-ognized in giving thought to its potential role in *architectural* design."[44]

Presciently and perceptively, Fisher openly declared the central-ity of representation—as opposed to technical knowledge—to urban, landscape, and architectural practice. This was SYMAP's great strength, and his own goal. The professions at the core of the GSD's mission, he argued in the same memorandum, had always been pri-marily concerned with visual communication. "It is unthinkable," Fisher contended "to try to communicate from one person to another information as to the complex variables existing in an urban area without the benefit of graphic display—or to communicate the facts regarding an architectural design of more than the most elementary simplicity."[45] Yet what interested him about graphic expression in design was as much its subtle complexity as its superficial clarity. Nowhere is his awareness of the subjectivity of visual representation, and so of mapping as well, more vividly shown than in what became one of his last, great obsessions—the visual perception of tone and color. (Or, in his painstakingly precise words, "the psychological eval-uation of color, as reflected from non-luminous surfaces."[46])

The preparation of a textbook on "mapping information" appears in Fisher's correspondence as early as 1965. He received a grant of $65,000 from Ford to complete work on this text in 1969; it was ulti-mately assembled after his death in 1979, appearing in 1982 as

44
Fisher, memorandum response, May 22, 1974, HTFP, I–5.

45
Ibid., 1–8.

46
Fisher to Don T. Hill, July 27, 1971, HTFP.

47

Howard T. Fisher,
Mapping Information
(Cambridge, MA:
Abt Books, 1982).

48

Fisher to William
Pendleton, November 25,
1970, HTFP.

49

Fisher, memorandum
response, May 22, 1974,
HTFP, I–8. The latter
term added on William
Warntz's directorship
in 1969, in recognition
of his background
in mathematics and
geography.

50

Fisher, memorandum
reponse, May 22, 1974,
HTFP, 2–3.

51

Carl Steinitz, "Hand-
Drawn Overlays: Their
History and Prospective
Uses," Landscape
Architecture 66, no. 5
(September 1976): 444–55.
As is convincingly argued
by Frederick R. Steiner,
McHarg never took credit
for overlay mapping, as
Steinitz suggests, but
rather recounted his own
exposure to the technique
as practiced by Charles
Eliot and Others.
See Frederick R. Steiner,
The Living Landscape:
An Ecological Approach
to Landscape Planning
(New York: McGraw-Hill,
1991), 200, 202.

52

Ian L. McHarg, Design
with Nature (Garden
City, NY: Natural History
Press, 1969), 20.

Mapping Information.[47] A great impediment to progress seemed to be Fisher's delight at the vagaries and subtleties of his subject. A November 25, 1970 letter to William Pendleton, Fisher's grant officer, records his growing obsession with "fundamental defects" in popular understandings of grayscale, as well as the widely used Munsell color chart. While Fisher boasts of having "slayed the color dragon" by 1971, his correspondence with experts in color theory continued for years afterward. ("In closing," he noted to Pendleton, "I don't believe I have ever had so much fun before."[48])

EXPANDING OVERLAYS

After Fisher, SYMAP was to become deeply influential both inside and outside the academy—even as the conceptual character of its use was to fundamentally, and influentially, change.

When the Laboratory for Computer Graphics and Spatial Analysis faced its most institutionally significant threat in his lifetime—a committee of faculty's recommendation of closure in 1974—Fisher attempted to survey the Lab's material impact on the school's teaching mission.[49] Applications in architecture had been limited, he admits, mostly to the visualization of perspectives. In planning, conversely, he believed they had been limited by a move "toward the traditional academic disciplines of economics, sociology, statistics, etc., and away from more 'design-oriented' thinking."[50] He reserves optimism, however, for the technology's adoption in the Department of Landscape Architecture.

One of Fisher's first hires on receipt of the Ford Foundation grant was a PhD student at MIT's School of Architecture and Planning, Carl Steinitz. Brought on as a research associate in the Laboratory, Steinitz would add an appointment as assistant professor in landscape architecture in 1966, and remain a full-time landscape faculty member at Harvard until 2007. Steinitz' particular contribution at this time was to connect the field established by Fisher with the emerging practice of overlay mapping as it was developing in landscape architecture, and the larger trend toward system-based approaches in urban design.

The use of overlays in landscape architecture was a direct result of their advocacy by the Scottish landscape architect and UPenn professor Ian McHarg—although Steinitz and his students, seeking to broaden the foundation of their own efforts, subsequently traced their use as far back as the office of Frederick Law Olmsted.[51] McHarg joined Steinitz in 1971 for one of a series of studios Steinitz led with procedural map-based techniques (the first of these, using SYMAP, had looked at the Delmarva Peninsula in 1967). At times unapologetically antiurban (the city is home to those "indistinguishable from the patients in mental hospitals," as well as "the bitch goddess of success"), McHarg's seminal 1969 *Design with Nature*—heavily featuring handdrawn map overlays—set itself squarely in the countercultural environmental movement, and sought above all a utopian merger of city and countryside.[52] Lewis Mumford, contributing an introduction,

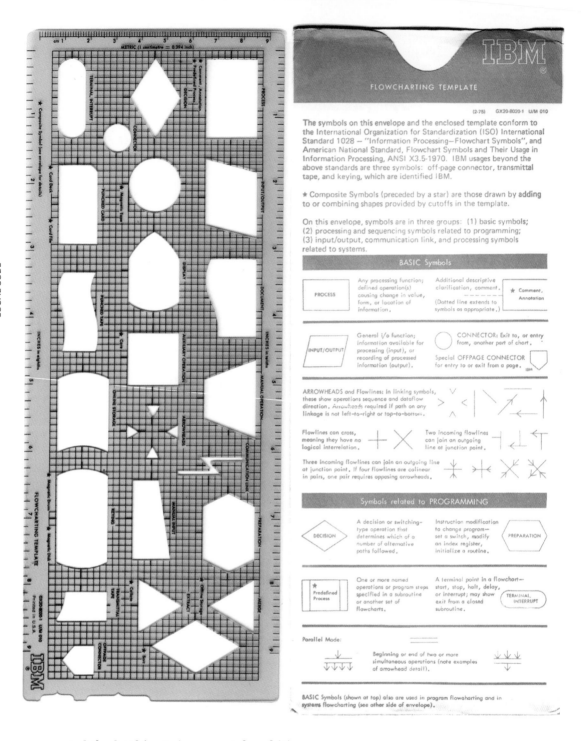

Fig. 6 — IBM flowcharting template, 1962
Collection of the author

connected the book's environmental ambition explicitly to his *New Yorker* colleague Rachel Carson's *Silent Spring*.

Yet map-based practice in this context developed into something distinct from the purely presentational tool that Fisher had originally envisioned, or the related gestalt approach of observation advocated by McHarg. In addition to a device for visual demonstration and subsequent intuition, the map became the framework for a systematic, procedural design process.

Part of this can be traced, somewhat unintentionally, back to Fisher's own graphic production. In his youth, particularly in the context of General Houses, he was guilty of utopian, system-based visions. But as a developer of GIS in his late sixties, he was well schooled in the awkward nature of reality, and advocated mapping chiefly as a tool to better perceive it.

Fisher was insistent, however, on a diagrammatic clarity when it came to preparing the conceptual outlines of a map for the SYMAP software, which was crucial for the intense structuring of data and calculation involved in the map's punch card–based production. To this end, he borrowed the visual language of the programming flow-charts often used in the preparation of FORTRAN code to explain the procedural steps of mapmaking, and their translation into code. Such symbols had been developed as early as John Von Neumann's first writings on computer logic in the 1940s, and were so essential to the preparation of code in the 1960s (before higher-level coding and development environments gained widespread use) that IBM distributed plastic drawing templates to allow their efficient if-this-then-that construction.

In this progression, we see first the flowchart of SYMAP's operations, prepared by Fisher in 1968, and then Fisher's later diagram of the strategic preparation of data and map design. The symbols, and logics, are precise—and near identical.

Yet in Steinitz work, and in the larger field of systems-based urban planning, we see an extension of the logic of such diagrams; not stopping, as they did in SYMAP, with the map itself, but flowing out and around the map into the landscape of practice, in a series of ambitious simulations and design strategies. The result was a hybrid of counterposed cultures—an ostensibly open, ecological approach with military-industrial origins that belied the utopian ecological language it harnessed—just as Buckminster Fuller's army-funded geodesics belied the draft-dodging hippies that sheltered beneath them. In the report of the 1970 studio, designed by Steinitz as a model for future practice inside the GSD and in the fields it sought to lead, we see a flattening of the diagram, leading directly from the ingesting of data at one end to the implementation of actions within it (if, for the sake of the studio, in the bounds of simulation). In such a diagram, the map is not the end to a process, but merely a productive symptom of it.[53] The territory of action is inside the machine and out in the world—but barely observed in between.

There were several underlying causes of this shift. The first, a conceptual one, arose from the logical nature of McHargian overlay mapping—versus the smooth graduated surfaces at which SYMAP excelled (particularly after Donald Shepard, a student in one of Fisher's freshman seminars, took up and radically improved the interpolation algorithm used by SYMAP). Unlike the shadings of SYMAP, the superficial either-or-and logic of the overlay fit hand in glove with the on/off Boolean circuits of digital processing in the way that smooth surfaces—albeit crudely rendered in overprinted characters—did not.

53
Carl Steinitz and Peter P. Rogers, A Systems Analysis Model of Urbanization and Change: An Experiment in Interdisciplinary Education (Cambridge, MA: MIT Press, 1970). For a comprehensive explanation of Steinitz's activities in this period (albeit not mentioning Fisher), see Catherine F. McMahon, "Predictive Machines: Data, Computer Maps, and Simulation," in A Second Modernism: MIT, Architecture, and the "Techno-Social" Moment, ed. Arindam Dutta (Cambridge, MA: SA+P and MIT Press, 2013), 436–73.

LOCAL CODE

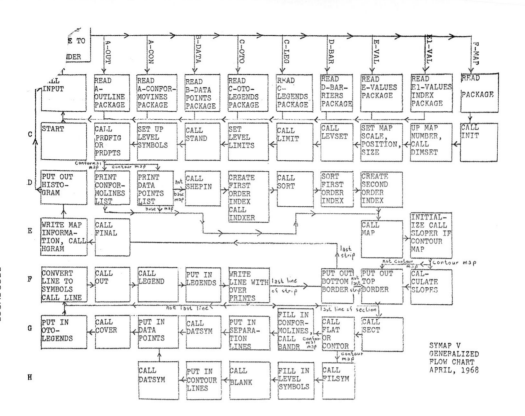

SYMAP V
GENERALIZED
FLOW CHART
APRIL, 1968

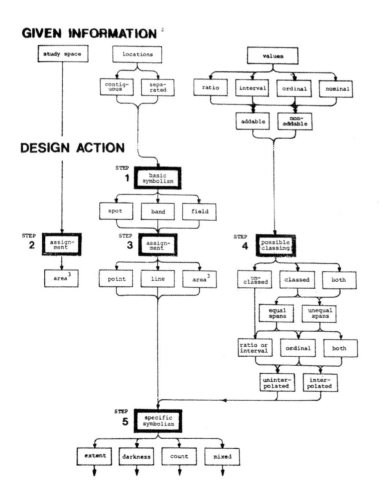

Fig. 7 — "SYMAP V Generalized
Flow Chart," 1968. A diagram of the
data processing of the SYMAP code
in FORTRAN. Harvard University
Archives, Howard T. Fisher Papers

Fig. 8 — "Flowchart for the Initial
Steps in Thematic Map Design,"
1969 Harvard University Archives,
Howard T. Fisher Papers

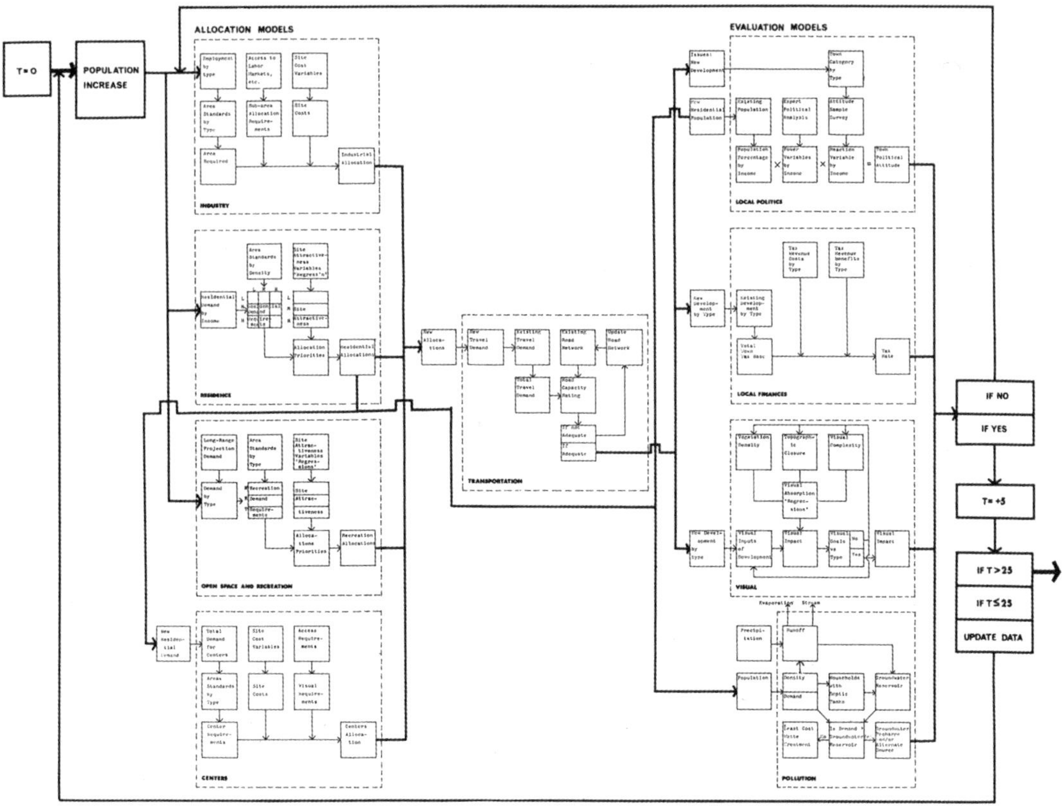

Fig. 9 — Flowchart showing software, simulation, and design, from Carl Steinitz and Peter P. Rogers, *A Systems Analysis Model of Urbanization and Change: An Experiment in Interdisciplinary Education* (Cambridge, MA: MIT Press, 1970) Courtesy MIT Press

The second was related to the media of programming itself, and the mental maneuvers that it encouraged. Those with a programming background especially tended to unsee the line between the strict, logical environment of the computer's programming, and the reality of the landscape outside of it. In this realm of overlaid areas (or, as it came to be known in GIS circles, topological mapping), the visual role of the map was secondary to its procedural origins, and the further procedures that it drives. (Such a prospect could already be glimpsed in a 1966 Steinitz-authored proposal to connect SYMAP calculations directly to game-theory programming for "conflict situations," in what is described as "an input-reaction-result, etc., cycle."[54])

This related in turn to the conceptual and institutional background from which Steinitz's work emerged, both at Fisher's Lab—renamed in 1968 after his retirement the Laboratory for Computer Graphics and Spatial Analysis—and later in the GSD's Landscape Architecture Research Office, or LARO (which formed separately from the Laboratory under Steinitz's supervision in 1970; Steinitz served on the committee in 1974 that recommended the Laboratory's closure). In this work, Steinitz was clearly influenced both by the more pragmatic data-driven approach advocated by his dissertation adviser, Kevin Lynch (whose *Image of the City* had been

54
Carl Steinitz, "A Research Proposal to Develop the Capabilities of the SYMAP Computer Graphics Program into a General System for the Analysis and Solution of Conflict Situations," April 25, 1966, HTFP.

funded by Rockefeller alongside Jacobs's *Death and Life*), but also by more theoretical work in urban simulation—in particular that of SAGE's original developer, Jay Forrester, who by the 1960s was also at MIT, actively preparing his manuscript on urban simulation, 1969's *Urban Dynamics*.

In such a systems-planning context, the computer map was only one point of feedback in a larger superprocess of cybernetic planning and feedback. Indeed, the report of Steinitz's 1970 studio—*A Systems Analysis Model of Urbanization and Change*—explicitly advocates for a procedural, systems-based approach not just to the practice of design, but to its education as well.

This procedural and Boolean bent was to receive further reinforcement by another departure from SYMAP's original template; this related not just to GIS's conceptual architecture, but to its literal ownership and distribution as well.

ESRI

"Really now—who is or what is ESRI?" wrote Fisher on the twenty-fourth of January 1973 to Laura Dangermond, the partner in marriage and business to one of Fisher and Steinitz's students at Harvard, Paul Jack Dangermond.[55]

Dangermond, known as Jack, had come to Harvard in 1968 from Redlands, California, some eighty miles east of Santa Monica in the Inland Empire east of Los Angeles (where his Dutch immigrant parents owned a landscaping supply store). After undergraduate studies in landscape architecture and environmental science at California Polytechnic State University, Pomona, Dangermond completed a one-year course in urban design at the University of Minnesota and an MLA in landscape architecture from Harvard; the latter specializing in "systems for geographic information."[56] He then returned to Redlands to found what was initially billed as a nonprofit consultancy: the Environmental Systems Research Institute, or ESRI. Most of its early work was conducted using SYMAP.[57]

While the Harvard Lab had charged money to distribute copies of the program on punch cards, especially after the depletion of the Ford Foundation grant, its code was open and modifiable by its users, and in the public domain. By 1970 Fisher was recommending the "extremely inventive and competent" Dangermond and ESRI as a consultant on SYMAP and related software.[58] Shortly afterward, Dangermond approached him about taking on responsibility from Harvard for the correspondence lessons for SYMAP and SYMVU ("SYMbolic VU," a Lab-authored follow-up to SYMAP that allowed depiction of continuous surfaces using a pen plotter). "Wouldn't it be great," Dangermond proposed, "if one organization were responsible for standardization and distribution of the various forms of computer graphic systems…?" adding, "I think I am very interested in grabbing a hold and assuming responsibility of this project, if you feel…I am capable."[59]

55
Fisher to Mrs. Jack [sic] Dangermond, January 24, 1973, HTFP.

56
Jack Dangermond C.V., 1970, HTFP.

57
Jack Dangermond C.V., 1970, HTFP. Of the twelve projects listed, four are described as using SYMAP; as discussed below, SYMAP also served, certainly in Fisher's opinion, as the basis for much of the other work as well.

58
"SYMAP and…one or more programs that are based on SYMAP." Fisher to Dr. D. R. F. Taylor, Department of Geography, Carleton University, June 2, 1970, HTFP.

59
Dangermond to Howard T. Fisher, July 27, 1970, HTFP.

Fisher was in turn so convinced of Dangermond's skills that he strongly encouraged him to take the position of Lab director after William Warntz resigned suddenly in 1971. "You are," Fisher wrote to Dangermond in May 1971, "the single best living person for this job."[60] While Dangermond had initially demurred, he finally came to Cambridge with Fisher's encouragement to speak with then GSD dean Maurice Kilbridge. However, he wrote shortly after to both Fisher and Kilbridge, "I would like *at this time* to say no to your offer, but would very much like in the future to participate in the Laboratory's activities."[61]

And yet a different, and more difficult, tone enters into the conversation between teacher and student starting in late 1972: within the space of several months, ESRI would shed its nonprofit status and begin selling its own proprietary GIS software to government and industrial organizations. Dangermond publicly announced this strategy in a paper presented at the Urban and Regional Information Systems Association (or USIRA, founded by Edgar Horwood) conference in the late summer of 1972; his submission announced a new program, Automap 1, for sale by ESRI, that "does everything that SYMAP does and also fits on small computers."[62] Especially given the two program's shared FORTRAN code, this produced a pointed, if mannerly, response from Fisher: "I think your failure to give full and proper credit to SYMAP as the source of your endeavors has prejudiced a number of people against you in an unfortunate way" ("I never felt personally upset," Fisher hastily adds).[63]

SOFTWARE ARCHITECTURE

Writing in 1959 about a new machine developed to replace the 7090 on which SYMAP was developed, the IBM engineers F. P. Brooks Jr., G. A. Blaauw, and Werner Buchholz were the first to apply the word *architecture* to the relative arrangement of computer components.[64] The computer in question, the IBM 7030, or "Stretch," proposed a rearrangement of the computer's interior circulation of information to achieve greater usefulness and functionality that—argued Brooks—was analogous to the rearrangement of physical space designed to achieve the same goal. (While a commercial failure, Stretch provided essential technology for the real-time computing of NASA's Mission Control Center, and also led directly to the highly successful System/360 product line.[65])

In the case of SYMAP, ESRI, and modern GIS, two questions about the software become relevant: First, its internal architecture—the way, that is, that the software draws in and treats the world. And second, its external

60
Fisher to Jack Dangermond, May 17, 1971, HTFP.

61
Dangermond to Dean Maurice Kilbridge, Graduate School of Design, June 7, 1971, HTFP.

62
Jack Dangermond, "A Classification and Review of Coordinate Identification and Computer Mapping Systems," in Urban and Regional Information Systems: Information Research for an Urban Society; Papers from the Tenth Annual Conference of the Urban and Regional Information Systems Association, August 28–September 1972, San Francisco, CA, vol. 2 (Claremont, CA: Claremont College Printing Service, 1973), 185.

63
A subsequent exchange of letters then takes place between ESRI and a "distressed" Laura Dangermond (with Jack Dangermond abroad in Japan at the time, by her telling). Fisher presses Dangermond most of all on whether ESRI was, or remained, a nonprofit, thus the question that opened this discussion. "To fail to give full credit to SYMAP in accordance with customs and traditions of the academic world gives the impression that you are trying to take credit for something improperly....Of course, if you are a strictly business enterprise—and that is [made] obvious—then people wouldn't expect you to have the same standards, but the title of your organization is definitely such as to imply that you are above the mere...standards of the marketplace...." Fisher to Jack Dangermond, January 8, 1973, HTFP. In fact, ESRI had reconstituted itself as a for-profit corporation only three days prior. "Business Incorporation Certificate for Entity # C0672337, Environmental Systems Research Institute, Inc.," California Secretary of State, accessed June 30, 2015, http://kepler.sos.ca.gov.

64
F. P. Brooks Jr., G. A. Blaauw, and W. Buchholz, "Processing Data in Bits and Pieces," and F. P. Brooks Jr.,"Architectural Philosophy," in Planning a Computer System: Project Stretch, ed. Werner Buchholz (New York: McGraw-Hill, 1962), 5–17.

65
Ceruzzi, History of Modern Computing, 151–57.

architecture—how the software itself is shaped and distributed. From an Inland Empire storefront, the privately held ESRI has grown to control more than 40 percent of the now enormous global market for GIS software and services, and far higher within the military and large corporations; this dominance proving resistant even to the disruption of digital mapping resulting from more freely available tools like Google Earth.[66] (The Dangermonds' resulting financial worth is currently estimated at $2.9 billion.[67])

However—reflecting both the larger intellectual trend at Harvard during Dangermond's tenure, the limited processing capacity of the minicomputers on which ESRI software was adapted from SYMAP in the 1970s, as well as the nature of the clients to whom ESRI software was marketed—the ESRI-driven version of GIS hewed closely not to questions of surfaces and their display, as had been SYMAP's original concerns, but rather to the simpler, Boolean logic that replaced it, in Steinitz' work and others. This remains true to this day, when ESRI ArcMAP provides a visual editor of GIS procedures that deploys the arrows, decision points, and outlines of latter-day programming flowcharts. The firm's subsequent success has been less in promoting the use of GIS by designers (few of whom can afford the full software's expensive license) than in selling software and services to more deeply pocketed local governments, corporations, and the military. (This despite a recent marketing effort around so-called "GeoDesign," complete with a Steinitz-authored textbook.[68]) As at the outset in SAGE, the ultimate procedure is not so much representing the world and its possibilities for change, but targeting the resources of its powerful actors.[69]

SOFTWARE AND ARCHITECTURE

"The fact that you do not give credit to me personally in regard to SYMAP," Fisher wrote Dangermond in 1973, "doesn't really worry me very much because nobody else seems to do that either except occasionally."[70] In today's landscape of mapping, however, we might usefully, and properly, remember several lessons from the career of Howard Fisher.

Whatever its origins in an American *noblesse oblige*, the vision of GIS he promoted—unambiguously public-spirited, yet equipped best of all for shades of gray—remains an indispensable ideal for both our public spaces and the new tools and practices that shape them. For the techniques and tools with which we shape our environment shape it far more than our own conscious craft.

In an influential set of essays written in 1999, the open-source developer Eric Raymond compares two competing models of software development to singular urban spaces—the cathedral and the bazaar. Both are actually collaborative environments; in the cathedral, however, a master mason (thus *archi-tect*, chief of builders) directs stages of work, with massed energy flowing efficiently according to a centralized plan that few are able to observe or understand until its completion. In the bazaar, by contrast (an environment likened especially

66
Michael Helft, "You Can't Kill Jack Dangermond's Company. Try, And It Will Only Get Stronger," Forbes, March 31, 2015, http:// www.forbes.com/sites/ miguelhelft/2015/03/31/ you-cant-kill-jack-dangermonds-company-try-and-it-will-only-get-stronger/.

67
"#628: Jack Dangermond," Forbes, accessed June 30, 2015, http:// www.forbes.com/profile/ jack-dangermond/.

68
Carl Steinitz, A Framework for Geodesign: Changing Geography by Design (Redlands, CA: Esri Press, 2012). Full disclosure—I was invited as a speaker to the "Geodesign" meeting held at ESRI in 2011, where I received an audience-voted award.

69
To its great credit, especially given the $10,000+ cost, ESRI has consistently allowed free or heavily discounted use of its desktop software by non-profits and academics—including me. This has not incidentally served to cement the software's ubiquity.

70
Fisher to Jack Dangermond, January 8, 1973, HTFP.

by Raymond to the environment created around the open-source Linux operating system), everything, for better or worse, gets negotiated in public—for the messy, but ultimate, good.

Today, however, we are confronted with the translation between real space and that of computing not through an elaborate system of metaphor, but rather through our daily, lived reality. Yet here the choice set out metaphorically and architecturally by Eric Raymond is all the more important. Nowhere is this larger shift so present as in the transition of digital mapping from the realm of research into an essential, complex part of our urban and ecological metabolism. In this transition are hidden fundamental choices—not so much about the future of data, but the future of cities themselves.

THE MAP AND THE TERRITORY

In 1931 the Polish-American scholar Alfred Korzybski coined the phrase "the map is not the territory" to describe the seemingly inevitable semantic and structural gap between the description of a landscape—of thought or earth—and its representation.[71] With today's ubiquitous encounter with digital cartography, however, we are experiencing an ever-accelerating collision of these two conceptual extremes. This rapid collapse is not limited to the design professions, but is transforming them just as surely nevertheless. And so, to a large part, our territory has become the map, and the map itself an essential kind of territory. Thus, perhaps the final and most essential lessons from the story of Howard Fisher are these:

First, maps remain at their most powerful when used not as instruments of unattended action or procedure, but rather as devices to change our perception of the world, and understanding of its possibilities.

And second, that architecture matters—inside and outside of the computer, and in particular the connection between the two. Particularly as the distinction between the space of information and the space of our own cities is subject to its own, evermore complex shades of gray, we need to be mindful in a new way. We need to remember that the way in which we would seek to operate in the city—carefully, transparently, collaboratively, and creatively—must hold true in the irreversibly interlinked space of city and data as well.

71
The phrase appears in Alfred Korzybski, "A Non-Aristotelian System and its Necessity for Rigour in Mathematics and Physics" (paper presented at a meeting of the American Association for the Advancement of Science, New Orleans, December 28, 1931). Reprinted in Alfred Korzybski, Science and Sanity (Lakeville, CT: International Non-Aristotelian Library, 1933), 747–61.

New York
Case Study 2012–2015

In collaboration with **Timon McPhearson,**
Director of the Urban Ecology Lab,
Parsons the New School for Design

This work is a collaboration with the urban ecology laboratory of Timon McPhearson at Parsons the New School for Design. Since 2009, McPhearson and his colleagues have cataloged over thirty thousand vacant and underutilized parcels in New York City, many of which are city-owned, and estimated their specific potential for a variety of ecosystem services.[1]

Especially since Hurricane Sandy flooded the city's landscape and infrastructure in 2012, New York City has been the focus of a variety of design efforts aimed at building urban resilience. Yet most of these proposals recapitulate the historic tendency to invest vast resources in already well-off neighborhoods, or to produce readily comprehensible, singular artifacts such as levees (the ribbon cuttings for which provide evidence of political action).

Our proposals, by contrast, focus on the distributed potential of vacant and underutilized land to form a network of physical resilience, and afford an equally important investment in the social and economic resilience of the city's most at-risk neighborhoods. Combining stormwater and heat-island mediation with the creation of shared public space, the investment proposed here is one equally focused on the everyday resilience of communities as in episodic resilience to disaster.

1
See Timon McPhearson, Peleg Kremer, and Zoé A. Hamstead, "Mapping ecosystem services in New York City: Applying a social-ecological approach in urban vacant land," *Ecosystem Services* 5 (2013): 11–26.

28474 209 EAST 125TH STREET

209841 WEST 20TH STREET

523245 THURSBY AVENUE

235112 PROSPECT PLACE

568467 21ST STREET

7980 154 ELDRIDGE ST

14584 548 WEST 53RD STREET

245504 1717 LINCOLN PLACE

LOCAL CODE

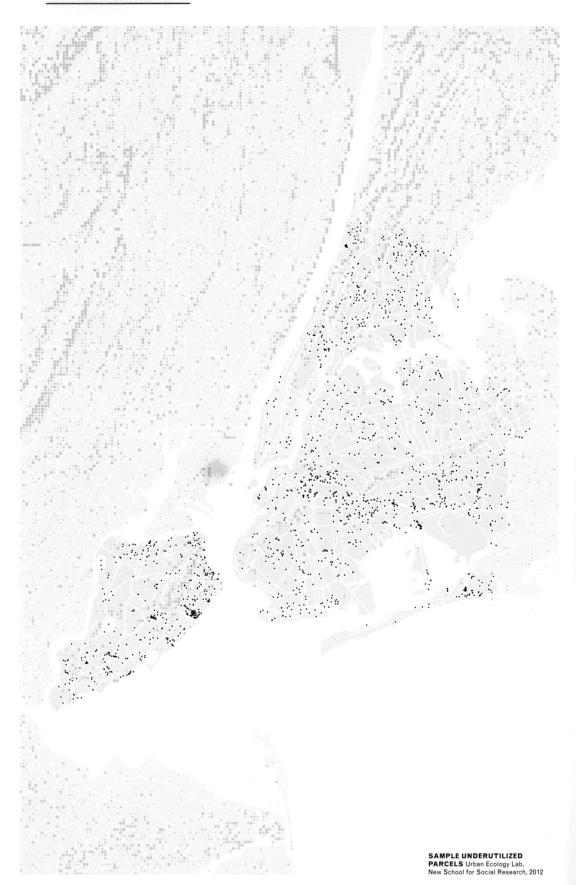

**SAMPLE UNDERUTILIZED
PARCELS** Urban Ecology Lab,
New School for Social Research, 2012

HOUSEHOLDS IN POVERTY
% US Census, 2010

**RESPIRATORY
ILLNESS** INCIDENCE,
% US Census, 2010

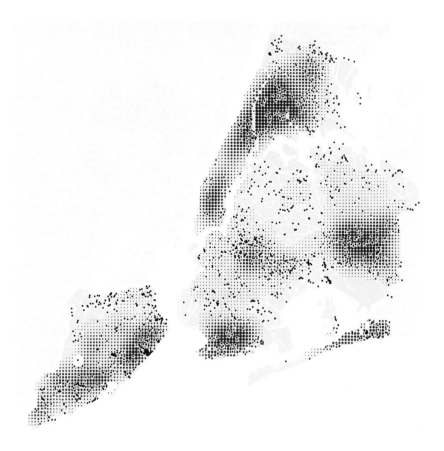

REPORTED CRIME
INCIDENT COUNT, NYPD, 2014

IMPERVIOUS SURFACES
LAND COVER ANALYSIS
City of New York, 2010

URBAN HEAT ISLANDS
Landsat Infrared image, 2014

URBAN GROUND COVER
ASTER image analysis, 2014

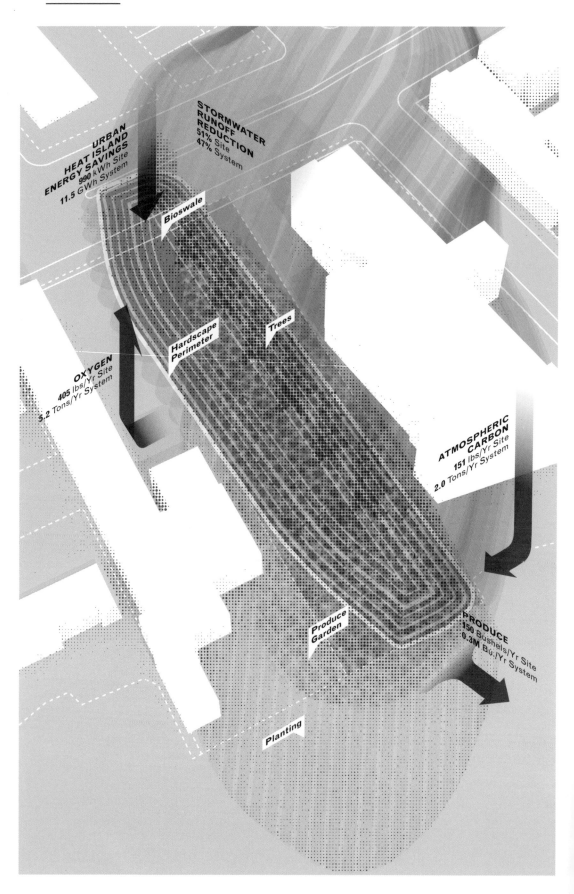

URBAN
HEAT ISLAND
ENERGY SAVINGS
990 kWh Site
11.5 GWh System

STORMWATER
RUNOFF
REDUCTION
51% Site
47% System

Bioswale

Hardscape
Perimeter

Trees

OXYGEN
405 lbs/Yr Site
5.2 Tons/Yr System

ATMOSPHERIC
CARBON
151 lbs/Yr Site
2.0 Tons/Yr System

Produce
Garden

PRODUCE
150 Bushels/Yr Site
0.3M Bu./Yr System

Planting

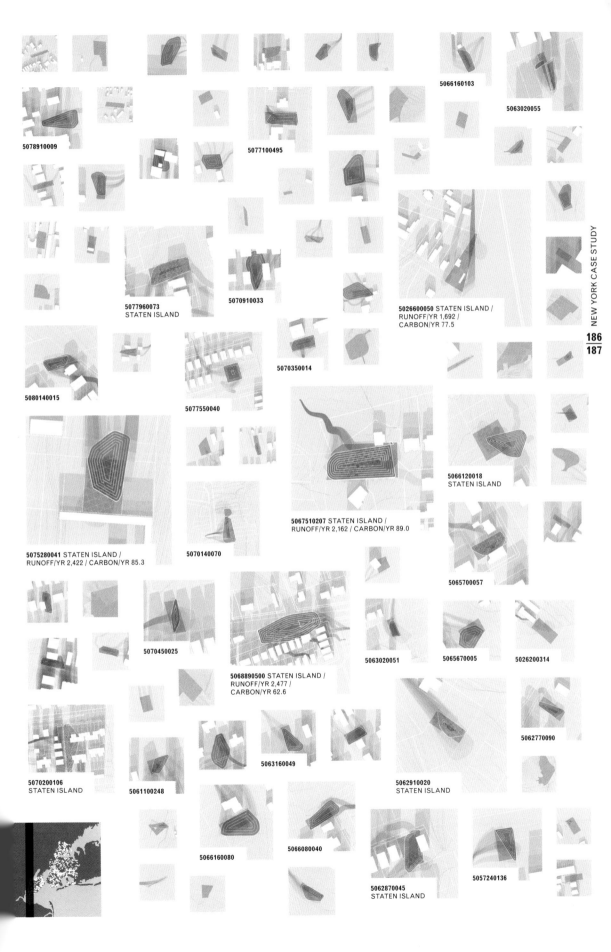

5066160103

5063020055

5078910009

5077100495

5077960073
STATEN ISLAND

5070910033

5026600050 STATEN ISLAND /
RUNOFF/YR 1,692 /
CARBON/YR 77.5

5080140015

5077550040

5070350014

5075280041 STATEN ISLAND /
RUNOFF/YR 2,422 / CARBON/YR 85.3

5070140070

5067510207 STATEN ISLAND /
RUNOFF/YR 2,162 / CARBON/YR 89.0

5066120018
STATEN ISLAND

5065700057

5070450025

5068890500 STATEN ISLAND /
RUNOFF/YR 2,477 /
CARBON/YR 62.6

5063020051

5065670005

5026200314

5062770090

5070200106
STATEN ISLAND

5061100248

5063160049

5062910020
STATEN ISLAND

5066160080

5066080040

5062870045
STATEN ISLAND

5057240136

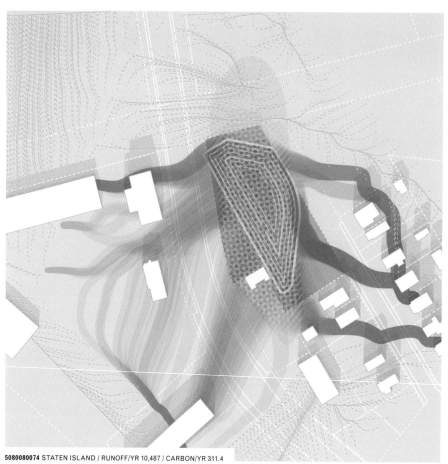

5080080074 STATEN ISLAND / RUNOFF/YR 10,487 / CARBON/YR 311.4

5062760011

5062280001

5062440026

5056510150

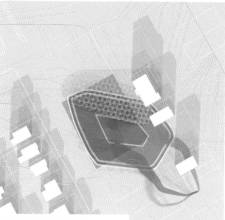

5065630034 STATEN ISLAND /
RUNOFF/YR 4,308 / CARBON/YR 160.4

5053550070

5063530057

5062910004 STATEN ISLAND /
RUNOFF/YR 4,454 / CARBON/YR 170.0

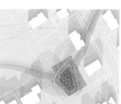

5064540030 STATEN ISLAND /
RUNOFF/YR 2,976 /
CARBON/YR 64.5

5013180144

5063510021

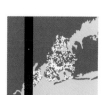

5017170070
STATEN ISLAND

5026380063 STATEN ISLAND / RUNOFF/YR 13,022 / CARBON/YR 298.8

5012460022

5012430086

5054210068

5054470011

5012000055

5017040008

5046160037
STATEN ISLAND

5011550005

5062570084 STATEN ISLAND /
RUNOFF/YR 3,229 / CARBON/YR 104.0

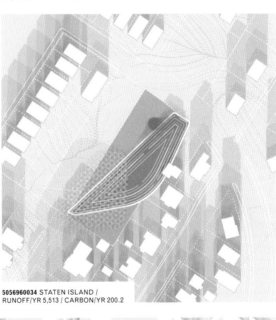

5056960034 STATEN ISLAND /
RUNOFF/YR 5,513 / CARBON/YR 200.2

5055200032 STATEN ISLAND /
RUNOFF/YR 5,338 / CARBON/YR 77.4

5052820040

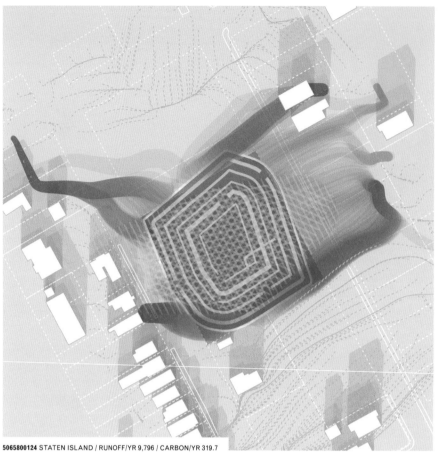

5065800124 STATEN ISLAND / RUNOFF/YR 9,796 / CARBON/YR 319.7

5053280037
STATEN ISLAND

5063510003
STATEN ISLAND

5015600080
STATEN ISLAND

5052990019

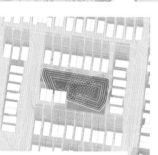

5016740007 STATEN ISLAND /
RUNOFF/YR 4,055 / CARBON/YR 83.1

5024500239 STATEN ISLAND /
RUNOFF/YR 3,434 /
CARBON/YR 60.4

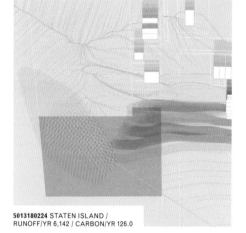

5013180224 STATEN ISLAND /
RUNOFF/YR 6,142 / CARBON/YR 126.0

5045720004   5052980032

5019650044

5012130078
STATEN ISLAND

5011720241 STATEN ISLAND /
RUNOFF/YR 3,675 /
CARBON/YR 66.2

5011400069

5011260084

5010610047

5044270032

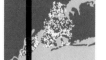

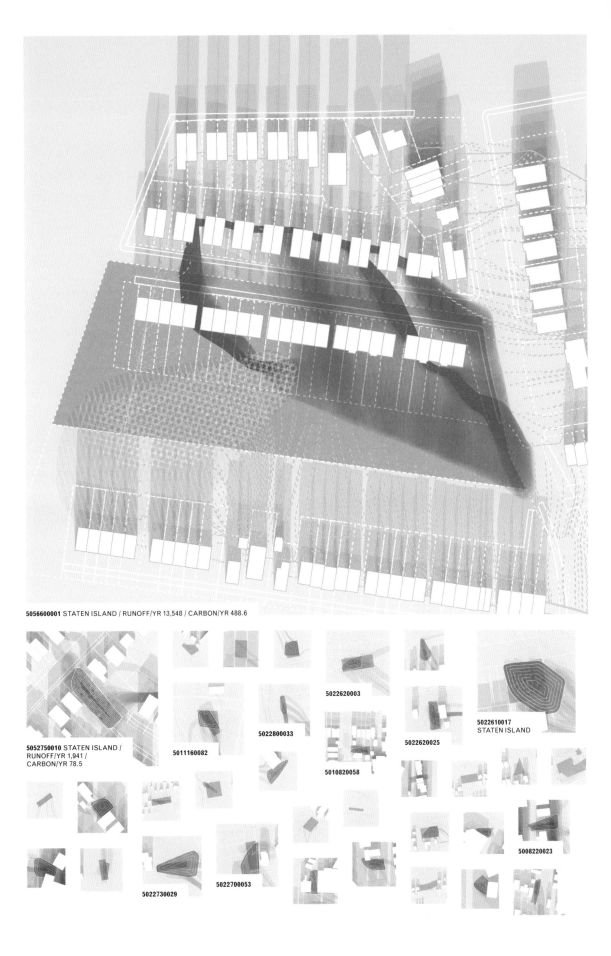

5056600001 STATEN ISLAND / RUNOFF/YR 13,548 / CARBON/YR 488.6

5052750010 STATEN ISLAND /
RUNOFF/YR 1,941 /
CARBON/YR 78.5

5022620003

5022800033

5011160082

5010820058

5022620025

5022610017
STATEN ISLAND

5008220023

5022730029

5022700053

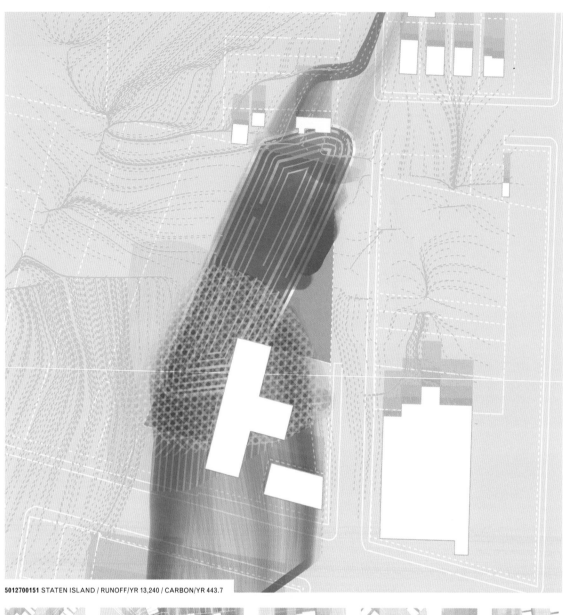

5012700151 STATEN ISLAND / RUNOFF/YR 13,240 / CARBON/YR 443.7

5010390025

5019850074 STATEN ISLAND / RUNOFF/YR 5,136 / CARBON/YR 69.9

5003950002
STATEN ISLAND

5049850021

5002220070

5047460048

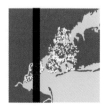

5046860022

5001860043

5042660049

5008110005

5010260001
STATEN ISLAND

5009480114 STATEN ISLAND /
RUNOFF/YR 3,805 / CARBON/YR 100.7

5042780001 STATEN ISLAND /
RUNOFF/YR 6,234 / CARBON/YR 165.9

5022420071

5046880001

5007600050

5001770078 STATEN
ISLAND / RUNOFF/YR 2,297 /
CARBON/YR 54.5

5006810150
STATEN ISLAND

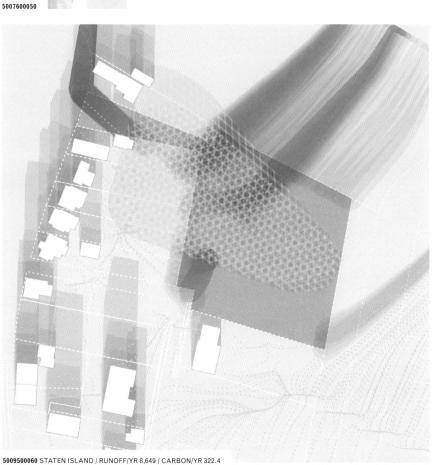

5009500060 STATEN ISLAND / RUNOFF/YR 8,649 / CARBON/YR 322.4

5002630023

5008830017

5035440025
STATEN ISLAND

5006720016

5035440043

5008430150 STATEN ISLAND /
RUNOFF/YR 1,333 /
CARBON/YR 63.7

5035500021 STATEN ISLAND /
RUNOFF/YR 2,374 / CARBON/YR 90.4

5035450041
STATEN ISLAND

5000720025

5036580073

5036610049
STATEN ISLAND

5008580147

5005900095

5033190065

5000860089

5000850009

5000940011

5031670020

5037900001
STATEN ISLAND

5006180332
STATEN ISLAND

5037640035
STATEN ISLAND

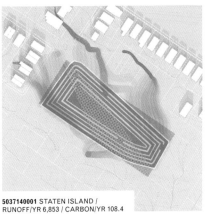

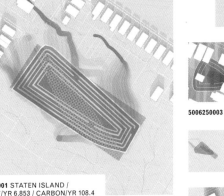

5006250003

5036630001 STATEN ISLAND /
RUNOFF/YR 7,555 / CARBON/YR 162.3

5033360044

5000850013

5037140001 STATEN ISLAND /
RUNOFF/YR 6,853 / CARBON/YR 108.4

5032110012

5033710021

5038640100

5000450037

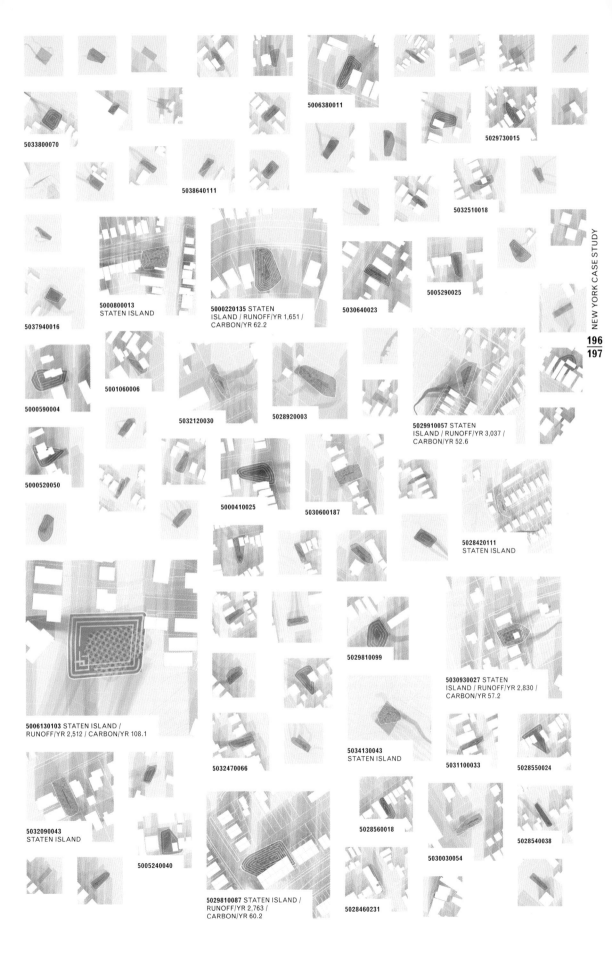

5033800070

5006380011

5029730015

5038640111

5032510018

5000800013
STATEN ISLAND

5000220135 STATEN
ISLAND / RUNOFF/YR 1,651 /
CARBON/YR 62.2

5030640023

5005290025

5037940016

5001060006

5000590004

5032120030

5028920003

5029910057 STATEN
ISLAND / RUNOFF/YR 3,037 /
CARBON/YR 52.6

5000520050

5000410025

5030600187

5028420111
STATEN ISLAND

5029810099

5030930027 STATEN
ISLAND / RUNOFF/YR 2,830 /
CARBON/YR 57.2

5006130103 STATEN ISLAND /
RUNOFF/YR 2,512 / CARBON/YR 108.1

5032470066

5034130043
STATEN ISLAND

5031100033

5028550024

5032090043
STATEN ISLAND

5005240040

5028560018

5028540038

5030030054

5029810087 STATEN ISLAND /
RUNOFF/YR 2,763 /
CARBON/YR 60.2

5028460231

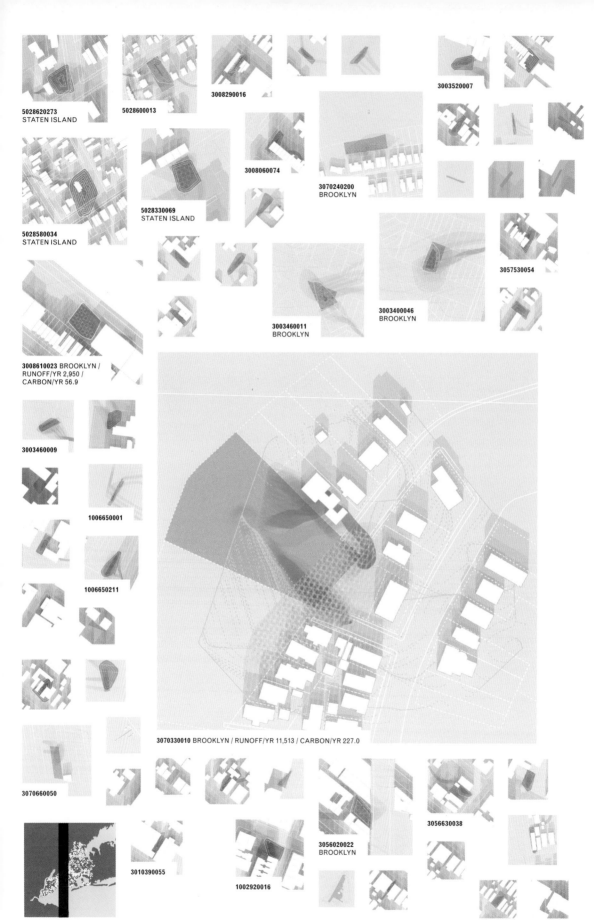

5028620273
STATEN ISLAND

5028600013

3008290016

3003520007

5028580034
STATEN ISLAND

5028330069
STATEN ISLAND

3008060074

3070240200
BROOKLYN

3057530054

3008610023 BROOKLYN /
RUNOFF/YR 2,950 /
CARBON/YR 56.9

3003460011
BROOKLYN

3003400046
BROOKLYN

3003460009

1006650001

1006650211

3070330010 BROOKLYN / RUNOFF/YR 11,513 / CARBON/YR 227.0

3070660050

3010390055

1002920016

3056020022
BROOKLYN

3056630038

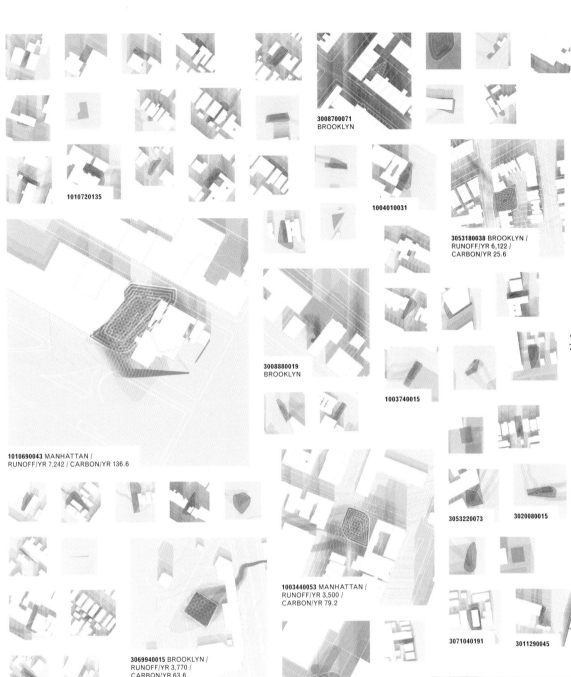

3008700071
BROOKLYN

1010720135

1004010031

3053180038 BROOKLYN /
RUNOFF/YR 6,122 /
CARBON/YR 25.6

3008880019
BROOKLYN

1003740015

1010690043 MANHATTAN /
RUNOFF/YR 7,242 / CARBON/YR 136.6

3053220073

3020080015

1003440053 MANHATTAN /
RUNOFF/YR 3,500 /
CARBON/YR 79.2

3071040191

3011290045

3069940015 BROOKLYN /
RUNOFF/YR 3,770 /
CARBON/YR 63.6

1012690006
MANHATTAN

3070740006

3052670018

1004010025

3009270026

3072120050

3020330006 BROOKLYN /
RUNOFF/YR 2,971 /
CARBON/YR 51.7

3071510065 BROOKLYN /
RUNOFF/YR 1,777 /
CARBON/YR 78.7

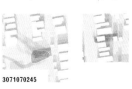

3071070245

3053200055 BROOKLYN / RUNOFF/
YR 6,389 / CARBON/YR 104.0

3019180051
BROOKLYN

3021570002

3019620069

3019180067
BROOKLYN

3071310028

3051990125

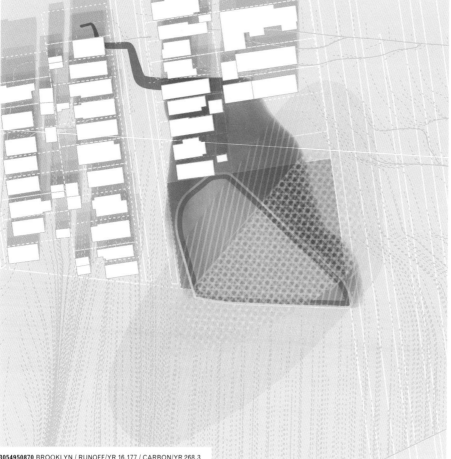

3054950870 BROOKLYN / RUNOFF/YR 16,177 / CARBON/YR 268.3

3019190100
BROOKLYN

3011400055

3066850001

3050240053

3019660031

1018280010

3074110033

3011490036

3019900014

3022320169

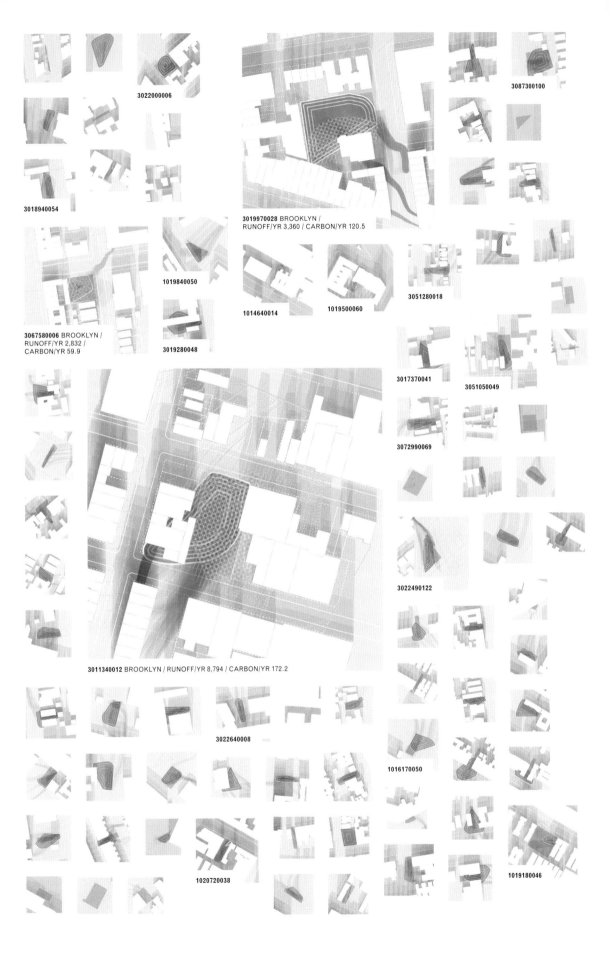

3022000006

3018940054

3019970028 BROOKLYN /
RUNOFF/YR 3,360 / CARBON/YR 120.5

3087300100

1019840050

3067580006 BROOKLYN /
RUNOFF/YR 2,832 /
CARBON/YR 59.9

3019280048

1014640014

1019500060

3051280018

3017370041

3051050049

3072990069

3022490122

3011340012 BROOKLYN / RUNOFF/YR 8,794 / CARBON/YR 172.2

3022640008

1016170050

1020720038

1019180046

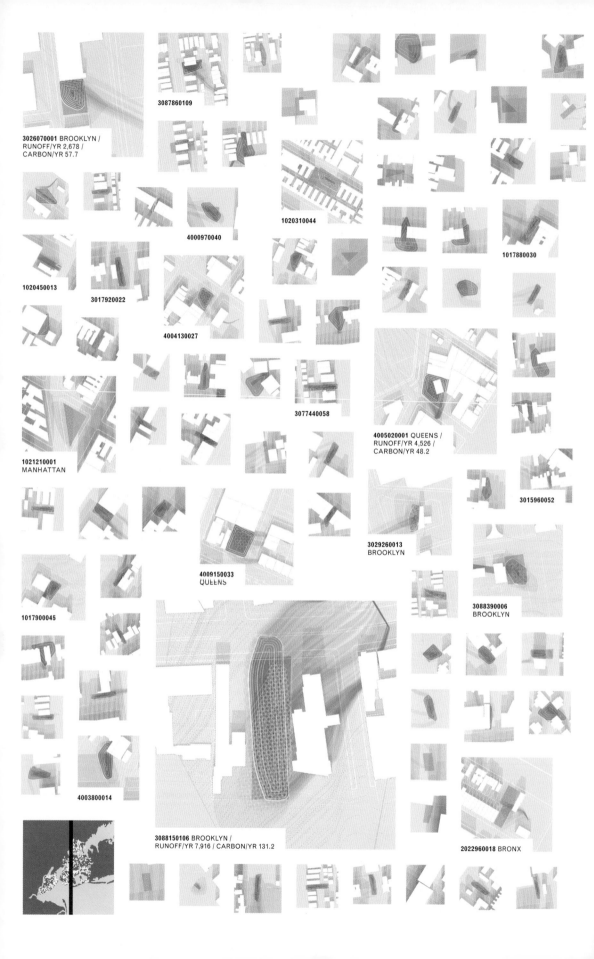

3026070001 BROOKLYN /
RUNOFF/YR 2,678 /
CARBON/YR 57.7

3087860109

1020310044

4000970040

1017880030

1020450013

3017920022

4004130027

3077440058

4005020001 QUEENS /
RUNOFF/YR 4,526 /
CARBON/YR 48.2

1021210001
MANHATTAN

3015960052

3029260013
BROOKLYN

4009150033
QUEENS

1017900045

3088390006
BROOKLYN

4003800014

3088150106 BROOKLYN /
RUNOFF/YR 7,916 / CARBON/YR 131.2

2022960018 BRONX

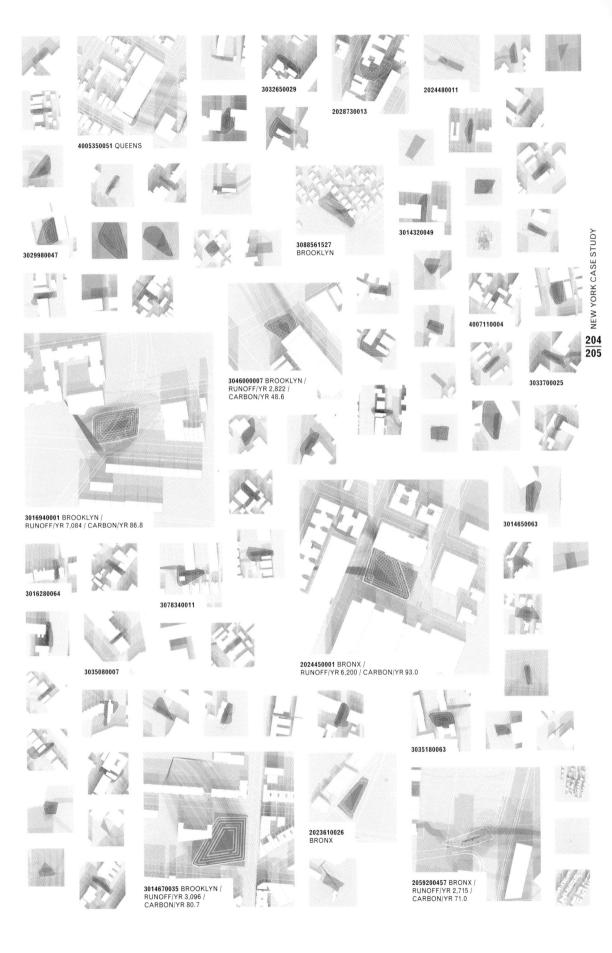

4005350051 QUEENS

3032650029

2028730013

2024480011

3029980047

3088561527
BROOKLYN

3014320049

4007110004

3033700025

3046000007 BROOKLYN /
RUNOFF/YR 2,822 /
CARBON/YR 48.6

3016940001 BROOKLYN /
RUNOFF/YR 7,084 / CARBON/YR 86.8

3014650063

3016280064

3078340011

3035080007

2024450001 BRONX /
RUNOFF/YR 6,200 / CARBON/YR 93.0

3035180063

2023610026
BRONX

3014670035 BROOKLYN /
RUNOFF/YR 3,096 /
CARBON/YR 80.7

2059200457 BRONX /
RUNOFF/YR 2,715 /
CARBON/YR 71.0

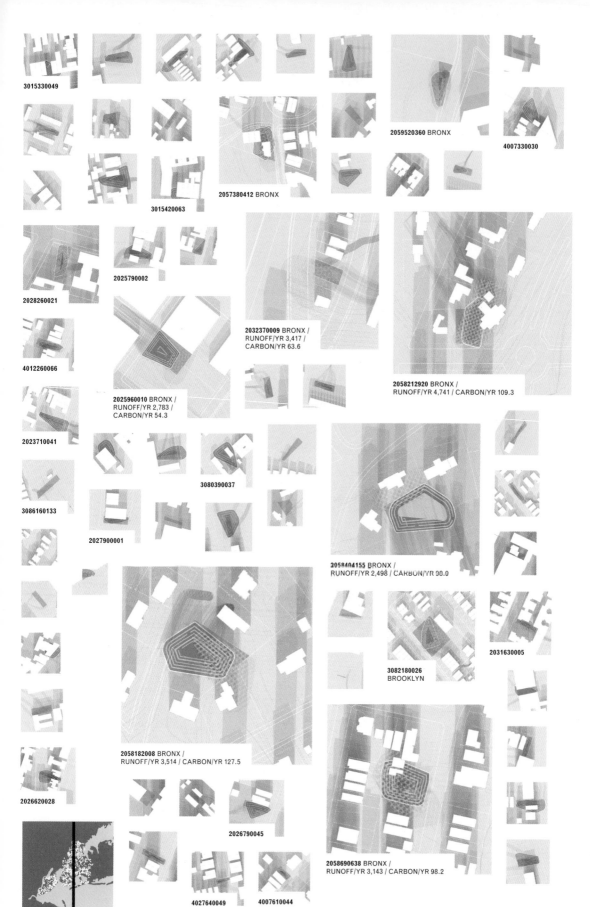

3015330049

2059520360 BRONX

4007330030

2057380412 BRONX

3015420063

2025790002

2028260021

2032370009 BRONX /
RUNOFF/YR 3,417 /
CARBON/YR 63.6

2058212920 BRONX /
RUNOFF/YR 4,741 / CARBON/YR 109.3

4012260066

2025960010 BRONX /
RUNOFF/YR 2,783 /
CARBON/YR 54.3

2023710041

3080390037

3086160133

2027900001

2058404155 BRONX /
RUNOFF/YR 2,498 / CARBON/YR 90.0

2031630005

3082180026
BROOKLYN

2058182008 BRONX /
RUNOFF/YR 3,514 / CARBON/YR 127.5

2026620028

2026790045

2058690638 BRONX /
RUNOFF/YR 3,143 / CARBON/YR 98.2

4027640049   4007610044

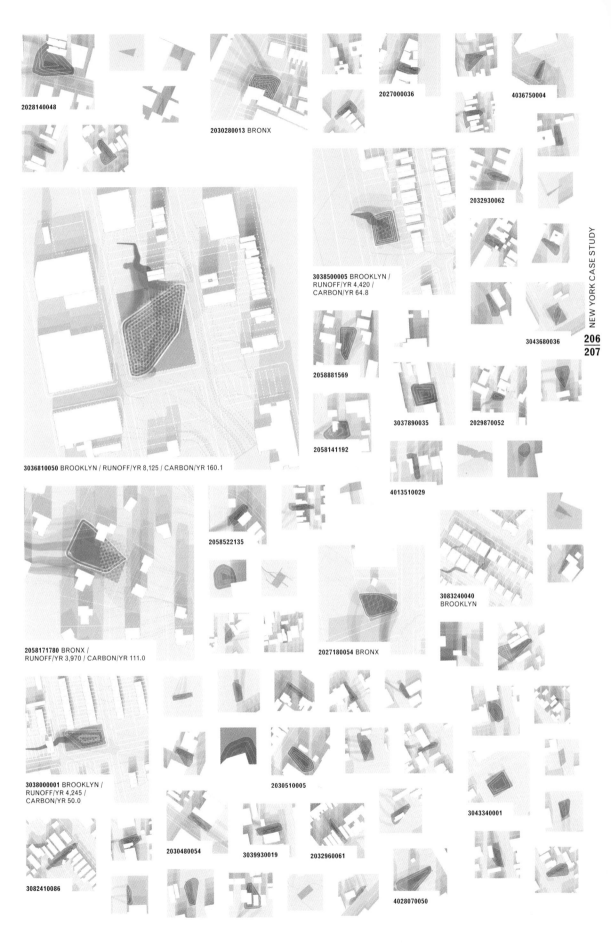

2028140048

2030280013 BRONX

2027000036

4036750004

2032930062

3038500005 BROOKLYN /
RUNOFF/YR 4,420 /
CARBON/YR 64.8

2058881569

2058141192

3037890035

2029870052

3043680036

4013510029

3036810050 BROOKLYN / RUNOFF/YR 8,125 / CARBON/YR 160.1

2058522135

3083240040
BROOKLYN

2058171780 BRONX /
RUNOFF/YR 3,970 / CARBON/YR 111.0

2027180054 BRONX

3038000001 BROOKLYN /
RUNOFF/YR 4,245 /
CARBON/YR 50.0

2030510005

3043340001

3082410086

2030480054

3039930019

2032960061

4028070050

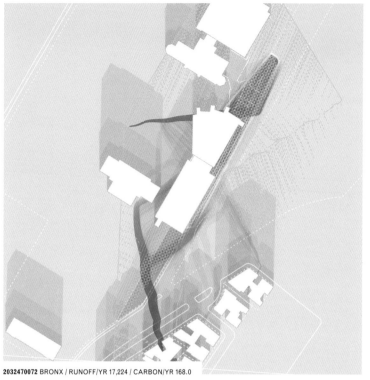

2032470072 BRONX / RUNOFF/YR 17,224 / CARBON/YR 168.0

4011000101
QUEENS

4030570072

3040860001

4028920012 QUEENS

3043150017 BROOKLYN /
RUNOFF/YR 3,507 /
CARBON/YR 73.0

4015360013 QUEENS /
RUNOFF/YR 6,983 / CARBON/YR 117.5

4036670445

3043390011

2036520026 BRONX /
RUNOFF/YR 4,074 /
CARBON/YR 58.5

4014260014

4010720053

2039080063

2042570056

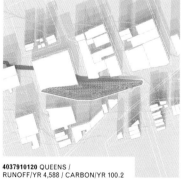

2033690032

4037910120 QUEENS /
RUNOFF/YR 4,588 / CARBON/YR 100.2

2035210016

2040050012 BRONX /
RUNOFF/YR 7,774 / CARBON/YR 125.2

4031030050

2038740051

4016570118

3042910135

3042570035

2034960017

2042730060

2046860018

2046320012 BRONX

2042640019

2050650053
BRONX

2044530043

2050400010

4021160058

2036850016

2050070031 BRONX /
RUNOFF/YR 4,278 /
CARBON/YR 43.2

2036860022

2050490025

2041070047

4040400048

96 Riverdale A

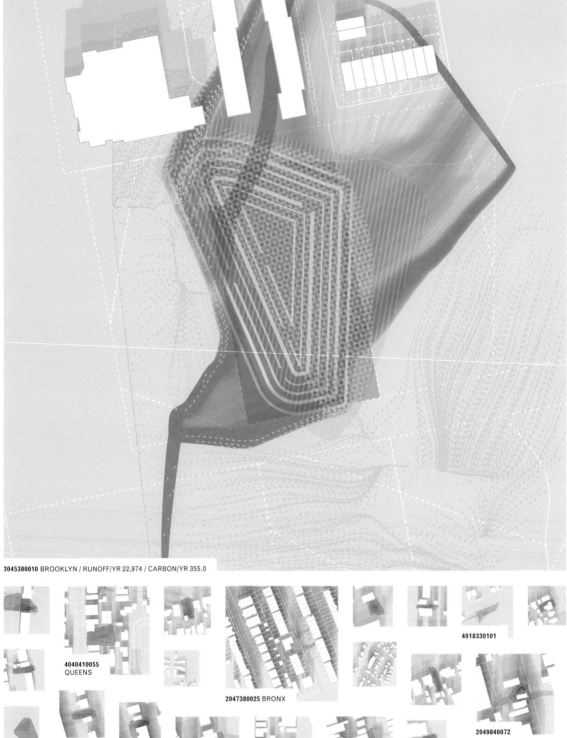

3045380010 BROOKLYN / RUNOFF/YR 22,974 / CARBON/YR 355.0

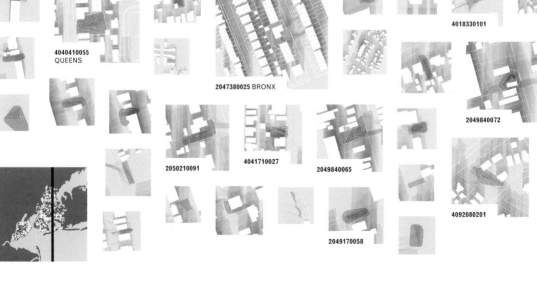

4040410055
QUEENS

4018330101

2047380025 BRONX

2049840072

2050210091   4041710027   2049840065

4092080201

2049170058

2049840007

4115490012

4141510016
QUEENS

4041160046

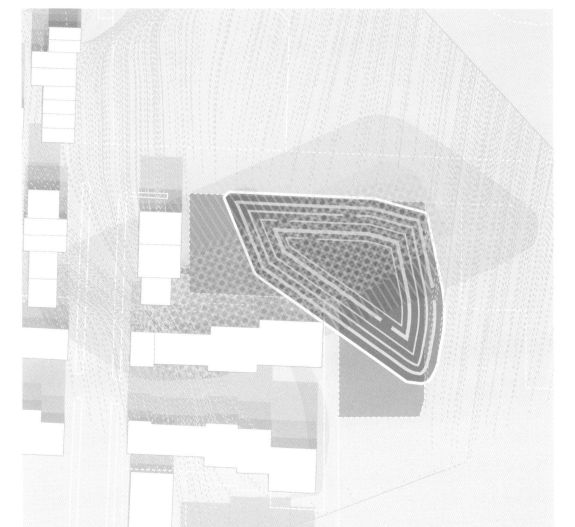

4039160119 QUEENS / RUNOFF/YR 17,001 / CARBON/YR 331.0

2048810124 BRONX /
RUNOFF/YR 2,052 /
CARBON/YR 65.2

4115350136

2053750040

2049450009

4115620159
QUEENS

2041920022

2049630037

4049620012

2049640024

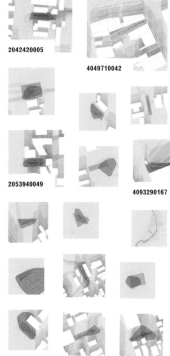

2042420005

4049710042

2053940049

4093290167

4032660019 QUEENS / RUNOFF/YR 9,889 / CARBON/YR 264.5

4142280274

4063860023

2052710060

4115720135 QUEENS /
RUNOFF/YR 9,754 / CARBON/YR 104.8

2049530137

2054260025

4094390060 QUEENS

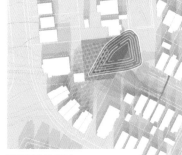

2054080418 BRONX /
RUNOFF/YR 3,139 / CARBON/YR 107.7

4065370206

4153040004

4051250027

4094500080 QUEENS /
RUNOFF/YR 3,837 /
CARBON/YR 53.2

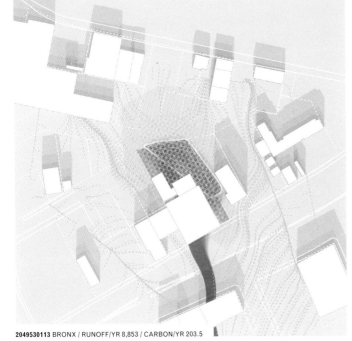

2049530113 BRONX / RUNOFF/YR 8,853 / CARBON/YR 203.5

4051540009 QUEENS

2055210258

4117850040

4100420015

4047890081 QUEENS /
RUNOFF/YR 3,639 / CARBON/YR 85.5

2055771112 BRONX /
RUNOFF/YR 1,660 /
CARBON/YR 67.5

4047050009

4153060005

2054150069

2056030038

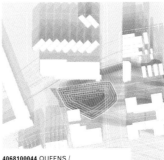

4068100044 QUEENS /
RUNOFF/YR 6,053 / CARBON/YR 73.2

4047320049

4117710086

4048590066

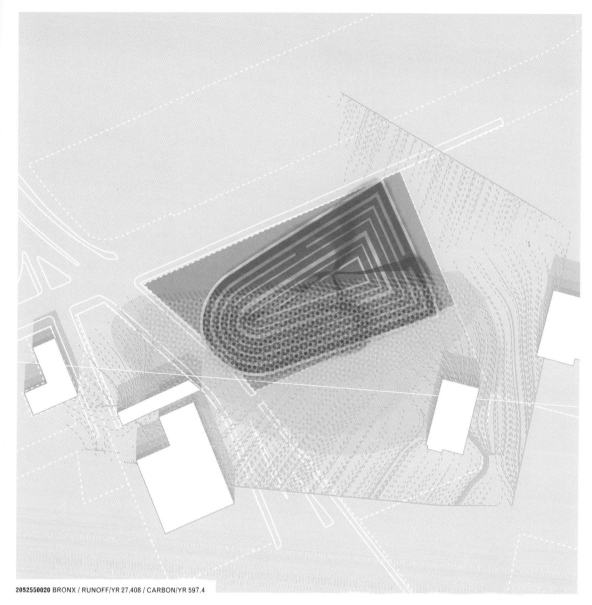

2052550020 BRONX / RUNOFF/YR 27,408 / CARBON/YR 597.4

4047220001 QUEENS /
RUNOFF/YR 3,915 / CARBON/YR 84.1

4121560007

4070750045

4101920051 QUEENS /
RUNOFF/YR 2,708 /
CARBON/YR 54.9

2056420005

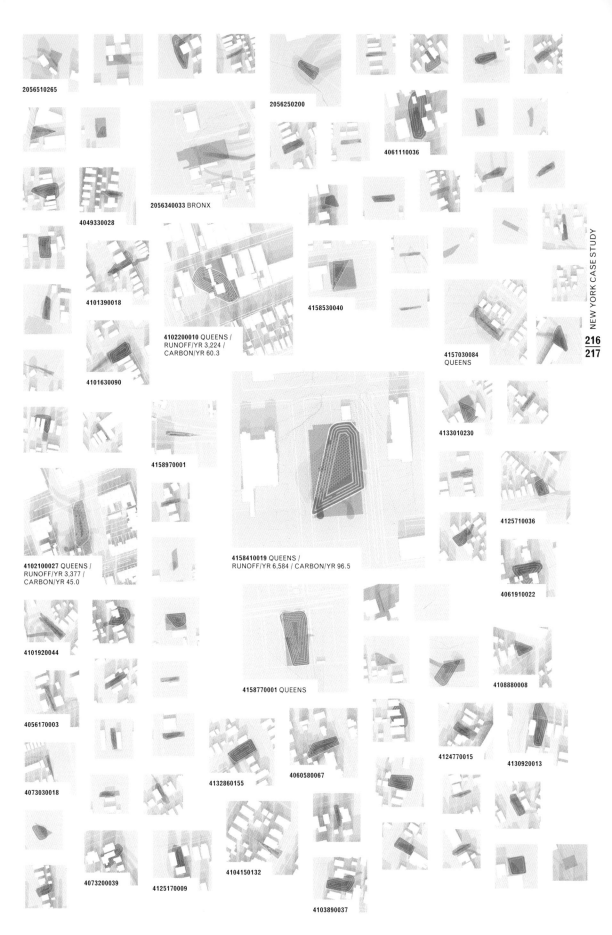

2056510265

2056250200

2056340033 BRONX

4049330028

4061110036

4101390018

4101630090

4102200010 QUEENS /
RUNOFF/YR 3,224 /
CARBON/YR 60.3

4158530040

4157030084
QUEENS

4133010230

4158970001

4125710036

4102100027 QUEENS /
RUNOFF/YR 3,377 /
CARBON/YR 45.0

4158410019 QUEENS /
RUNOFF/YR 6,584 / CARBON/YR 96.5

4061910022

4101920044

4056170003

4158770001 QUEENS

4108880008

4073030018

4124770015

4130920013

4132860155

4060580067

4073200039

4125170009

4104150132

4103890037

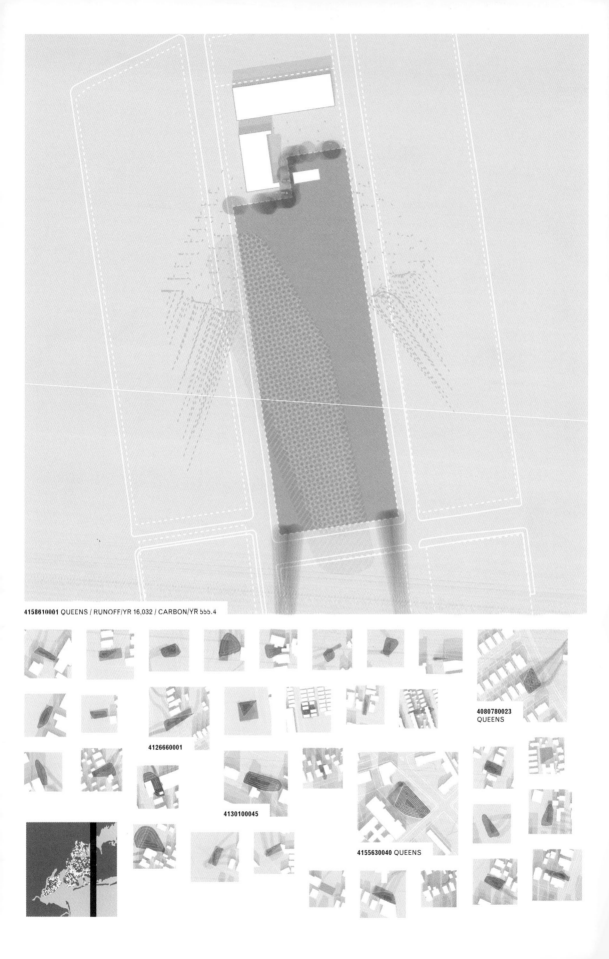

4158610001 QUEENS / RUNOFF/YR 16,032 / CARBON/YR 555.4

4080780023 QUEENS

4126660001

4130100045

4155630040 QUEENS

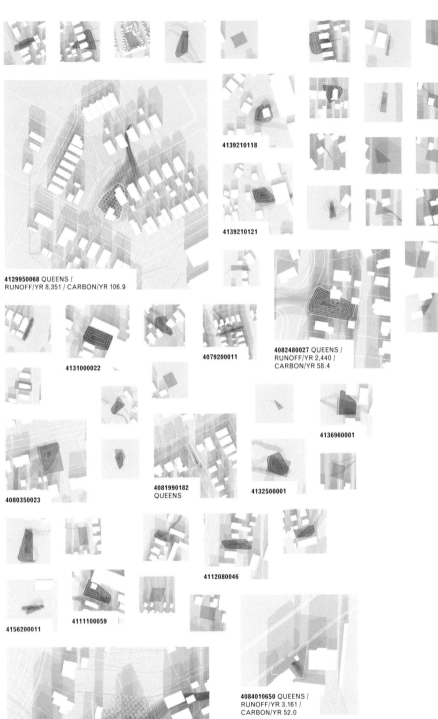

4139210118

4139210121

4129950068 QUEENS /
RUNOFF/YR 8,351 / CARBON/YR 106.9

4131000022

4079200011

4082480027 QUEENS /
RUNOFF/YR 2,440 /
CARBON/YR 58.4

4080350023

4081990182
QUEENS

4132500001

4136960001

4112080046

4156200011

4111100059

4084010650 QUEENS /
RUNOFF/YR 3,161 /
CARBON/YR 52.0

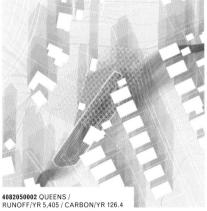

4082050002 QUEENS /
RUNOFF/YR 5,405 / CARBON/YR 126.4

We Are All Made of Stars

In the five seconds you might devote to reading this sentence, the heat and pressure of the Sun's center transforms three billion tons of hydrogen into a fractionally smaller mass of helium. The difference—twenty million tons—is unchained as an enormous amount of energy, following the improbable and immutable proportion $E=MC^2$.

At the moment this energy is created in the Sun's core, the same amount is displaced, like water in a hose, from its surface: blasting forth as a sphere of photons on a sudden, endless journey through the universe. A miniscule proportion—some five millionths—of this expanding sphere is, eight-and-a-half minutes later, interrupted by the sunward surface of Earth.[1] This incidental harvest, in one way or another, powers all life and civilization.[2]

"WHERE DOES THE ENERGY COME FROM?"

We have only recently come to understand the sun. As late as 1932, the famed physicist Neils Bohr remarked, "I cannot be really sympathetic to work in astrophysics because the first question I want to ask when I think of the Sun is where does the energy come from? You cannot tell me where the energy comes from, so how can I believe all the other things?"[3] Until the late nineteenth century, astronomy was almost entirely "positional"—concerned only with the location of stars in the sky.

Beginning in 1885, however, astronomers at the Harvard-Smithsonian Observatory, making use of glass prisms and a telescope not much larger than a trashcan, began to produce a catalog of tens of thousands of stars and their color and apparent luminosity in the sky. At a meeting of the Royal Astronomical Society in 1912, Bohr's fellow Dane, the astronomer Enjar Hertzsprung, presented a novel graphic treatment of this data, plotting the absolute brightness of a variety of stars (their distance delicately computed by the tiny parallax created by the movement of Earth around the Sun) against their luminosity. When plotted against each other, the stars revealed an unexpected figure: a band of values, termed the main sequence, stretching from upper left to lower right, with a slope somewhat higher than 1/1. Because it is how Hertzsprung originally assembled his plot, the slope, while positive, is forever mapped upper left to lower right. Groups of bright, large red stars float above the main sequence, and a band of small, blue-white stars below. Together with his American collaborator, Henry Norris Russell, the Danish astronomer's name became attached to the now common chart, dubbed the Hertzsprung-Russell diagram.[4]

Beginning in the late 1920s and 1930s, with the discovery of nuclear reactions, the main sequence was revealed not to be (as was initially speculated) a chart of the lifecycle of every star (so "sequence"),

---

1

On average. Earth's orbit is an ellipse, but the average radius is 93 million miles. Earth is almost circular, with a radius of nearly 3,950 miles. The area of a circle radius 3,950 miles (49,016,699) divided by the area of a sphere radius 93 million miles (108,686,539,000,000,000 square miles) = .000000045 percent.

2

The energy of nuclear fuel, and the proportion of Earth's own geothermal heat that comes from the decay of heavy elements such as uranium, are exceptions—but only by a degree. See below.

3

In memory of the famed astrophysicist Subrahmanyan Chandrasekhar, see K. C. Wali, Chandra: A Biography of S. Chandrasekhar (Chicago: University of Chicago Press, 1991), 102.

4

See M. S. Longair, The Cosmic Century: A History of Astrophysics and Cosmology (Cambridge: Cambridge University Press, 2006).

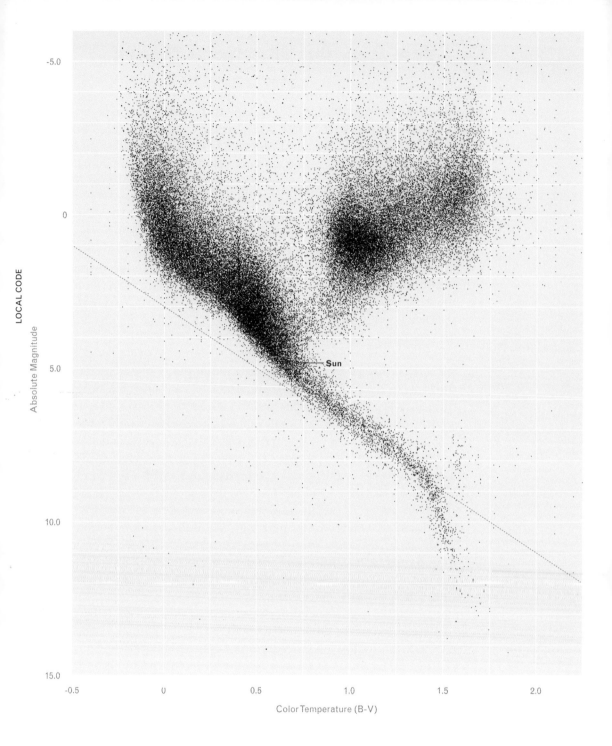

Fig. 1 — **Stars from the Hipparcos Catalog, Yale Bright Star Catalog (5th Edition), and the Gliese Catalog of Nearby Stars (3rd Edition), plotted according to absolute magnitude and color temperature; an illustration now termed the Hertzsprung-Russel Diagram. Shown are the 87,476 stars brighter than a magnitude of 9.0, or closer than 50 parsecs. The main figure on the graph is those stars burning hydrogen—the so-called Main Sequence identified by Hertzspring and Russell. Stars above and to the right are burning heavier elements. The dotted line shows the expected proportion if stars' brightness and temperature were proportional; they are not, rather scaling super-linearly.** Drawn by the author

but rather the result of a remarkable, superlinear relationship between the amount of hydrogen in a star and the amount of energy produced via the fusion of that hydrogen into helium. As a star coheres from interstellar hydrogen, gravitational pressure causes nuclear fusion to begin at the star's new core; the larger the star, the greater the pressure at the star's center and the amount of hydrogen to fuel the process of fusion. Larger stars burn hydrogen far hotter and more briefly than their smaller cousins, and it is the subtle shift in these proportions that produces the main sequence's shape.

And so every hydrogen-burning star occupies a point on the main sequence's slope. Yet when a star begins to exhaust its hydrogen, or if it is massive enough to generate the fusion of the growing core helium it has created by fusing hydrogen, it departs. Smaller stars become relatively dim white "dwarves," cooling to invisibility over time and never creating elements more massive than helium (these lie at the bottom left of the H-R diagram.)

Larger stars can continue to fuse elements created in their centers, the largest all the way up to massive iron at atomic number 26 (such supermassive stars float above the main sequence on the H-R diagram). But after this fifty-four-proton landmark, the fusion of elements stops producing energy and, instead, requires it to proceed. When lighter-than-iron fuel is exhausted at the core of such supergiants, the stars are no longer kept inflated by the fusion at their cores; they suddenly, and spectacularly, collapse. For an instant, the resulting supernova burns brighter than ten thousand suns—and it is only in the chaotic furnace of a supernova that atoms collide and combine to create all the elements in the universe that are heavier than iron, sitting above it on the periodic table. (A single 4.6-billion-year-old supernova in our own stellar neighborhood is thought to have created all the heavy elements we can see, touch, and even are made from. In this way even energy from nuclear fission—from the decay of uranium in an atomic reactor to the radiation-produced geothermal energy of our Earth's crust—is a kind of solar power.)[5]

THE SHINING METROPOLIS

But while we are made of stars, we do not think of ourselves as being like them. And yet, in at least one sense, we are. Only one other thing in the universe outputs energy at a scale that more than doubles with each doubling in size: our cities, which burn with a different but no less exceptional intensity. And the reason lies not in the subatomic nucleus, but in the equally uncanny nature of networks, and their remarkable, aggregated entwining of social, physical, and informational threads in the dense fabric of urban life.

In the same vein, the life-imbued networks that compose you and I—self-contained, water-sodden assemblies of circulatory, respiratory, neural, and metabolic systems—also exhibit remarkable properties. We humans are many times bigger than a mouse, but we have far fewer meters of blood vessels, nerves, and intestines than a human-sized mouse would have. It turns out that as we organisms

5
A remarkable exception to this rule of thumb occurs when dim, dense white dwarves steal mass from a nearby companion star. When this happens, the dwarf will explode in a supernova once its mass rises to about 1.4 times that of the Sun, through a reaction that differs fundamentally from that of the immense stars described here. A standard supernova gets much of its energy from the collapse of its outer layers. A Type 1a supernova derives all of its energy from the heating of the inner, carbon core of a white dwarf through this increased mass. Because the luminance of a supernova is closely tied to its mass, and the mass of Type 1a supernovas is consistent, these superbright explosions form a so-called standard candle throughout the universe, allowing measurements of their relative movement and position to be possible. In 1998 Saul Perlmutter, Brian P. Schmidt, and Adam Riess, together with their large teams of collaborators, used these stars to show that the universe is expanding, and that the acceleration of its expansion is increasing. We do not yet know why. See James Glanz, "Breakthrough of the Year, Astronomy: Cosmic Motion Revealed," Science 282, no. 5397 (1998), 2156–57.

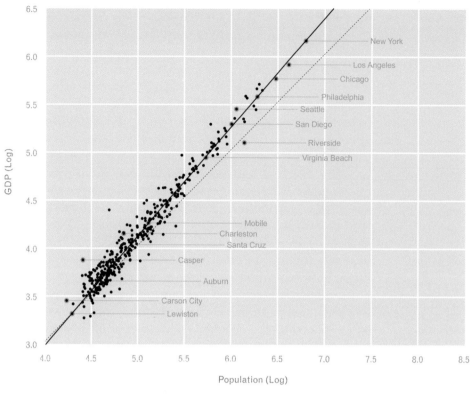

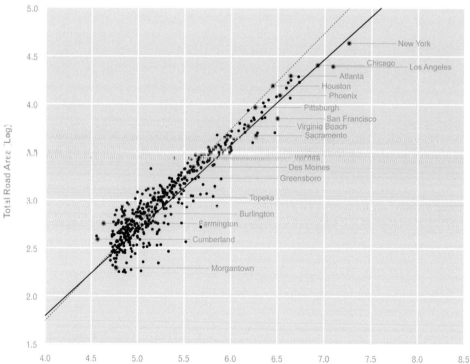

Fig. 2 — The relationship between the population of US Metropolitan Statistical Areas (MSAs) and GDP (left). The relationship between MSA population and infrastructural scale (shown as road area in M2). One/one scaling is shown with a dotted line in each case, the best-fit curve as a solid. In each case, the best fit is close to the theoretical prediction for a network model of urban infrastructure and growth, $\beta={}^7\!/_8$ for economic output and $\beta={}^5\!/_8$ for infrastructure. Data from the US Bureau of Economic Analysis (2013) and US Department of Transportation. A version of this data originally appeared in Luís M. A. Bettencourt, "The Origins of Scaling in Cities," *Science* 21 (June 2013): 340 (6139), 1438–1441. Data courtesy of Professor Bettencourt. Drawn by the author

6
See John R. Speakman, "Review: Body Size, Energy Metabolism and Lifespan," *The Journal of Experimental Biology* 208, 1717–30.

7
See Luís M. A. Bettencourt, "The Origins of Scaling in Cities," *Science* 340, no. 6139 (2013): 1438–41.

8
Stephen J. Gould and Richard C. Lewontin, "The Spandrels of San Marco and the Panglossian Paradigm: A Critique of the Adaptationist Programme," *Proceedings of the Royal Society of London, Series B, Biological Sciences* 205, no. 1161 (September 1979): 21.

9
Gould, the disciplinary interloper, incorrectly terms the curved pendentives "spandrels," traditionally the architectural term for the flat bridging between a wall and a curved opening. There is an extensive and entertaining literature arguing this point within the sphere of evolutionary biology; see Stephen Jay Gould, "The Exaptive Excellence of Spandrels as a Term and Prototype," *Proceedings of the National Academy of Sciences USA* 94 (1997): 10750–55.

become larger, the total length and overall complexity of our constituent metabolic networks do not increase proportionally with size. Instead, these networks increase their efficiency—all the way up to the three-hundred-eighty-thousand-pound blue whale.[6] Cities—perhaps as no surprise—share this quality. A larger city makes do with fewer gas stations, sewer pipes, and police stations (relative to size) and is so able to operate less expensively than a small town (which is a large part of why shrinking cities have such deep difficulties). But as cities get bigger, something quite different also happens.

While you and I are larger than a housecat, we are cooler (and much more so than a mouse). But as cities expand, they also get far hotter. The heat of a city is not physical heat (though the actual heat of cities is a pressing environmental problem), but rather the subtle metabolism of the city itself. Like the fusion of a star, this metabolism is measurable only indirectly; in the case of cities it is detected through the pace of patents, the number of ballet companies, the profusion of newspapers, and even the speed of bodies on the sidewalk. All these numbers, it turns out, are more than doubled with each doubling of urban size—especially once the makeshift logic of administrative boundaries is adjusted for (for example, Hoboken is not New York de jure, but is de facto). In the end, as cities go, twice as big is more (about 15 percent more) than twice as hot.[7]

That cities are complex, emergent metabolisms, and that a particular kind of energy is produced from their ordered, chaotic mixing of viewpoints, techniques, and cultures is, one would hope today, not such a revolutionary observation. But it would seem particularly important when we think about the very qualities of cities with which we began at the start of this volume—robustness and resilience—and about how to bring them better into.

THE PANGLOSSIAN PARADIGM

"Everything is made for the best purpose. Our noses were made to carry spectacles, so we have spectacles. Legs were clearly intended for breeches, and we wear them"—so the paleobiologist Stephen Jay Gould quoted Voltaire, via *Candide*'s Dr. Pangloss, to caution his colleagues against seeing perfection in nature. The setting was an influential 1979 essay, "The Spandrels of San Marco and the Panglossian Paradigm: A Critique of the Adaptationist Programme."[8] To advance the essay's argument further, Gould uses an architectural metaphor. Under the then prevailing "adaptionist" viewpoint, he imagines, the pendentives of the Cathedral of San Marco would not be taken to be (as they are) a necessary leftover of the superimposition of a dome on a quadripartite vault, but rather (as they are not) perfect adaptations to the display of triangular paintings of angels.[9] As Gould would later point out, however, many of the most robust features of evolution derive from such unlikely origins, reappropriated, remade, and reconstituted, and from leftovers most of all. For it is the case, according to the habit of evolutionary change, that a normally secondary or peripheral feature of a complex organism is likely to come to the fore through exaptive transformation; precisely because of its seeming uselessness, it is most ripe for experimentation and change.[10] In a 1982 article, Gould and the paleontologist Elisabeth S. Vrba proposed the neologism *exaptation* to describe such transformation. From eardrums (ex-reptilian jawbones) to wing feathers (duvets for freezing dinosaurs), "exaptations" far outnumber pure adaptations in our ecology. Even when a trait, like our skeleton, seems incontrovertibly perfected for its current use, there is likely still a surprising shift at play. For our supporting bones, we must thank our Cambrian ancestors for laying up phosphates inside the body for

Fig. 3 — The Spandrels of San Marco, Venice
© Photograph by the author

metabolic purposes; these deposits were adapted for structural purpose many millions of years later. Such adaptation, or exaptation, is particularly relevant in the current discussion.

CONSERVATIVE SURGERY

As it is in cities, so it is in organisms. This in itself is not a new idea; indeed, one of the very first theorists of urban metabolism, Sir Patrick Geddes, would distinguish himself equally as an urban designer, a theorist, and an evolutionary biologist. In his own work in complex cities, Geddes would stress the importance of distributed, subtle "conservative surgery" over the graphic and intellectual appeal of root-and-branch de novo design.[11] (Even as his life's work, the combination of exhibit, architecture, and viewing devices known as the Outlook Tower sought to connect the local and global in the citizen's gaze.)[12]

And yet, how to radically increase the robustness of cities by "conservative" means? Far from emphasizing optimization, recent work in evolutionary biology has stressed the role of "compartmentation, redundancy, robustness and flexibility" in evolutionary change.[13] At the macroscopic scale, the view of an organism—even a human being—as a single thing adapting to new environments is itself being supplanted by the idea of bodies, including our own, as a "mini-ecosystem, or economy," in which competing forces populate redundant systems to produce a far more robust, resilient and adaptable whole than any single, optimized outcome could ever provide."[14] (Ninety-nine percent of the genetic material in our bodies, it has only recently been discovered, belongs not to us but to the complex microfauna of

10
Stephen Jay Gould and Elisabeth S. Vrba, "Exaptation—A Missing Term in the Science of Form," Paleobiology 8, no. 1 (Winter 1982): 4–15.

11
See Patrick Geddes and Jaqueline Tyrwhitt, "Conservative Surgery," ther Air Datrish Geddes in India (London: L. Humphries, 1947).

12
Sonja Dümpelmann, "Air-minded Visions: The Aerial View in Early-Twentieth-Century Landscape Design and Urban Planning," Flights of Imagination: Aviation, Landscape, Design (Charlottesville: University of Virginia Press, 2014), 75–118.

13
See Marc Kirschner and John Gerhart, "Evolvability," Proceedings of the National Academy of Sciences USA 95 (July 1998): 8420–27.

microbes that support our metabolism, without which we would quickly perish.[15])

Much discussion of resilience in contemporary urban discourse emphasizes the importance of redundancy.[16] But again, to borrow from biology, it would seem that "not redundancy of parts but distributed robustness is the major cause of robustness in living systems."[17] In particular, it is has been observed of natural systems that "the absence of completely rational, premeditated system design may favor the origin of distributed robustness."[18]

Too much of our contemporary discourse around cities and technology emphasizes the ability (indeed, the inherent bias—see "The Map and the Territory") of technological systems and networks to find optimal solutions. And this seductive tendency brings us back to the fourth, constant character in this story: systems-based planning, with its dream of reducing the complexity of the city to the precise logic of the computers increasingly used to address it.

Yet against this grain, what we find when we examine the nature of resilience is that calculated, "optimal" solutions are by their nature suboptimal for the creation of robustness and evolvability. This gulf is particularly evident in the claims made for technocratically inflected, large-scale solutions to urban problems—whether in 1965 or 2015. A 100-meter floodgate in Venice (or New York), however well constructed, provides no deliverance against a 1,001-centimeter flood. And, we must constantly be reminded, the chief characteristic of climate change, beyond our certainty about its cause and reality, is uncertainty about its effects. Above all, we must in this context remember that our true knowledge about the city is itself astonishingly limited. Or, to put it another way, the limits to what we can know about such a complex, dynamic system are both subtle and immense.

CITIES AND UNCERTAINTY

In the last several years, the rise of urban data together with scientific work on urban scaling has given rise (though not so much from its own authors) to speculation, yet again, that the city can be understood and influenced through precise, scientific means.[19] If we return to the surface of the Sun, however, we can find an appropriate analogy for the fundamental incompatibility of control and urban life in the quite different life of our speeding photon before it speeds from the solar surface.

It turns out that although we know for near certain what happens to a photon once it blasts forth on its way across the universe (including

14
David Krakauer, "Cellular Struggle at Heart of Variety," review of The Plausibility of Life, Resolving Darwin's Dilemma, by Marc W. Kirschner and John C. Gerhart, The Times Higher Education Supplement, November 27, 2006.

15
See Jeremiah J. Faith, Janaki Lelwala-Guruge, Mark Charbonneau, Sathish Subramanian, Henning Seedorf, Andrew L. Goodman, Jose C. Clemente, Rob Knight, Andrew C. Heath, Rudolph L. Leibel, Michael Rosenbaum, and Jeffrey I. Gordon, "The Long-Term Stability of the Human Gut Microbiota," Science 341 (2013), doi: 10.1126/science.1237439.

16
See, for example, Ove Arup & Partners and the Rockefeller Foundation, "The City Resilience Framework," The Rockefeller Foundation, April 2014, accessed June 30, 2015, http://assets.rockefellerfoundation.org/app/uploads/20150530121930/City-Resilience-Framework1.pdf.

17
Andreas Wagner, Robustness and Evolvability in Living Systems (Princeton, NJ: Princeton University Press, 2005), 14.

18
Wagner, Robustness, 315. See also Erica Jen, ed., Robust Design: Repertoire of Biological, Ecological, and Engineering Case Studies (New York: Oxford University Press, 2005), 218.

19
Jonah Lehrer, "A Physicist Solves the City," New York Times Magazine, December 17, 2010. "A Physicist Solves the City" trumpets a 2010 New York Times Magazine profile of Geoffery West. As attractive as it might be to urban administrators (not least of which the Michael Bloomberg Administration in New York, which invested $15 million in a physicist-led Center for Urban Science and Progress at NYU; see New York City Office of the Mayor Press Release, "Mayor Bloomberg, New York University President Sexton and MTA Chairman Lhota Announce Historic Partnership to Create New Applied Sciences Center in Downtown Brooklyn," April 23, 2012), the notion that the city can in any way be solved by science may well be just as fabulistic as many others penned by the author of the New York Times Magazine article in question—now disgraced journalist Jonah Lehrer.

the remote possibility of its energy being captured here on Earth), we know almost nothing about its life beforehand—and cannot begin to guess. For while we know that the photon's energy was created in the Sun's core, the nature of the path it takes from the star's center to its surface is, in fact, incalculable. Like a path through an urban network, it is, in statistical terms, a "random walk"; in the dense environment of the Sun's plasma, the photon is constantly absorbed and reemitted by hydrogen atoms in random directions, resulting in a theoretical trajectory that would put even the most extensive pinball machine to shame. And so, much like our uncertain path through the city on a given lazy Sunday, the photon's walk can only be approximated; guesses as to the duration of its passage through the Sun—depending on assumptions—range from one thousand to as much as one hundred and fifty thousand years.[20]

It is hard, yet essential to divorce the practice of design from certainty. Here, we might remind ourselves not so much of biological metaphors in architecture, but rather of architectural metaphors in biology: "foundations," "building blocks," "blueprints," and the German "Bauplan," or body plan, for the fundamental architecture of life. As Adrian Forty has observed, the consistent application of natural, and particularly biological, language to architecture has served in actuality as a persistent barrier to considering the manifold natural systems to which architecture is actually connected.[21] Most problematically, such metaphors tend to buttress the enduring fallacy of architecture as an independent object, innocent of its impact on the world at large.

Yet, fascinatingly, the inverse is also true in biology. The deployment of design language in biology has served generally to perpetuate an idealized, overly deterministic vision of the operations of genetic systems. Ironically, these have served to mask the qualities of natural processes that are also inseparable from the reality of crafting buildings and landscapes: chance, contingency, complexity, and luck. (To those who began to ascribe a universal and ubiquitous power of optimization to the operations of natural selection in Darwin's own lifetime, the master himself lamented, "Great is the power of steady misinterpretation."[22]) It is to this vision of indirect causation, and inescapable complexity, that *Local Code* aspires. In reality, the code of DNA—and, likewise, the coded urban proposals contained herein—become much more like a real architectural blueprint than the architect's idealized vision of it. Which is to say that in nature, as in the city, we can only aspire for such singular texts to have a subtle, if salutary, effect on the world as it comes into shape.

20
Frank H. Shu, The Physical Universe: An Introduction to Astronomy (Mill Valley, CA: University Science Books, 1982), 89–90.

21
See "Nature," in Adrian Forty, Words and Buildings: A Vocabulary of Modern Architecture (New York: Thames and Hudson, 2000), 220.

22
Charles Darwin, On the Origin of Species by Means of Natural Selection: Or, The Preservation of Favored Races in the Struggle for Life (Chicago: Rand McNally, 1872), 395.

Ideas, particularily in and about cities, are not the work of individuals but rather the web of connections and encounters that brings them into being. Here I attempt (but undoubtedly do not succeed in) thanking and recognizing all those who brought this work into being. When I use "our" and "we" in these acknowledgments, and in discussing the drawings within it, it is in recognition that this book is the work of many hands, and that the support offered by those below came by and to all of us.

The software at the heart of this book involved collaborations with many advisers and co-coders. However, several people are particularly worthy of my thanks for their persistence and commitment to the project. The first is David Lung, who programmed the first working model of Local Code with me in Visual Basic in the summer of 2009, and who has continued to add his wit and encouragement to the endeavor ever since. The next is Shivang Patwa, who managed the work through its first iterations with dedication and skill. The third is the remarkable Benjamin Golder, whose optimism, brio, and technical skill have seen the project through many dark nights—including some spent in Denver rail yards. The fourth is Carlos Sandoval, whose skill and intelligence made much of what you hold in your hands become real on the page. Rudy Letsche and Miles Stemper provided crucial assistance with final production. And finally, Sara Jensen Carr—once a student and coteacher at Berkeley, now a colleague at the University of Hawaii—whose thoughtful and precise thinking form the basis of much of our claim to environmental and scientific rigor.

Of particular note as well is the team who first put the San Francisco case study together as part of the WPA 2.0: Working Public Architecture competition—a remarkable opportunity for which Dana Cuff and Roger Sherman merit enormous thanks. The team included not only Ben, David, Sara and Shivang, but also Matt Smith, Laurie Spitler, and Marina Christodoulides.

The germ of the San Francisco case study is also rightly mapped to conversations with John Peterson and John Cary, who not only brought my attention to the city's database of unaccepted streets but provided an essential sounding board and encouragement for the work's position in the landscape of policy and practice. And Mike Farrah, at the time a special assistant in the San Francisco Mayor's office, provided crucial access to data. Two graduate studios at Berkeley helped me develop my thinking and understanding of the residual and abandoned in San Francisco. This work is therefore also that of those students—Edwin Agudelo, Matthew Baran, Maria Carrizosa, Nicole Cousino, Christian Cutul, Christopher Dobosz, Elizabeth Harrington, Lan Hu, Nicholas Karklins, Gavin Knowles, Peter Lingamfelter, Cindy Liu, John McGill, Taylor Medlin, Cindy Moon, Shivang Patwa, Hua Shen, Matt Smith, Sarah Smith, Nicolas Sowers, Laurie Spitler, Kim Suczynski, and Jung Mi Won.

In Los Angeles in 2010, we were very fortunate to collaborate with the remarkable Amigos de los Rios, led by Claire Robinson. We are grateful for their patience, support, and belief in our then nascent working method.

My particular thanks go to Fabio Carrera in Venice, not only for supporting this work in 2012 but also for introducing me to the world of GIS in 2004. Alberto Gallo and Tiberio Scozzafava-Jaeger provided particular support to the Venice-related design work you hold here, and Jane da Mosto and Maria Allesandra Segatini provided welcome support to and conversation at a workshop held at the US Pavilion of the 13th Architecture Biennale, from which this work emerged. We are also enormously grateful to Cathy Lang Ho for not only the invitation to the pavilion but also her support of our larger work in

Venice. And finally, my enduring gratitude goes to my dear friend and indomitable lagoon navigator, Sandro Bisa.

Back on these shores, thanks go to Timon MacPhearson at the New School in New York City, for both sharing and supporting over the last three years a vision of the centrality of the city's peripheral spaces and communities. Eric Sanderson at the Wildlife Conservation Society shared data and thoughts selflessly, and Lisbeth Sheperd and Erika Symmonds of Green City Force helped us remember what it is to do real work in New York.

Alongside this incalculable assistance in each of the places we have worked, there is the help and support given to the project in the spaces of ideas and drawing, which it just as firmly seeks to inhabit. An early chance to develop the work physically and representationally came from the 2010 Biennial of the Americas. I am particularly grateful to my colleague and friend Ron Rael, whose support of this work throughout has been selfless and incalculable. I am also enormously grateful to Paola Santoscoy for her belief and support in the work and its complex installation.

My initial opportunity to develop the intellectual atmosphere surrounding this work into a critical position and historical excavation alongside its technical development came from another friend, colleague, and supporter, David Gissen. An invitation to present in the 2011 Phyllis Lambert Seminar gave essential annealing to this argument as well, and for this, as well as for prompting my interest in landscape and entropy to begin with, I remain enormously grateful to Allesandra Ponte.

To the extent that I have a capacity to think and act beyond buildings, these abilities flow from my influential years at the University of Virginia School of Architecture. Particular thanks go, as ever, to Julie Bargmann, Elizabeth K. Meyer, and William R. Morrish for expanding my sense of how it was possible to talk, think, and act in cities and landscapes.

Much of the graphic thinking around this book happened through the singular experience of a 2013–2014 fellowship at the American Academy in Rome (AAR). My thanks go to the reviewers and jury for the fellowship, to AAR president Mark Robbins, and to the colleagues and supporters in Rome who are innumerable, and in particular those who took time to help me think about cities, time, and drawing in studio visits and conversation: Kim Bowes, Brad Cantrell, Lindsay Harris, Thomas Kelly, Peter Benson Miller, Catie Newell, and Ruth Noyes.

At Berkeley, I am deeply grateful to my valued colleagues in the College of Environmental Design, beyond those already named, who provided essential support to this project. Jennifer Wolch, as a dean as well as a colleague, helped give the project meaning and depth in the realm of geospatial calculation and policy. In recent years, chair of architecture Tom Buresh has catalyzed an environment in which this work, and that of my colleagues, has been able to grow and prosper. Walter Hood has, as ever, helped keep me honest about landscape.

The Berkeley Art Museum and Pacific Film Archive, on whose board it has been my great pleasure to serve since 2012, has provided a welcome home to conversations about Local Code's position within the space of culture and practice, and I am grateful to Larry Rinder for his support and conversation in this regard. Lucia Jacobs provided particular insights from her own expertise, and that of her remarkable family. The Environmental Design Library, as always, provided incalculable assistance, both through the volumes it holds and through its painstaking assistance in tracking down the most obscure of sources; particular thanks go to David Eifler and Molly Rose.

Three archives provided crucial materials for the historical research in this book: the Gordon Matta-Clark collection at the Canadian Centre for Architecture in Montreal, where Renata Guttman receives special thanks. Thanks go also to the Jane Jacobs Papers at Boston College and to the Howard T. Fisher Collection in the archives of Harvard University.

Local Code received crucial early support, both material and intellectual, from the Berkeley Center for New Media. I am particularly grateful to Ken Goldberg for his belief and early interest. Further essential support came from the Hellman Family Fund, the Graham Foundation for Advanced Studies in the Fine Arts, and the Center for Information Technology Research in the Interest of Society. A 2011 residency in the Autodesk Idea Studio at One Market proved catalytic and expansive; we are grateful especially to Kimberly Whinna for her help and support in this regard. I also extend deep thanks to current and former colleagues at San Francisco's Urban Planning + Research Association (SPUR), particularly Allison Arieff and Gretchen Hilyard. Only a few blocks from SPUR, SFMOMA curator Jennifer Dunlop Fletcher and associate curator Joseph Becker have my enormous gratitude for their interest and support of the project, and to their staff for its painstaking installation at the museum in 2012.

I am grateful, further afield, to my friends and colleagues at the Santa Fe Institute, which since my first visit in 2001 has provided an essential underpinning of my understanding and thinking of all that is complex and interconnected in the world, including cities. Most recently, I am especially grateful to Geoffrey West and Luís Bettencourt for our ongoing collaborations and discussions about the particular science of cities.

In the world of policy and government, I single out for particular thanks Benjamin de la Peña, now of the Knight Foundation, and Jason Shubpach of the National Endowment for the Arts, who at various times have provided essential support and criticism.

At Princeton Architectural Press, thanks go to my old friend and newfound publisher, Kevin Lippert, as well as Jennifer Lippert, for their support and belief in this work. I am very grateful, too, for the tolerance, intelligence, and support of Barbara Darko. And beyond the realm of thanks when it comes to my remarkable collaborators on this book, Catalogtree: Daniel Gross, Joris Maltha, and their remarkable team, who have engaged the work and improved more than I even could have imagined.

Finally, several parts of the text of this book were originally published, and so strengthened, elsewhere. Portions of each of the chapters originally appeared in an essay solicited by David Gissen for *Architectural Design* in 2010, and were also developed for a presentation, solicited by Aaron Sprecher, for the 2010 Association for Computer-Aided Design in Architecture (ACADIA) conference in New York. Portions of the final chapter were developed first for an invited presentation at the Harvard GSD for a course taught by Kiel Moe and Sanford Kwinter on thinking about energy in 2013, and will appear as well in the resulting ACTAR volume.

Closer to home, I would like to extend continually incalculable thanks to my brother, Thomas de Monchaux, who continues to serve as an extra brain, proofreader, and essential interlocutor; and to my father, John de Monchaux, whose urbane career and intuitive understanding of urban situations—crossing at many moments the histories examined in this book— has made it possible for me to begin to understand cities. My mother, Suzanne de Monchaux, passed away during the preparation of this book, and her legacy remains an essential part of its creation.

Finally, and above all, I thank Kathryn Moll, whose collaboration, deep intelligence, and amazing love make this and so much of what I do possible, and my son, Charles de Monchaux, whose continued curiosity and delight in the world make it impossible not to feel the same. More than anyone else, they have made this book possible. It is to them that it is dedicated, with love.

Addicott, John F., M. F. Antolin, J. S. Richardson, D. K. Padilla, J. M. Aho, and D. A. Soluk. "Ecological Neighborhoods: Scaling Environmental Patterns." Oikos 49, no. 3 (1987): 340–46.

Ahern, Jack. "From fail-safe to safe-to-fail: Sustainability and resilience in the new urban world." Landscape and Urban Planning 100, no. 4 (2011): 341–43.

Akbari, Hashem, and Steven J. Konopacki. "Calculating energy-saving potentials of heat-island reduction strategies." Energy Policy 33, no. 6 (2005): 721–56.

Alberti, Marina. "The Effects of Urban Patterns on Ecosystem Function." International Regional Science Review 28, no. 2 (2005): 168–92.

Bender, Darren, Lutz Tischendorf, and Lenore Fahrig. "Using Patch Isolation Metrics to Predict Animal Movement in Binary Landscapes." Landscape Ecology 18, no. 1 (2003): 17–39.

Bolund, Per, and Sven Hunhammar. "Ecosystem Services in Urban Areas." Ecological Economics 29, no. 2 (1999): 293–301.

Bonometto, Lorenzo. "Functional characteristics of salt marshes (barene) in the Venice Lagoon and environmental restoration scenarios." In Flooding and Environmental Challenges for Venice and its Lagoon: State of Knowledge, edited by Caroline A. Fletcher and Tom Spencer, 473–85. Cambridge: Cambridge University Press, 2005.

Cadenasso, Mary L., Steward T. A. Pickett, and Kirsten Schwarz. "Spatial heterogeneity in urban ecosystems: reconceptualizing land cover and a framework for classification." Frontiers in Ecology and the Environment 5, no. 2 (2007): 80–88.

Cecconi, Giovanni. "Morphological restoration techniques." In Flooding and Environmental Challenges for Venice and its Lagoon: State of Knowledge, edited by Caroline. A. Fletcher and Tom Spencer, 461–72. Cambridge: Cambridge University Press, 2005.

Chen, Wendy Y., and C. Y. Jim. "Assessment and Valuation of the Ecosystem Services Provided by Urban Forests." In Ecology, Planning, and Management of Urban Forests, edited by Margaret M. Carreiro, Yongchang Song, and Jianguo Wu, 53–83. New York: Springer, 2008.

Cheng, Shuiping, Wolfgang Grosse, Friedhelm Karrenbrock, and Manfred Thoennessen. "Efficiency of constructed wetlands in decontamination of water polluted by heavy metals." Ecological Engineering 18 (2002): 317–25.

Collinge, Sharon K. Ecology of Fragmented Landscapes. Baltimore: Johns Hopkins University Press, 2009.

De Groot R. S., R. Alkemade, L. Braat, L. Hein, and L. Willemen. "Challenges in Integrating the Concept of Ecosystem Services and Values in Landscape Planning, Management and Decision Making." Ecological Complexity 7, no. 3 (2010): 260–72.

Di Silvio, Giampaolo. "Sediment balance, morphodynamics and landscape restoration." In Flooding and Environmental Challenges for Venice and its Lagoon: State of Knowledge, edited by Caroline. A. Fletcher and Tom Spencer, 359–68. Cambridge: Cambridge University Press, 2005.

Donovan, Geoffrey. H., and David T. Butry. "Market-Based Approaches to Tree Valuation." Arborist News 17 (August 2008): 52–55.

Donovan, Geoffrey. H. "The Value of Shade: Estimating the Effect of Urban Trees on Summertime Electricity use." Energy and Buildings 41, no. 6 (2009): 662–68.

Dwyer, J. F., E. Gregory McPherson, Herbert W. Schroeder, and Rowan A. Rowntree "Assessing the Benefits and Costs of the Urban Forest." Journal of Arboriculture 18 (1992): 227–34.

Evans, J. P. "Resilience, Ecology and Adaptation in the Experimental City." Transactions of the Institute of British Geographers 36, no. 2 (2011): 223–37.

Forman, Richard T. Land Mosaics: The Ecology of Landscapes and Regions. Cambridge: Cambridge University Press, 1995.

Gozzi, Antonio, and Giselle Menel Lemos, "Application of hydrodynamic and morphological models." In Flooding and Environmental Challenges for Venice and its Lagoon: State of Knowledge, edited by Caroline A. Fletcher and Tom Spencer, 391–400. Cambridge: Cambridge University Press, 2005.

Grimm, Nancy B., J. Morgan Grove, Steward T. A. Pickett, And Charles L. Redman. "Integrated Approaches to Long-Term Studies of Urban Ecological Systems: Urban Ecological Systems Present Multiple Challenges to Ecologists-Pervasive Human Impact and Extreme Heterogeneity of Cities, and the Need to Integrate Social and Ecological Approaches, Concepts, and Theory." Bioscience 50, no. 7 (2000): 571–84.

Holling, Crawford Stanley. "Understanding the Complexity of Economic, Ecological, and Social Systems." Ecosystems 4, no. 5 (2001): 390–405.

Kremer, Peleg, Zoé Hamstead, and Timon McPhearson. "A Social-Ecological Assessment of Vacant Lots in New York City." Landscape and Urban Planning 120 (2013): 218–33. doi: 10.1016/j.landurbplan.2013.05.003.

Kuo, Frances E., and William C. Sullivan. "Aggression and Violence in the Inner City: Effects of Environment Via Mental Fatigue." Environment and Behavior 33, no. 4 (2001): 543–71.

McGarigal, Kevin, Barbara J. Marks, and Pacific Northwest Research Station. FRAGSTATS: Spatial Pattern Analysis Program for Quantifying Landscape Structure. Portland, OR: US Department of Agriculture, Forest Service, Pacific Northwest Research Station, 1995.

McPhearson, Timon, Erik Andersson, Tomas Elmqvist, and Niki Frantzeskaki. "Resilience of and Through Urban Ecosystem Services." Special issue, Ecosystem Services 12 (2015): 152–56.

McPhearson, Timon, Zoé Hamstead, and Peleg Kremer. "Urban Ecosystem Services for Resilience Planning and Management in New York City." Special issue, AMBIO: Journal of the Human Environment 43 (2014): 502–15.

McPhearson, Timon, Peleg Kremer, and Zoé Hamstead. "Mapping Ecosystem Services in New York City: Applying a Social-Ecological Approach in Urban Vacant Land." Ecosystem Services 5, no. 10 (2013): 11–26.

McPherson, E. Gregory. "Accounting for Benefits and Costs of Urban Greenspace." Landscape and Urban Planning 22, no. 1 (1992): 41–51.

McPherson, E. Gregory, and Rowan A. Rowntree. "Energy Conservation Potential of Urban Tree Planting." Journal of Arboriculture 19 (1993): 321–31.

McPherson, E. Gregory, James R. Simpson, Qingfu Xiao, and Chunxia Wu. "Million Trees Los Angeles Canopy Cover and Benefit Assessment." Landscape and Urban Planning 99, no. 1 (2011): 40–50.

McPherson, E. Gregory. "Northern California coast community tree guide: benefits, costs, and strategic planting." Albany, CA: US Department of Agriculture, Forest Service, Pacific Southwest Research Station, 2010, http://www.fs.fed.us/psw/publications/documents/psw_gtr228/psw_gtr228.pdf.

Newman, Peter, Timothy Beatley, and Heather Boyer. Resilient Cities: Responding to Peak Oil and Climate Change. Washington, D.C.: Island Press, 2009.

Niemelä, Jari. Urban Ecology: Patterns, Processes, and Applications. Oxford: Oxford University Press, 2011.

Nowak, D. J., and D. E. Crane. "The Urban Forest Effects (UFORE) Model: Quantifying Urban Forest Structure and Functions." In Integrated Tools for Natural Resource Inventories in the 21st century, IUFRO Conference. St. Paul, MN: US Department of Agriculture, Forest Service, North Central Research Station, 2000.

Nowak, D. J., R. Hoehn, and D. E. Crane. "Oxygen production by urban trees in the United States." Arboriculture & Urban Forestry 33, no. 3 (2007): 220–26.

Odum, Howard T. Ecological and General Systems: An Introduction to Systems Ecology. Niwot, CO.: University Press of Colorado, 1994.

Pickett, S. T. A., M. L. Cadenasso, J. M. Grove, C. H. Nilon, R. V. Pouyat, W. C. Zipperer, and R. Costanza. "Urban Ecological Systems: Linking Terrestrial Ecological, Physical, and Socioeconomic Components of Metropolitan Areas." Annual Review of Ecology and Systematics 32 (2001): 127–57.

Rowntree, R. A., and D. J. Nowak. "Quantifying the Role of Urban Forests in Removing Atmospheric Carbon Dioxide." Journal of Arboriculture 17, no. 10 (1991): 269–75.

U.S. Department of Agriculture Natural Resources Conservation Service. "Community Garden Guide: Vegetable Garden Planning and Development." http://www.nrcs.usda.gov/Internet/FSE_PLANTMATERIALS/publications/mipmcot9407.pdf, accessed April 15, 2015.

Wolch, Jennifer, Josh Newell, Mona Seymour, Hilary B. Huang, Kim Reynolds, and Jennifer Mapes. "The Forgotten and the Future: Reclaiming Back Alleys for a Sustainable City." Environment & Planning A 42, no. 12 (2010): 2874–96. doi: 10.1068/a42259.